Nonfiction Mentor Texts

Teaching Informational Writing Through Children's Literature, K–8

Lynne R. Dorfman & Rose Cappelli

Foreword by Tony Stead

Stenhouse Publishers
Portland, Maine

Stenhouse Publishers
www.stenhouse.com

Credits
Page 20: Excerpt from *Water* by Cassie Mayer, copyright © 2008 by Heinemann Library. Reprinted with permission.

Library of Congress Cataloging-in-Publication Data
Dorfman, Lynne R., 1952–
      Nonfiction mentor texts : teaching informational writing through children's literature, K–8 / Lynne R. Dorfman and Rose Cappelli.
          p. cm.
          Includes bibliographical references.
          ISBN 978-1-57110-496-0 (alk. paper)
          1. English language—Composition and exercises—Study and teaching (Elementary) 2. English language—Composition and exercises—Study and teaching (Middle school) 3. Exposition (Rhetoric)—Study and teaching (Elementary) 4. Exposition (Rhetoric)—Study and teaching (Middle school) 5. Children's literature—Study and teaching (Elementary) 6. Children's literature—Study and teaching (Middle school) 7. Mentoring in education. I. Cappelli, Rose, 1950– II. Title.
          LB1576.D635 2009
          372.62'3—dc22   2008054528

Cover, interior design, and typesetting by Martha Drury
Photographs by Pat Cleveland, Lynne R. Dorfman, and Ralph Abbott
Cover photo by Jon DeMinico

Manufactured in the United States of America on acid-free, recycled paper
21 20 19 18 17   11 10 9 8 7

In memory of Julianne (Judy) Gehman and
Francine Perrine-Wittkamp:
mentors, colleagues, friends.

Contents

Chapter 1

The Value of Nonfiction: Imagining the Possibilities   1

Defining Our Thinking • Choosing Nonfiction Mentor Texts • The Importance of Nonfiction Writing • The Teacher as Writer of Nonfiction • The Your Turn Lesson: A Gradual Release of Responsibility • Imagining the Possibilities • An Author's Voice: Advice for Teachers

Chapter 2

Establishing the Topic and Point   13

Forming an Essential Question • Narrowing the Topic • Expert Lists: Writing About What We Know • Using Anchor Charts • Begin with Noticing • Making a Point • Capturing the Focus • Final Thoughts • An Author's Voice: Sharpening Subject Focus—and Bringing in Depth

Chapter 3

Building Content   37

Building Content with Rich Description • Using Numbers and Comparisons in Descriptions • Creating Content with Examples and Explanations • Quotes and Dialogue Create Interesting Content • Anecdotes Are a Breath of Fresh Air • Cartoon Drawings Help Readers Visualize Text • Features Fit the Facts • Bringing Nonfiction to Life • An Author's Voice: A Good Storyteller Doesn't Have to Be a Good Writer, but a Good Writer *Must* Be a Good Storyteller

Chapter 6

Nonfiction Writing in the Real World (and Other Interesting Formats to Engage Student Writers)   **135**

Postcards, Letters, and Email—Familiar Formats • Nature All Around Us • Up Close and Personal • Using Interviews to Create Family Histories • ABC Study: A Useful Organizational Format • Using Primary Source Documents • Newspapers as Mentor Texts: Writing an Obituary • How-To: Writing Recipes, Poems, and Procedures • Survival Guides: Practical Advice in Practical Formats • Opportunities Abound • An Author's Voice: Some Tips for Writers

Chapter 7

Voice, Syntax, and Conventions in Nonfiction   **187**

The Importance of Oral Writing to Establish Voice • The Conversational Tone • The Poetic Voice • Establishing an Audience Connection: Writing in the Second Person • Purposeful Use of Fragments • Finding a Toe-Tapping Tempo to Share Information • Writers Love Words! • Author Study: An Investigation into Craft and Conventions • Tying It All Together • An Author's Voice: Bringing Your Writing to Life—Painting a Clear Picture

Nonfiction writing has always been my passion, so whenever I happen upon a publication that highlights the power of and necessity for teaching children to be active writers of informational texts, I take a particular interest. What a delight it was to read this book by Lynne and Rose. This is a long-overdue and much-needed publication. The authors' understandings and practical insights about how to effectively make nonfiction writing a pleasurable and achievable experience for all students are welcoming.

It is easy to espouse the importance of writing nonfiction, but to have practical ways to make this a reality is another thing entirely. Lynne and Rose achieve a mix of theory and practice wonderfully with the "Your Turn" lessons in the second part of each chapter. It is in these lessons that teachers will find a wealth of ideas on how to assist students in becoming successful writers of nonfiction. That their ideas and suggestions come directly from classroom practice shows that these ideas work and can be successfully implemented by all teachers. I love the way they explain that in order to be successful teachers of nonfiction writing, we as teachers must also be writers of nonfiction.

Lynne and Rose have clearly shown than nonfiction is far more than simple narrative texts that present a series of facts. They demonstrate that nonfiction comes in a variety of formats. They impress upon their readers that mentor texts need to include recipes, persuasive writing, maps, email, and so forth as models for writing nonfiction. They provide practical suggestions on how to assist students to write for a variety of purposes and in a multitude of formats. Their chapter on writing persuasive texts is particularly innovative. This is a genre that is crucial for students to master, yet there are few publications that highlight this text type. They also provide wonderful insights into how fiction can be used to help students understand point of view and take this into their own writing.

As I read through this book, I was heartened to see how Lynne and Rose impress upon their readers that students need to write nonfiction with passion. They make a valid and timely point when they say that students need to raise questions as readers and writers of nonfiction. It is when writers actively research to investigate their own wonderings about a particular topic that writing with passion is optimum.

Lynne and Rose are right in saying that nonfiction writing can be challenging for students, for they can become overwhelmed with too much content to research and present. Their suggestions on how to get students to narrow their focus and become specific about what they want to tell their readers is poignant. The chapter on adding details is brimming with great ideas, as is their chapter on how to encourage students to add strong beginnings and conclusions.

I was delighted to see a chapter that addressed voice in nonfiction. For too long, nonfiction has been viewed as simply presenting a series of facts in a logical order. Lynne and Rose dispel this myth and show how important it is for writers to engage their readers. In their words, "It is the voices of the nonfiction writers that draw us into their world. Their interests and the things they know best can also become things we know and love if we hear their voices in our head and in our heart."

The final chapter in the book is a real gem. Lynne and Rose provide an extensive list of mentor texts that can be used to show students how to be effective writers of nonfiction. Teachers are going to find this list invaluable. What I particularly like about the list provided is that Lynne and Rose highlight particular aspects of nonfiction that can be explored with each mentor text. I was thrilled to see the inclusion of poetry in this list, and for that matter, throughout the book. For the most part, poetry is nonfiction as it deals with real people, real events, and our physical world. To use examples of poetry as mentor texts as a means of teaching children how to express their informational writing is powerful.

Readers of this book are going to be enlightened, invigorated, and empowered to make nonfiction writing a core part of their instruction. When I finished reading this book, I immediately wanted to find the nearest classroom and begin implementing all their wonderful ideas. It is a book you will treasure and revisit time and time again.

Tony Stead

Acknowledgments

Katie Wood Ray (1999) tells us:

> *When students are taught to see how writing is done, this way of seeing opens up to them huge warehouses of possibilities for how to make their writing good writing.* (11)

For us, our mentors have opened up a warehouse of possibilities for how to link the teaching of writing with children's literature. We are especially grateful to our nonfiction writing mentors for this endeavor. The work of Tony Stead, Barry Lane, Nell Duke, Laura Robb, JoAnn Portalupi, Ralph Fletcher, Janice Kristo, and Rosemary Bamford has been extremely informative and helped us see nonfiction writing in a different light. These authors have stretched us to think outside the box so that we can offer our students new possibilities for their writing. A special thank-you goes to Tony Stead for writing the foreword to this book. We are truly honored. Of course, we also would like to thank our tried and true mentors who have made us better writers and teachers of writers: Katie Wood Ray, Regie Routman, Shelley Harwayne, Donald Graves, Lucy Calkins, and Nancie Atwell.

We offer heartfelt thanks to our friends from the Keystone State Reading Association. You have been our greatest cheerleaders. We have had the opportunity to visit and share our thinking with reading councils across the state of Pennsylvania, and your members have made us feel welcome and valued. A big thanks to Patti Sollenberger and everyone at Reading Matters for your constant support and encouragement.

Thank you to everyone involved with the Pennsylvania Writing and Literature Project at West Chester University. Our involvement with PAWLP has provided a network of colleagues and opportunities to continue to grow professionally. Through the project we have met educators—teachers and administrators—who have welcomed us into their school districts, participated in our graduate courses, and shared their thinking.

A big thank-you to our author friends who have contributed words of wisdom and advice to teachers and students: Jen Bryant, Sneed B. Collard III, Andrea Fishman, Jane Kirkland, Frank Murphy, Trinka Hakes Noble, Steven Swinburne, and Wendy Towle. We appreciate the time you have taken from your busy schedules to help make our book special.

Of course, this book could not have been imagined or completed without the support and collaboration of the teachers and students at Fern Hill Elementary School in the West Chester Area School District and the Upper Moreland Intermediate School in the Upper Moreland Township School

District. In particular, we are grateful to our principals, Dr. Sara Missett and Dr. Joseph Waters. Additionally, we would like to thank Tammi Florio, Cheryl Ash, Jenny Lehman, Jacqueline Sham, and our superintendents, Dr. Alan Elko and Dr. Robert Milrod.

To our families and friends—thank you for putting up with our long hours and weekend writing marathons. You have all been understanding, patient, and considerate of our need to write, write, write. A special thanks to Allan and Ralph.

Finally, we are forever grateful to our Stenhouse family—each and every member. Bill Varner is our trusted editor, and we are happy to also be able to call him our friend. Thank you, Bill, for your solid belief in our ability to get the job done and for the right words at the right time. Thanks also to Chris Downey, Erin Trainer, Jay Kilburn, Doug Kolmar, Nate Butler, Martha Drury, and Gina Gerboth. You are all wonderful people—it's a pleasure to work with you!

To all the authors of nonfiction children's literature, we are constantly amazed by your voices and the way you have captured the minds and the hearts of teachers, parents, and children. You have given the nonfiction genre new life with your dazzling craft, your attention to detail, and your enthusiasm for your subject area. You are the mentors who stand beside teachers in their classrooms and help them inspire young writers. Thank you.

Lynne and Rose

The Value of Nonfiction: Imagining the Possibilities

Teachers are the great translators of theory into practice.

Writing instruction does not look exactly the same in one classroom

as it does in another.

—Tom Romano, *Blending Genre, Altering Style: Writing Multigenre Papers*

Defining Our Thinking

Have you ever picked up a child's piece of writing and known immediately what it is he or she has recently been reading, or who he or she values as an author? Take, for instance, this beginning to an informational piece about spring from Carson, a first grader. (Note: Throughout the book, primary students' original spelling has been retained for authenticity.)

> It was a horible tarible no good winter but yesterday night a very very good thing happened to me! Spring finally came! It felt like it had bin winter for a year. I was so happy I felt like shouting "spring is here" as loud as I could.

It is evident that the words of Judith Viorst from *Alexander and the Terrible, Horrible, No Good, Very Bad Day* have influenced who Carson is as a writer. Viorst created a character this first grader could relate to, so the words Alexander used became the words Carson chose to use as he made a connection to his own life. That is the power that mentor texts can have in influencing the writing of our students in our classroom communities.

It is unlikely that Carson opened his journal, then opened up Viorst's book and copied her words. More likely, Carson was first introduced to Alexander in a read-aloud, either at home or at school (maybe both). Perhaps he loved that well-known repeated refrain so much that he asked for the book to be read again and again. Perhaps it is a book he later returned to as a reader, reacquainting himself with his old friend in a new way, hearing the words again, and thinking more deeply about Alexander's plight. Perhaps one day in a writing workshop lesson or conference, Carson's teacher returned to the book to point out an aspect of the author's craft. That is just how we define mentor texts—as pieces of literature you and your students can relate to, fall in love with, and return to and reread for many different purposes. They are the books whose words resonate in the minds and hearts of our writers. They provide the models for the types of writing that can be studied and imitated and that will allow our students to move forward as writers.

It is important to remember that finding a mentor, whether it be a teacher, an author, or a text, involves bonding. If students don't see themselves or the relevance to their own lives in the books we make available to them, it will be hard for them to form the kind of relationship that will allow them to grow. As teachers, we must make it a point to know our students well—as individuals with specific interests and as writers with specific needs. We need to understand their strengths and needs as readers and writers, acknowledge these strengths and needs, and find the authors and texts that will provide them with just the right models. Tony Stead (2002) explains it this way:

> *If we are to truly assist children in their quest to become better writers for many purposes, we need to acknowledge what they already*

know as writers and base our demonstrations around what they need. (18)

As we work on nonfiction in our writing workshops, we need to take advantage of the power of the reading-writing connection. Kristo and Bamford (2004) urge teachers to use mentor texts over and over again throughout the day in all types of reading and writing lesson formats. Doing so will give students opportunities to learn firsthand how an author crafts nonfiction or uses a particular feature of nonfiction. "Your constant reference to these books will be contagious," Kristo and Bamford explain. "You'll find students taking their cue from favorite authors in no time" (81).

Students need to immerse themselves in the reading, writing, and inquiry work of nonfiction in order to be successful with the full range of informational texts. If our students are writing poetry, we would expect them to be reading and hearing lots of poetry as well. So it makes sense that if we want our students to write good nonfiction, we need to immerse them in the work of good nonfiction authors. Portalupi and Fletcher (2001) remind us: "As students try to create their own information texts, they need to spend time apprenticing themselves to the finest nonfiction writers around" (83).

Choosing Nonfiction Mentor Texts

As you look through the books that occupy your classroom library shelves or the favorites you stash on a special shelf behind your desk as your indispensable read-aloud selections, how many of them would count as nonfiction texts? In the nonfiction count, how many are narrative nonfiction texts, such as biographies and autobiographies, or selections that read more like narratives, such as *Bat Loves the Night* or *One Tiny Turtle* by Nicola Davies? How often are your students writing nonfiction during your writing workshop time? How do you choose a nonfiction mentor text for the young writers in your class?

Kristo and Bamford (2004) define nonfiction as the literature of facts. They describe the main purposes of nonfiction writing: to deliver information, explain, argue, and/or demonstrate. In this book, we are defining nonfiction texts in a much larger sense than as informational trade books and picture books. We are also including other kinds of expository texts, such as cookbooks, newspapers, magazines, brochures, and travel guides, as well as Internet selections.

Portalupi and Fletcher (2001) discuss the importance of familiarizing our students with high-quality nonfiction literature and the subgenres that have developed within the informational picture book selections. Kristo and Bamford (2004) discuss several types of nonfiction books that writers consider depending on purposes, intended audiences, and possible use by those audiences. Authors can present a topic narrowly but in great depth or they can broadly cover a topic. It is important to learn about the different kinds of nonfiction books that are available to our students in order to make sensible selections for mentor texts.

Many of the nonfiction books we are recommending are life-cycle books, such as *One Tiny Turtle* by Nicola Davies and *Monarch and Milkweed* by Helen Frost, or survey books, such as *All About Frogs* by Jim Arnosky. We also have used many how-to books, such as *A Kid's Guide to Washington, D.C.* by Diane Clark. Identification books (field guides), such as Jane Kirkland's Take a Walk Books, and photographic essays, such as *Lincoln: A Photobiography* by Russell Freedman, are other types of promising nonfiction books to use as mentor texts. We are also impressed with the wonderful selection of picture book biographies, such as *Thomas Jefferson: A Picture Book Biography* by James Cross Giblin, *Into the Woods: John James Audubon Lives His Dream* by Robert Burleigh, and *Rachel: The Story of Rachel Carson* by Amy Ehrlich.

In order to create an energizing sense of freedom within writing workshop and opportunities to write nonfiction across the content areas, we can make use of a variety of types of nonfiction books depending on our purposes for writing. When we allow our students to make decisions about how they will deliver and present information, we provide them with a sense of ownership, so vitally important to the notion of commitment to the process and product of writing nonfiction.

We have found that fiction books can also serve as mentors when writing informational and persuasive texts. *Hey, Little Ant* by Phillip and Hannah Hoose and *The Seashore Book* by Charlotte Zolotow are two examples. Informational picture storybooks, such as *All in Just One Cookie* by Susan E. Goodman, *Everglades* by Jean Craighead George, and *Penny: The Forgotten Coin* by Denise Brennan-Nelson show students yet another way to present information in a friendly and interesting format.

Sometimes we need a fiction book to serve as a catalyst to write about a topic or to imitate the form, voice, or syntax of an author. Consider the fiction books *Dear Mr. Blueberry* by Simon James, *Tuck Everlasting* by Natalie Babbitt, *Click, Clack, Moo: Cows That Type* by Doreen Cronin, or *Charlotte's Web* by E. B. White to find ideas, formats, and even strategies for writing persuasively. *Around the World: Who's Been Here?* by Lindsay Barrett George is written in the form of letters from a teacher to her class. Sometimes a fiction story presents facts through a unique voice, as in Pamela Duncan Edward's *Barefoot: Escape on the Underground Railroad*, told in the voices of the woodland and marsh animals.

Sometimes we select mentor texts to provide a clearer picture of our multicultural society and the distinctive voices that can be heard in these books. Consider *Voices of the Alamo* by Sherry Garland, *Through My Eyes* by Ruby Bridges, *Teammates* by Peter Golenbock, *Baseball Saved Us* by Ken Mochizuki, *Virgie Goes to School with Us Boys* by Elizabeth Howard, and *Hiroshima No Pika* by Toshi Maruki. It is important to find mentor texts that help us recognize and imitate qualities of good writing while at the same time fairly representing the diversity that exists in our country. These texts can build bridges to new understandings about ourselves and others. They provide us with models of high-quality literature to help us learn how to write about diversity issues with dignity, style, and grace.

Duke and Bennett-Armistead (2003) advise teachers to expose their students to a variety of texts, because research suggests a reciprocal relationship between the kinds of texts children become familiar with and the kinds of texts they choose to write and are able to write well. They write, "Children who are not exposed to much informational text are not likely to develop informational writing skills as quickly as children who are" (129). Shelley Harwayne (2008) states that kids need mentor texts that are distinctive. At Celebrate Literacy 2008, a conference sponsored by the Pennsylvania Writing and Literature Project in West Chester, Harwayne suggested that we should help our students borrow techniques that are distinctive—that our young writers need mentor texts that are distinctive. She talked about the importance of reading-writing connections and reminded us that Peterson (2007) described reading and writing as good neighbors with a big hole in the hedge that separated their properties to allow them to pass freely back and forth. Kristo and Bamford (2004) would concur; they elaborate on this same idea:

> *Teachers work hard from the beginning of the school year to "marinate" their students in good nonfiction. They read aloud high-quality nonfiction so that students develop an ear for how good expository writing sounds. Their lessons about reading and writing nonfiction scaffold their learners so they feel accomplished with what they can do all along the way.* (166)

We agree completely! Writers begin to understand that from the moment they begin to think about writing a text (finding a specific topic and engaging in prewriting) until long after the writing of the first draft (talking about it with others, revising it, and reflecting on how the writing has changed and grown in sophistication), they are beginning a journey. This journey will take them to and connect them with subsequent mentor texts and new writings—and, consequently, will lead them to new journeys. We know that students become better writers of nonfiction because they try out new things and take responsible risks (try out or imitate the writing techniques in mentor texts that they are capable of doing with a little practice and guidance). It is only through risk taking and experimentation that our writers will continue to grow and become better writers tomorrow than they are today.

The Importance of Nonfiction Writing

Laura Robb (2004) discusses the importance of writing nonfiction in order for our students to refine their thinking skills and organize their ideas and understandings about their world. Calkins and Pessah (2003) discuss the importance of engaging students in nonfiction writing in order for them to read nonfiction texts with a deep understanding. From a writer's point of view, they will at the same time acquire an understanding of features, structures, point of view, and voice. Kletzien and Dreher (2004) tell us that just as most of the reading we do as adults is informational texts, so is most of our writing. They believe that informational writing involves young writers expressing their interests and expertise from both personal knowledge and experience. Students can read widely to become experts on topics of interest before writing about them. The authors state:

> *Whenever children are expected to write in a particular form, they need to be provided with many examples to explore. For example, if children are asked to write procedural text, teachers can read several procedural texts along with them, inviting them to notice how the authors have written the text and having them identify particular characteristics of those texts.* (96)

Pike and Mumper (2004) remind us that it wasn't so long ago when most of the nonfiction reading used in schools was found only in textbooks. They talk about the importance of nonfiction writing to address issues of audience, purpose, and form.

Tony Stead (2002) presents a useful table that lists all the purposes and many forms of nonfiction writing. He says that one look at such a list can make it clear to educators that fictional narratives cannot begin to provide all the opportunities our writers need to record our life's journey. Stead cautions us that nonfiction writing involves a lot more than writing reports about animals (something that seems to be very popular among educators and students alike, regardless of grade level!).

Stead instructs us to seize moments when we can harness our students' natural curiosity to provide the energy they need to read and write about their world. Stead feels that we may have placed too much emphasis on narrative writing, perhaps because we are more comfortable with the roadmap for narrative—its language and structures—and because of our unfamiliarity with different writing genres and how they work. We would like to add to this notion that we, as teachers of young writers, are too often unfamiliar with rich models for the many forms and structures of informational texts. In the words of Tony Stead, "We need to . . . open the door to a wide world of possibilities" (11).

Here, in descending order, are our top ten reasons to write nonfiction:

10. To share our expertise with others and develop self-confidence and self-esteem.
 9. To write for wider audiences with authentic purposes.
 8. To obtain a thorough understanding of a topic of study.
 7. To enhance our vocabulary, visual literacy, and use of technology.

6. To demonstrate our ability to write in different text forms.

5. To take ownership for learning about our world and being able to share that knowledge with others.

4. To make use of powerful scaffolds to help create new and enjoyable patterns for our writing.

3. To develop myriad strategies for building content and to find ways to organize and synthesize our learning.

2. To continue to build our curiosity for our world by promoting a spirit of inquiry.

1. To provide choice—especially for those of us who would prefer reading and writing nonfiction over reading and writing fiction.

The Teacher as Writer of Nonfiction

In order to build a strong writing community, we as teachers must be a central part of that community. That means that we must demonstrate to our students that we are writers, too. It is only through the act of writing that we can show students that we value writing and see it as both an interest and an essential skill to use outside of the academic classroom. Informational writing gives us the chance to write for many purposes and audiences. Routman (2005) says: "The simple fact is we have to see ourselves as writers if we are to teach writing well" (35). She goes on to detail what we do in our daily lives and how that applies to the concept of teacher as writer in our classrooms:

> *In the course of living and working, we write communications of all kinds: notes, cards, e-mails, faxes, lists, plans, parent newsletters, college papers, journals, letters, and more. When we begin to take a close look at how we think, compose, revise, edit, and publish, we inform our teaching.* (36)

Writing informational text gives us opportunities to go beyond our classroom walls and make connections with global ideas fashioned by people who might not even live in our country. Regardless of whether we are writing from our own knowledge base and expertise or whether our burning desire to learn more about a topic leads us to read widely, ask questions, and seek out other experts, when we write about our world, we enlarge our universe as we discover new meanings. Graves (1994) tells teachers that nonfiction is the genre in which students will read and write the most throughout school and their careers. He suggests that teachers deliberately navigate their way through all kinds of nonfiction writing with their students:

> *Once again, we need to do reporting assignments right along with the children, showing them how to look at a subject, read picture books, raise questions, take notes, and write a discovery draft.* (324)

There is no need to worry about doing it "right" the first time. As a matter of fact, everyone deserves a chance to struggle and be challenged. When our students see the uncertainties we may go through as writers, they are better able to accept their own struggles because they view them as part of the writing process. When we write along with our students, we become part of the community of writers and learn from each other. The experiences we gain from writing ourselves lead us to better conferences, more informed instruction, and endless opportunities to reflect on practice. Tom Romano (2004) talks about three hats he wears in the classroom:

> *I have in mind readers who look at themselves as writers. I have in mind students, too. I look at myself as a mixture of those identities: teacher, writer, student. I write for my job and my pleasure. I teach for my job and my pleasure. And I am ever a student. I learn from what I read and watch and write and listen to. I learn from my students, whom I accompany on their writing journeys. (9)*

So don't be afraid to pick up your pen and start the journey!

The Your Turn Lesson: A Gradual Release of Responsibility

The Your Turn lessons that are included at the end of each chapter offer opportunities for you to practice a lesson format that follows the optimal learning model promoted by Regie Routman (2003, 2005). Our Your Turn lessons are often designed to take longer than the traditional mini-lesson, sometimes spanning a few days. When trying something new, students need time to observe how it is done and then try it out together with a partner or perhaps the class—maybe even more than once. The last step in the Your Turn lessons—reflecting on the effectiveness of the strategy and when and where it could and should be employed again—is all-important. It is through reflection that students will come to independently own a strategy, which, through repeated use, will become an automatic skill. Without the reflection component, students frequently hand back the responsibility to the teacher, who often must reteach something again and again.

The first step in a Your Turn lesson is to model with appropriate mentor texts that will support your students as they try out new strategies and take risks. As teachers, we make our thinking public—that is, we share our thinking about the writing and what we are noticing that deserves our attention. Revisiting these mentor texts to reflect on the hows and the whys of the author's craft helps us provide a powerful instructional framework that empowers our young writers. In our classrooms, students study mentor texts that offer challenges and opportunities to learn new strategies that, through practice, will become skills employed effortlessly.

Stead (2002) advises teachers to give students multiple demonstrations and models and to provide extra support when it is needed. We believe this support can be offered within a flexible grouping structure, during writing conferences, and even in whole-group shares. Stead says that sometimes we even "need to jump into the swimming pool with them and hold them up until they feel confident enough to let go and swim for themselves" (21). Ultimately, what students learn in their shared and guided writing experiences are applied to their independent writing. Our student writers develop entire systems of strategies that push them to expand their writing abilities by writing daily (or at least three times each week) in a writing workshop format and reflecting on how the strategies they tried out worked for them.

In this book and our previous book, *Mentor Texts: Teaching Writing Through Children's Literature, K–6,* we use structures of the Your Turn lesson to scaffold the gradual release of responsibility model in order to deepen our writers' understanding of *what* they do, *how* they do it, and *why* they do it. It is our thinking about our own thinking—metacognition—that is our end goal. But we realize that in order to be very effective with this kind of self-evaluation, we need our young writers to think and read like writers. As they encounter texts as read-alouds, shared reads, independent reads, and the work of author study and/or genre studies, they should view mentor texts in all of these contexts as significant to their own work as writers and share their latest thinking with the members of their writing community. According to Shelley Harwayne (2008), if you deeply understand the *why*, you can invent the *how!*

We hope the architecture of our Your Turn lessons will provide a dependable approach to help you provide the nudges your students need to envision themselves as effective writers and develop their writing talents. Although we often recommend a mentor text for our lessons, we list several options and welcome you to find new ones in our Treasure Chest selections (see Chapter 8) or use your own favorites.

Your Turn Lesson Format

Hook:	Use literature to invite participation.
Purpose:	Tell what you will do.
Brainstorm:	Invite writers to sketch, list, talk, create word storms, and so on to generate ideas.
Model:	Use a mentor text, your own writing, or sometimes a student sample to demonstrate a writing technique or strategy.
Shared/Guided Writing:	Writers actively participate in the modeled technique or strategy individually, in partnerships, or as a whole class through a shared writing experience. Use partner or group sharing and roving conferences to guide writers.

Independent Writing:	Writers compose a new piece or return to a published piece or notebook entry to try out the strategy.
Reflection:	Writers consciously reflect on how the writing worked. Reflection is an important step that helps students view themselves as writers and become aware of the strategies that work for them and that move them forward. All writers should reflect first on the strategy that was demonstrated and tried out, then on the piece as a whole, and finally on themselves as writers. Self-reflection can be guided through the use of key questions such as the following:

How did today's strategy work?
Additional questions can be varied according to the level of the writer and the purpose of the lesson:

What do I do well as a writer? What are the unique characteristics that set my writing apart from others (my fingerprints)?

If I were to revise, what is one thing I would absolutely change, omit, or add?

Would this piece of writing work better in a different format? A different tense?

Optional Steps in the Your Turn Lesson Format

Write and Reflect Again:	Writers rewrite their entry or piece using the revision strategy from the reflection. Writers ask themselves if this is a piece they wish to continue to work on for publication.
Goal Setting:	Writers use input from peer and teacher conferences as well as self-reflection to set personal goals.

Imagining the Possibilities

Fletcher and Portalupi (2001) recognize the value of literature as part of the writing workshop:

> *Literature isn't only used to teach about the writer's craft. Early in the workshop you will find that literature is valuable simply for modeling the possibilities open to writers.* (81)

Throughout our book we will introduce you to many of the mentor texts we have used successfully with our students. There is no set list, no specific order of introduction, and no blueprint for success. We encourage you not only to explore our titles but also to think about the books that you love and that contain the kinds of words, rich language structures, and organizational patterns you want from your students.

Chapter 8 offers a treasure chest of possibilities. We have annotated each book with suggestions for how it can be used to teach the strategies identified in that particular chapter. You will find many books listed in more than one section. These are the books that we return to over and over again because they are so rich in possibilities for our students—the true mentor texts. Our list is always growing as we find new books or return to our familiar friends and look at them in new ways, discovering even more possibilities.

At the end of each chapter, the Author's Voice sections offer advice for young authors that you can share with your students. We are very fortunate that some of our favorite nonfiction authors have provided us with insights into their process in the writing of nonfiction texts. We think your students will like hearing from them too.

It was rewarding to rediscover the inspirational work of Rachel Carson, environmentalist and author, through *Rachel: The Story of Rachel Carson* by Amy Ehrlich. This picture book biography captures Rachel's sense of wonder and curiosity about the world. It begins with an anecdote about Rachel as a young girl. Even though Rachel lived in the woods of western Pennsylvania, far from any ocean, one day she found a fossil near her home. Her mother helped her identify it as a sea creature.

Imagine! Beyond the fields and orchards, beyond the woods where she played with her dogs, beyond the Allegheny and the town of Springdale and the city of Pittsburgh, there was a vast ocean even now. At night Rachel lay in bed, her thoughts turning like waves.

That is the kind of curiosity we hope this book will help you spark in your students: curiosity about themselves, their world, and the possibilities open to them as writers. As Portalupi and Fletcher (2001) state, "We should look at research and nonfiction writing as our chance to extend their [students'] deep wonder and curiosity about the world in which we live" (20). All it takes is a little imagination!

An Author's Voice: Advice for Teachers

Andrea Fishman
Director, PA Writing and Literature Project
West Chester University, West Chester, PA
Author of *Amish Literacy: What and How It Means*

Playing acoustic guitar. Quilting. Creating a website. Improving your tennis serve. Painting with watercolors or sketching with charcoal. What was your most recent real-life learning experience? Not learning from a textbook, but learning that involved knowledge *plus* art, craft, and skill?

No matter what you wanted to learn, you probably had a teacher—or wished you had one. And that teacher was someone with experience and some mastery of what you wanted to learn.

That's why teachers of writing should be writers themselves.

How many ways are there to discover content? To find a focus? To organize ideas? To turn a phrase? To deal with writer's block? What does it look like and feel like to be inside a writer's skin when she or he faces a blank page or a draft that just doesn't sound right? Teachers who haven't had these experiences and solved these problems—and struggled with them—can't understand what students go through as they learn to become writers in their classrooms. Nor can they understand the joy of the aha! moment when writers discover the answer to their "So what?" and suddenly realize they do have something to say that's worth the struggle.

That's why readers of *Nonfiction Mentor Texts* should take advantage of the "Your Turn" opportunities Lynne and Rose provide. And why they should write with their students. Because the best teachers of mentor texts are mentor teachers, teachers who write.

Establishing the Topic and Point

The best nonfiction writing begins with a writer's passionate curiosity

about a subject.

—JoAnn Portalupi and Ralph Fletcher, *Nonfiction Craft Lessons:*
Teaching Information Writing, K–8

Writers are curious creatures. They notice things about the world around them and start to ask many questions. An author, for example, might be fascinated with size. In Steve Jenkins's *Actual Size*, readers can delight in the illustrations (drawn at actual size!) that accompany a sentence followed by measurements such as length, weight, and height. In his book *How Big Is It? A Big Book All About Bigness*, Ben Hillman illustrates how a text can be focused around one common denominator, such as size, even though the subjects are very different (for example, the egg of the elephant bird and the Arecibo Radio Telescope!). He writes about the Goliath bird-eater, a spider measuring almost a foot across; the German airship Hindenburg, more than three times longer than a Boeing 747; Hyperion, a redwood that is currently the tallest tree in the world, as well as many other big things.

Another author may come to an interesting realization—we all leave home at some point in our lives. Sneed B. Collard III, in *Leaving Home*, makes the point that all animals (including people) leave home—it's just that we leave in different ways and at different times.

Other authors find one characteristic to examine, as Yvonne Winer demonstrates in *Frogs Sing Songs*, a book that celebrates the varied voices of frogs all over the world. We might assume that David Rice was curious about life spans— what is the lifetime for a shark, an African crocodile, or a giant sequoia? In *Lifetimes*, we learn the answers to these questions as Rice takes us from the shortest lifetime (that of a mayfly), to the longest one (that of our universe).

What questions did Karin Ireland ask herself before writing *Wonderful Nature, Wonderful You*? Sometimes our curiosities lead us to new understandings, often about ourselves. As Ireland observed or read about the wonderful creatures in our environment, she must have imagined the life lessons they provide for both adults and children. In this excerpt, she talks about nature's successes and what we can learn from them:

> *A green sea turtle returns to the beach where it was hatched to lay its eggs. The beach may be several hundred miles away. But when it's time to migrate, the turtle simply begins its trip.*
>
> *When it's time for a baby parrot to fly, it spreads its wings and flies.*
>
> *Nature expects to succeed in doing what it's there to do.*
>
> *You can do anything you set your heart and mind to do. You really can.*

So how do these authors get started? What is the first thing they do? Most authors start with a keen interest or curiosity about something—like an itch they need to scratch. They may read, travel to a location for personal observations, or talk to experts. From there, they narrow their research and/or plan for writing by coming up with a lot of questions—but they probably choose the one important question that they really want to answer. That question may provide the global structure for an entire book, even though many secondary questions may also be raised and answered. But it is that one question that provides an author with a focus, even if he or she is going to write a three hundred page book!

Forming an Essential Question

Informational writing can prove to be very challenging for elementary and middle school students. Many texts are set up to cover a wide range of topics that answer myriad questions rather than one essential question. While these texts are books students can dip into and out of to find specific information to answer an essential question, as a whole they don't provide the writing model students can grasp to grow as writers of nonfiction. As writing teachers, it is our job to show students how to handle these texts by looking at a specific chapter or at content under one heading or subheading and then thinking about the question the author posed for that particular part.

Imagine that your students are discussing the different ways animals can defend themselves. Using Etta Kaner's *Animal Defenses: How Animals Protect Themselves*, you or your student may examine the four-page spread that shows how living things can be copycats in order to keep their predators away. In fact, Kaner begins with an interesting question and answer:

> *Is being a copycat always a bad thing? Not if you're an animal.*

Another student may choose his or her five-page spread that answers this essential question:

> *If an animal is not a fast mover, what does it do when a predator is close by? It hides . . . This is called camouflage.*

In addition to modeling essential questions, this book is an excellent example for the type of focused research we want our students to do in order to help them become mini-experts and write with voices of authority about a specific topic. Each short section focuses on one particular form of defense and includes such features as headings, captions, illustrations, and sidebars that represent the "wow" facts (facts that Kaner dubs "strange but true") students love to collect and use in their writing—just the type of features writers can easily imitate.

Narrowing the Topic

After forming an essential question, the next step is to show students how they can study one topic across many texts. For example, if you've just read Kaner's section on camouflage to develop an understanding of how animals use camouflage to escape predators, you might use Rebecca Grambo's *Defenses* to further explore the topic. Belinda Weber's *Animal Disguises* offers a way to reframe the essential question to limit its scope. Weber's book is entirely about camouflage. Instead of asking how animals use camouflage to hide from their predators, a student might ask, more specifically, how animals use color to hide from their predators and use Weber's book to find information.

A student may choose to narrow his or her topic and only explore color disguises after reading all three texts. If that's the case, he or she might first want to read *Living Color* by Steve Jenkins. The author explores how color is used by animals as a way to hide from enemies, attract a mate, or even warn predators of the danger of eating them. As you can see, Jenkins focuses on many *purposes* for color (or the absence of color) in the natural world, but your students may zoom in on only one purpose—camouflage. After all, they are probably writing a report or informational essay, not an entire book!

As writing teachers, we quickly move our students away from bed-to-bed narratives to more focused stories that will include the rich details unfocused stories don't include. And yet, we often continue to assign broad topics that are beyond the scope of the nonfiction writer. These assignments can lead to writing that lacks intensity and specificity. Just as when they write a narrative, students must be able to wrap their arms around their topic.

Expert Lists: Writing About What We Know

One way to get started with nonfiction writing and topics that students can readily explore is to create an expert chart (sometimes called an authority list) and post it where students can see it and add to it. In *Nonfiction Craft Lessons: Teaching Information Writing K–8*, Portalupi and Fletcher explain: "More often than not, the writer already knows something about the subject. . . . Students need to first uncover the experiential knowledge they already possess" (2001, 9).

You can begin by pointing out to students that the authors of nonfiction that they love to read are experts in their fields. In the book jacket flap of *Bat Loves the Night*, we learn that the author, Nicola Davies, is a zoologist who has studied many kinds of animals, including bats. In fact, she lives in a cottage where pipistrelle bats (the subject of the book) roost in her roof. Another well-known author of nonfiction text, Jim Arnosky, is a dedicated naturalist. He not only writes but also draws the illustrations for his All About books based on something he has actually observed.

In one of Lynne's fourth-grade classrooms, the students were surprised by the length of their expert chart, the things they knew about outside of school, and the common interests they shared. Jake had firsthand experience with hermit crabs since he kept ten of them as pets. Sierra knew a lot about baking because she spent many weekends with her grandmother, who made delicious cakes and pies. She also volunteered to add cheerleading to the list because she planned to make the squad for middle school and high school and even try to continue cheerleading throughout her college years. Spencer added skate-boards, and Kiera offered gymnastics as her area of expertise. Shane's list included baseball, soccer, and football. Lynne took an area of expertise and showed the students how many different informational writing pieces she could pursue from the general topic of horses:

> grooming a horse
> caring for the equipment
> how William the Conqueror used his cavalry to win England
> dressage moves
> jumps for a hunter course
> divisions of a horse show
> open jumping
> Olympic competitions
> English vs. Western
> judging a horse show
> eventing
> throughbred racing
> caring for a mare and foal

Lynne encouraged her students to do the same. Josh's list about snakes included poisonous snakes, nonpoisonous snakes, how snakes help the environment, snakes of ancient Egypt, boa constrictors, how to care for a pet snake, and how snakes use their color for camouflage. When Josh began looking at snake books to add to his list, he discovered there were many more poisonous snakes than he realized. So he limited his research to discuss only poisonous snakes in Pennsylvania.

A student's expert list should include things that he or she may know something about but that lead him or her to want to know more. When talking with our students about expert lists for nonfiction writing, we like to share *Hummingbirds: Tiny but Mighty* by our good friend Julianne (Judy) Gehman. As a child, Judy was fascinated by a hummingbird she saw in her great aunt's garden. Many years later, she was entertained by the hummingbirds that visited her home in Sullivan County. These firsthand observations—these noticings— led her to research hummingbirds and write this book for children to enjoy. It is a good example of a mentor text, because Judy narrowed her topic to the ruby-throated hummingbird. Her book makes the point that even though they are tiny, hummingbirds are mighty. Perhaps the one question she decided on answering for children is, "How can such tiny creatures be so strong?" Her research and personal observations helped her write her book.

Sometimes we come to a topic as an expert without doing any reading, but we can still use mentor texts to help us define our scope and think about our purpose for writing a piece. Many students can write process pieces without doing more than surface reading or browsing of informational text. We often use counting books, such as *Soccer Counts* by Barbara Barbieri McGrath and Peter Alderman or *Quilt Counting* by Lesa Cline-Ransome, to demonstrate how to write a piece that explains a process or offers advice based on practical experience about how to do something. In the example that follows, Dean shares his expertise in sandwich making. He had enough personal experience that no additional research was needed.

How to Make the Perfect Sandwich
by Dean S., Grade 4

It is summer break and there is a good aroma in the kitchen. Your stomach is empty and lunch time is right around the corner. What will you have? Have you ever wanted to make the perfect sandwich? Then what you need is the right plan including food, utensils, and a focused mind. Now you're ready to make the perfect sandwich.

First, you'll need to get the right food. You can pick them up at any grocery store. You will also need a butter knife and a sharper kitchen knife. (Make sure to be careful.) Now you can lay the bread out on the kitchen counter. You can use any bread you want like rye (My favorite), white, wheat, or a roll. Anything.

Next, it's time for the lunch meat and cheese. I like ham but you can always try something new. Put the lunch meat on one piece of the bread. Try to put at least two pieces on the sandwich for a taste explosion. Now you add cheese. (Make sure the cheese is in slices.) You can choose any cheese you want like American, Swiss, or provolone. Note: Make sure the meat and cheese are on the same piece of bread.

Now what you need to do is get toppings. You can make it a healthier sandwich by adding lettuce and tomato. Also add mayo or mustard. Spread the mayo with the butter knife. Use the sharper knife to cut the sandwich in half. All sandwiches go good with something to drink. Also try a side of chips, fries, or goldfish crackers.

I don't know about you, but this is making me hungry. Grab a knife and get started. I know I am. Just don't leave the mess for mom to clean up. A sandwich just might be what you need to fill your hunger. Dig in!

Using expert lists is a way to help young writers tackle a very difficult genre. Instead of launching immediately into research of the unknown, let them write about the known. JoAnn Portalupi and Ralph Fletcher (2001) offer this advice:

The research world of picture books, articles, Weekly Reader, multimedia encyclopedias on CD-ROM, nature films, and so on can be overwhelming to young writers. As we immerse them in the voices of other experts, we should take care that their own voices, perceptions, and observations don't get lost in the process. As students begin investigating their subjects, we need to make sure they value their own experience of the world. (40)

Using Anchor Charts

When you move into research, it is better to first study something with the class, and then allow children to choose topics to write about that focus on an essential question—things they are still wondering about or things that have not been answered during discussions and readings. One way to accomplish this is through the use of an anchor chart, which reading/writing experts such as Lucy Calkins, Debbie Miller, and Stephanie Harvey advocate for classroom use regardless of grade level.

Fact-Question-Response

A fact-question-response (F-Q-R) chart (Harvey 1998) is an anchor that actively engages students in the reading of nonfiction material. The use of questioning and thinking strategies will help them identify what they still wonder about. We like to use three different colors of sticky notes to write down facts that are gathered, questions that arise, and responses to the reading that detail the reader's opinions and reactions to the text. As students gather their thoughts on sticky notes, they note whether a fact links with a question or response they have written. As they continue to read the selection to the end or make connections with a video, discussion, or other books used in class, they reread their questions to see if any of them have been answered. (See Your Turn Lesson 1 at the end of the chapter for a more detailed discussion.)

Some questions will be unanswered. These are the burning questions that students still wonder about and that can lead them to a focused piece of research. For example, Lynne's fourth graders read *Avalanche* by Stephen Kramer and came up with many great questions for research, such as "How are dogs trained to search for people buried beneath the snow in an avalanche?"; "What breeds of dogs are best for this kind of work?"; and "What was the worst avalanche ever recorded in history?"

Reading about some of the animal relationships highlighted in *Weird Friends: Unlikely Allies in the Animal Kingdom* by Jose Aruego and Ariane Dewey led to many questions with a group of Rose's second graders. They wondered, "How does the hermit crab grab the sea anemone without getting stung?" and "If the beetles clean the mouse's home for bugs, what if the bug is bigger than they are?"

K-W-L

In addition to the F-Q-R chart, another anchor chart that is familiar to many teachers is the K-W-L (what I know, what I wonder about, what I learned). Often teachers use a K-W-L anchor chart to begin a unit of study, asking students to activate their schema by thinking about what they already know about the topic to be studied. It is probably a good idea to start reading and talking about the topic (for example, earthquakes) before asking students to wonder, so that everyone has some background knowledge from which to work. This is where the importance of knowing your students comes into play. If students know nothing about a subject, it is much more difficult for them to think about what they might want to learn. Students in Florida may have a more extensive background in the Everglades ecosystem than students in the Southwest. At the end of the unit, students come together to share essential concepts and big ideas about what they learned. At this point, we like to add an "s" column for "Still Wondering." We believe that students can formulate specific, high-quality questions after engaging in a unit of study. These are the questions that can be used for a focused research project that could include essays, speeches, reports, feature articles, poems, journal entries, letters, and travel logs to name a few.

Begin with Noticing

For very young children, forming an essential question begins with noticing. They observe the world around them and notice things that elicit a stream of questions such as "Why is the sky blue?" or "How do birds build nests?" Books for emergent readers such as Cassie Mayer's *Water* or Lisa Bruce's *Yellow* can be mentor texts for helping students begin to think about the essential question that an author might consider before researching and writing. *Water*, and other books in the Materials series, contains essential questions that children can easily recognize (see Figure 2.1).

FIGURE 2.1
Pages 16 and 17 from *Water* by Cassie Mayer pose an essential question followed by details that answer the question.

How Can Water Change?

Water can change form.

Water can be a liquid.

Sometimes we can lead students to understand an author's process of forming the essential question through the discussions we hold after reading. Recently, Rose was working with a small group of kindergarten students using the book *What Lays Eggs?* by Katherine Gracestone. As part of the introduction to the book, Rose told the students that they would be reading a book about eggs. She asked them to consider what they might wonder about eggs. "How big is a dinosaur egg?" offered Nancy.

"What colors can eggs be?" added Bryce. The students continued to offer their ideas as Rose recorded them on chart paper. She explained that these were all wonderful questions about eggs that could be explored, and she asked them to think about what the author might have wondered as she wrote her book. (See Figures 2.2 and 2.3 for two students' explorations on the topic of eggs.)

After reading the title together (*What Lays Eggs?*), the students immediately were able to connect with the author's essential question, possibly because it was right there in the title, which was added to the chart. Rose explained to the students that authors need to have a purpose in mind as they write, and that in the case of authors who write nonfiction, the purpose often starts with a question. "Understanding the question the author was exploring will help us think about what the author wants us to know. It can also help us think about what questions we have that we can write about," she explained.

A few weeks after their exploration of eggs, Rose met with this group again to explore a different informational book: *Bears* by Amy Algie. *Bears* is an early concept book that uses photographs, labels, and simple text to explore the topic of what bears like to do. Since the title of this book was not in the form of a question, Rose wondered if the students would still be able to uncover the essential question. She was not disappointed. After the shared reading she asked, "So what do you think the author, Amy Algie, was wondering about bears?"

FIGURE 2.2
Alex explores topic and point. (Eggs: Many animals lay eggs.)

FIGURE 2.3
Nancy explores topic and point. (Eggs: Many animals lay eggs. Some animals look after their eggs.)

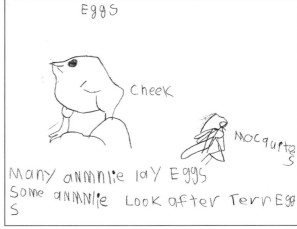

"I think she wanted to know what bears like to do," said Amber.

"I think so, too," said Evan. "Maybe she wanted us to know that different bears like to do different things. We should read some more books about bears." Later on, Rose brought in several more easy books about bears. After brainstorming some possible topics, the students decided to explore the essential question of what bears eat. With partners, they examined the pictures and worked together to read as much as they could to answer their essential question. Together, they composed a shared writing piece that detailed their discoveries.

What Bears Eat
Some bears like to eat berries.
Some bears like to eat fish.
Some bears like to eat grass.
Some bears like to eat pinecones.
Some bears like to eat animals.
Bears like to eat!

Making a Point

When writers zoom in to focus on a particular question, they must consider not only topic, but the point they are trying to make to their readers. It is important to teach young writers about point, because any writing worth its salt makes one, however subtle. Although narratives do offer a point, sometimes stated in a subtle way in a final paragraph, in an informational or persuasive piece, the point is much stronger. It is found in the introduction, controls the body of the piece, and is restated as powerfully as possible in the conclusion.

There are many examples of writing that are topic-based only. Let children examine encyclopedias to understand this kind of writing. You can familiarize your students with this concept of topic and point through picture books and books containing pieces of short texts by using them as read-alouds. *Chameleons Are Cool* by Martin Jenkins or *Living Color* by Steve Jenkins are two good choices.

When students read nonfiction to gather ideas for an informational report, they should ask themselves some key questions about what they've read:

1. What is the most important thing I want to tell my target audience?
2. What are the big ideas about the most important thing I need them to understand and remember?
3. What structure am I going to use to shape the information? (time sequence, compare/contrast, cause/effect, problem/solution, etc. [See Chapter 6.])

Children need to know that all good writing centers around a controlling point or "so what?" that makes content meaningful, powerful, and memorable. In the shared writing example about bears, the children explored the essential question of what bears eat. After the research, they all could agree that the point they wanted to make was that bears like to eat. Older students might make the point that because bears are willing to eat such a wide variety of food, they will never go hungry.

Lynne used David Hummon's *Animal Acrostics* to support nonfiction writing in several third-grade classrooms. This beautifully illustrated book uses acrostic poetry supported by additional facts about each animal named on the page. In addition, the book is organized around various biomes, such as the African savannah and the tropical rain forest. The book also includes a page of "wonderful words" (1999, 38)—nouns, verbs, and adjectives that add style to nonfiction writing. The third graders used this mentor text as a model to create acrostic poetry and highly focused research reports around an essential question about marine life. They were ready to do this because they had just completed a nonfiction unit of study on ocean creatures in their reading anthology. The students were so excited about *Animal Acrostics* after hearing it as a read-aloud that Lynne asked them if they would like to use it as a model to create their own class book about sea creatures. The book would be published for everyone in the class to share with family and friends. Knowing their purpose and audience added to the students' engagement in the project. As Regie Routman (2005) says, "Our students need to see that our purpose for writing is genuine, that we write with readers in mind even if the readers are ourselves" (42).

Lynne began this unit of study by using a set of books about whales and dolphins. The set included *Super Swimmers: Whales, Dolphins, and Other Mammals of the Sea* by Caroline Arnold and *Whales and Dolphins* by Susanna Davidson as well as many others (see the Treasure Chest for Chapter 2, found in Chapter 8). She had read these books and tagged certain pages with sticky notes of different colors to mark information around different key points or concepts about dolphins. She divided the class into six small groups for collaborative reading based on the different points the author was making about dolphins. The task set for each group was to come up with the point or big idea the author was sharing as well as an essential question that the author would have asked before writing the particular selection. After the students had read, talked, and reached consensus about the key concept or point, and had written an essential question, Lynne used a chart to display their thinking. As the students shared, they began to see that although they had all read information about dolphins, their selections were making different points about them. Lynne recorded each group's big idea and essential question.

Big Ideas	**Essential Questions**
Dolphins are intelligent creatures.	How do we know dolphins are intelligent?
Dolphins are mammals.	What are the characteristics that make dolphins mammals?
Dolphins are athletes.	What kinds of things can dolphins do that show they are muscular and fit?
Dolphins can communicate with each other.	What kind of communication system do dolphins use?
Dolphins help human beings in many ways.	Can dolphins be trained to help humans?
Dolphins are threatened by pollution and fishermen.	Are dolphins in danger of becoming extinct?

After the charting, Lynne explained their next task. She asked the students to think about the ocean creatures they had just finished studying before they read *Animal Acrostics* together. What more would they want to know, or what other creatures would they like to learn more about and report on for the class book they had decided to create? To help them find topics, she asked the students to read the books they had collected from home and from the school, classroom, and public libraries, as well as the books Lynne provided from her personal library. They orally shared possible topics of interest, and Lynne charted them. Each student was able to choose a topic to create his or her own section for the class book. Lynne told them they would have two days to browse books to find their topic before doing any careful reading or note taking. Once they had an appropriate topic (information was available and a limited number of students had chosen the topic), they could start reading across several books.

Lynne wanted to make sure they were familiar with their topic before doing research around one point, so the first assignment was to write an acrostic poem about their choice (they were familiar with this form), and to write, without looking at their books, a small paragraph in their own words that extended the information presented in the poem. When students have read enough and are able to wrap their arms around what it is they are writing about, they are much less likely to resort to copying information.

Now they were ready to look at their information again and find the big idea and point they wanted to make about their animal. A quick conference about topic and point was a good way to check in with each student. Lynne reminded them of the work they'd done as a whole class with the topic of dolphins. Students reread three or four texts to support the point they were trying to make. Using the information in their acrostic poems and their notes, students created a draft around their point. After revision and editing, students published the class book, complete with illustrations. In Ryan's piece, he makes the point that sharks are dangerous creatures. It is a good contrast to Matthew's piece, which informs the reader that sharks have a bad reputation, but that in truth, not all sharks are dangerous to people.

Danger!
by Ryan, Grade 3

Are you scared of SHARKS? Sharks attack fifty to seventy-five people each year world-wide. Divers get attacked each year. Sharks can be dangerous creatures. Almost any shark six feet long or longer is a potential danger. Three species are most likely to attack. They are the Great White, the Tiger Shark, and the Bull Shark.

The most shark attacks ever recorded were in the 1970's near Australia by sand bull sharks. Only thirty-two species of sharks have been documented to attack humans, but another thirty-six species are potentially dangerous.

Many shark attacks occur near shore waters typically inshore of a sandbar where sharks may be confined at low tide. Sharks may gather along steep drop-offs, and near channels or river mouths because their natural food items can be found there.

There may be a number of reasons why sharks attack humans in these areas. Whatever the cause, shark bites produce serious, sometimes life-threatening wounds.

Sharks aren't always a threat but they should be treated with caution. Sharks can be dangerous. When you're in the water, watch out for SHARKS!

Shark Attacks
by Matthew, Grade 3

Are sharks dangerous to humans? Shark attacks are increasing because more people are using the sea—swimming, fishing, boating—but chances of being attacked by sharks are slim. Millions of people use the sea every day but only about six people are killed each year by sharks. Lightning in North America caused 100 deaths each year.

Shark attacks occur sometimes because sharks get confused. For example, surfboards with a swimmer on top dangling his legs may look like a good meal. Their bite and spit method help sharks to recognize that people are not part of their regular diet, and they will let them go.

The simple truth is that sharks have a reputation as man-eaters, but out of the 200 varieties, only 25 species are dangerous to people. For example, whale sharks never hunt people and eat nothing but plankton.

Sharks have a bad reputation like the big bad wolf in the *Little Red Riding Hood* story. The truth is, most sharks are harmless. They are not after you. They are simply looking for dinner. Use caution whenever you are in the water, but remember that you have a better chance of being struck by lightning than being attacked by a shark!

All students were successful with this writing project because the writing was focused around a key point that limited the scope of the assignment and made it doable for third graders. In addition, they had a specific purpose and audience they were writing for. They weren't just writing for their teacher—they were writing for family, friends, the school librarian, and the school principal as well. A copy of the finished product was kept in the main office for visitors to the school, the classroom, and the school library, helping to make this project worthwhile and exciting for the students.

Capturing the Focus

Mentor texts can illustrate how an author can develop a piece of writing about a person around a quality he or she possesses. For example, in *The Bus Ride That Changed History: The Story of Rosa Parks*, Pamela Duncan Edwards uses the "house-that-Jack-built" scaffold to tell the story of the famous bus ride. On every page the repeated line ". . . which was overturned because one woman was brave" captures the focus of this book. The author chose to highlight Parks's bravery this way. In her author's note she concludes: "Sometimes it just takes one person to be brave." In Chapter 4, we discuss developing concluding remarks around "the way we are known." A biographical piece that is developed around a person's noteworthy characteristic can use this format for concluding remarks.

You can count on some authors to give you their point of view and the point they are making in the final pages of the text. In Jim Arnosky's All About series, the final pages are often devoted to his message and point of view. For example, in *All About Frogs*, Arnosky makes sure that you have fallen in love with frogs or at least have learned many interesting things about them before he steps out of third-person writing to assume the first person and write:

> *In the natural order of things, frogs can take care of themselves. But frogs cannot avoid or escape environmental dangers such as water pollution and the loss of wetland habitats. Sometimes I walk along a shoreline just to count the frogs that suddenly leap into the water. I always count more frogs than I imagined I would see. That's the way I like it. That's the way it should forever be.*

In Shelley Gill's *Alaska's Three Bears*, a last page is devoted to giving people advice about how to act when hiking and camping in bear country. Her point of view is simply stated in her last sentence:

> *Remember, the bears were here first. Please respect their home. It would be a shame to lose them.*

One of our favorite new finds is *Monumental Verses* by J. Patrick Lewis. In a poem of introduction, Lewis lets us know that his reason for choosing to write about monuments is to honor these great structures of art and science. He invites readers to compose a poem about additional monuments that they might be interested in and that may inspire them to write.

> *Pretend your pen is a camera: take a picture of the monument, but only with your words.*

Whether it is as a read-aloud, in guided reading, in content-area classes, or in writing workshop, we should always help students think about why the authors chose to write what they did—what their purpose was and what point they wanted to make. In this way, students can better internalize the importance of having a "so what?" and applying it to their own writing.

Final Thoughts

In nonfiction writing, it is better to let students begin with what they know. They all have areas of expertise. It is our job as teachers to find out what these are and to give students opportunities to write about them formally and/or informally. When we move into unknown areas, we can build schema by reading, talking, drawing, and sometimes observing before forming essential questions that students can research. They begin by reading about a focused topic across many texts so they can become "mini-experts" before writing. Choosing the right topic and being able to narrow it to a manageable size will help all students be more successful with informational writing.

An Author's Voice:
Sharpening Subject Focus—and Bringing in Depth
Sneed B. Collard III
Author of *Leaving Home* and *Teeth*

One of the most difficult aspects of writing is to narrow your focus or subject to something that you can tackle effectively. This process, though, is also a key to a writer's effectiveness.

A problem for many writers is that they pick topics that are too large or complicated. For instance, I love the ocean—so much, in fact, that I studied marine biology in college. As a writing subject, however, the ocean is too big. If I even *tried* to write about the entire ocean, I would quickly be overwhelmed by the vast amount of information I wanted to include. A second problem with this topic is that if you tried to write about it all, your information would be so general and shallow that your readers would soon be nodding off in their seats. How did I solve these problems?

By narrowing my topic.

For instance, I've always been especially interested in the deep sea, the parts of the ocean below the reach of sunlight. But even this subject is too big for a single book. Instead of trying to write all about the deep sea, I decided to write only about those animals that live on the actual bottom of the ocean. The result was my book *The Deep-Sea Floor* (2003). The topic is small enough that I could manage to cover it in one book. But the book also has enough focus to attract readers. Note that I went through two layers of narrowing here: from the ocean to the deep sea, and then from the deep sea to the deep sea floor. I could have gone even further and narrowed it down to animals that live only at deep sea vents or something like that, but for this book at least, I didn't want to.

A second book I wrote about the deep sea focused on bioluminescent animals—those that make their own light. I did not want to write about all of these animals. There are too many, for one thing. Also, I thought I might end up boring the reader. I solved this problem by narrowing down my topic to one particular scientist who studies these bioluminescent animals. By doing this, I not only sharpened my focus, but made my book more interesting by telling a story of her career. The result was a book called *In The Deep Sea* (2006).

You can see that narrowing my subject keeps me from being overwhelmed by an infinite amount of information. It also does something else very important. It adds, forgive the pun, *depth* to my work. Readers are very picky. They want to know a piece of writing will let them sink their teeth into something juicy right away. Narrowing your focus brings out the "juiciness" of a topic, making your work more fun—and more effective.

Your Turn Lesson 1

Using F-Q-R to Form an Essential Question

Fact-question-response (F-Q-R) is a strategy that helps students synthesize information as they read by asking questions, determining important facts, and integrating their own thoughts and opinions. It can also be an effective tool for helping students discover a focus for future research on a topic. With enough practice, students can eventually use this strategy in independent work during reading and writing workshop. There are many ways to conduct this activity. Sometimes students will just chart the questions they come up with, the responses they make, and the facts they learn in any order as they read. In the example here, the questions and responses are specifically linked with the facts recorded.

Hook: Return to some nonfiction books that you have used or that students have access to in which it is easy to pick out the essential question that the author explored. Some of our favorites include *Lifetimes* by David Rice, *Leaving Home* by Sneed B. Collard III, and *Animal Disguises* by Belinda Weber.

Purpose: *Questioning is at the heart of research. As you have seen from the books we've examined, many authors begin their study of a topic with a question they have. Today you will learn how to use the facts you know to form a question for more focused research.*

Brainstorm: Have students brainstorm a list of topics they might choose to research. This might come from a completed unit of study (they might list howler monkeys, endangered species, or medicinal plants after studying the rain forest), or from an expert list (see the discussion of expert lists earlier in Chapter 2).

Model: The use of short text is excellent for modeling. Books such as those in the Question Time: Explore and Discover series from Kingfisher or the Supersmarts collection from Candlewick Press have one- or two-page spreads that can be used to model various strategies, including F-Q-R. In addition, many classroom news magazines can also be used to model. In the following example, Rose introduced "Space Fakes" from *Seeing Stars* by James Muirden, part of Candlewick's Supersmarts collection. Display the selection on a visualizer or document imager and explain to the class what you will do.

A topic I am interested in exploring is stars. Today I'm going to read a section on comets and meteors. As I read I'm going to jot down some important facts. When I'm finished I'll go back and respond to some of those facts and see if any of them lead to more questions. I'll use this chart to help me organize my thinking.

In our example, the finished chart might look something like this:

Facts	Questions	Response
Stars are made of gas.		
Comets are made of snow and dust.	Where do the snow and dust come from?	I never thought of snow as part of space.
Comets turn to gas when they get close to the sun.	How long do comets and meteors live?	They must burn up—that's the end of them!
Meteors are pea-sized pieces of space rock.	Do meteor showers occur all over the world? Do meteor showers occur at certain times of the year?	I remember seeing a meteor shower.

Shared/Guided Writing: Together with the class, explore another short text (perhaps from the same book) and create a chart with facts, questions, and responses. When students can offer a response, it shows they are thinking about it and their thinking may lead to questions they want to research. Good questions come from reading and knowledge gathered from classroom discussions, videos, podcasts, current events, and personal experiences, or from considering something that has been left unanswered.

Independent Writing: Have students return to the brainstormed list of possible topics and choose one they might want to learn more about. Gather some resources and ask them to explore their topic as they list facts, questions, and responses. Depending on your grade level, you might create an F-Q-R chart for them to work from.

Reflection: After the students have completed their chart, gather them together to do some thinking about how this strategy worked for them. You can use the following questions as a guide:

How did the F-Q-R chart help you narrow your focus for research?

What did you discover about your topic that you might not have known before?

What are you still wondering about?

When could you use this strategy again? Could this strategy be useful in reading workshop as well?

Can you take one of your responses and change it into an essential question for further research?

Your Turn Lesson 2

The Point Is . . .

Hook: Gather together some books that address the same general topic but that focus on different things to make different points.

For example, there are many books written about Abraham Lincoln that make different points about him. *Abe Lincoln: The Boy Who Loved Books* by Kay Winters makes the point that Lincoln's love of books influenced many aspects of his life. In *Abe Lincoln's Hat* by Martha Brenner we learn something about Lincoln's personality—that he was sometimes forgetful, so he stored important papers in his hat to remind him of the things he had to do. *If You Grew Up with Abraham Lincoln* by Ann McGovern focuses on the many differences between present time and the time Lincoln lived, and *Abraham Lincoln* by Amy L. Cohn and Suzy Schmidt makes the point that Lincoln was a big man, not only in stature but also in the hearts of those who knew him.

Purpose: *Many authors write about the same topic. For example, there are lots of books about sharks, bears, Abraham Lincoln, and the rain forest. But each book might focus on a different aspect of that animal, person, place, or thing. Each author wrote with a different purpose in mind—they each made different points. Today I am going to show you how you can write an informational piece about the same topic as someone else but make different points.*

Brainstorm: Choose a topic that is common to the class and have your students brainstorm different points that could be made when writing about it. List the points on the board or on a chart. For example, if your topic is the best thing about school, you might list getting to see friends, learning new things, going to the library, talking to teachers, working with different materials in art class.

Model: Choose one of the points listed on the chart and write a short piece in front of the class. You can also do some oral writing to save time, but make sure the students get to watch how you formulate your thoughts. A piece written on a point from the preceding brainstormed list might go something like this:

> I love coming to school! The best part about it is the library. The first thing you see when you walk in is the display of new books. Those colorful covers in their crisp new jackets really grab me. I almost always check one out or put my name on a waiting list. There are so many wonderful titles that sometimes it is hard to decide which one to read next. Spending time in this room surrounded by books is usually the highlight of my day.

Shared/Guided Writing: Choose another point from the brainstormed list, then write from that perspective in a shared writing experience. Students could also work in pairs if you think they are ready.

Independent Writing: Ask students to turn to a territory list or heart map in their notebooks. (If they don't have a territory list or heart map, they can simply list possible topics for writing). Have them choose a topic that would lend itself to an informational piece, then brainstorm different points they could make about it. For instance, if soccer is a listed topic, they might describe how it requires a great deal of skill to play, or how important the rules are to follow, or how it is an excellent form of exercise. Ask them to choose one point and write. On another day, they can choose to write about the same topic but from a different viewpoint.

Reflection: Ask students to reflect on how brainstorming different points that could be made about a topic affected their writing.

> *How did thinking about the point you wanted to make in your writing help you focus your ideas?*

> *How could thinking about the point help you when you write in science or social studies?*

> *What could you do to help you decide on the point you want to make in your writing?*

Option: *The Important Book* by Margaret Wise Brown offers a useful scaffold for narrative or content-area writing that can also help students decide on the point they want to make. After describing what is important about the topic, any of the ideas can be expanded to a more complete informational piece.

Your Turn Lesson 3

Using a Scaffold for Point-of-View Poetry

This lesson will show your students how to create a nonfiction poem to illustrate a point of view using a simple scaffold. To prepare for this lesson, collect pictures from magazines or newspapers that are rich in detail and that might inspire places, characters, or events. Also, have a set of books on hand about an interesting topic for both boys and girls, such as sharks, bats, horseshoe crabs, or bees.

Hook: Introduce your topic to the students. It is helpful if you can tie it in with a unit of study in social studies, reading, or science. Read a picture book such as *Sharks* by Seymour Simon. If possible, display the stunning photos on a visualizer or document imager to enlarge it, or gather the students close enough to see the amazing photography.

Options: *The Shark: Silent Hunter* by Renee le Bloas and Jerome Julienne, excerpts from *Who's for Dinner? Predators and Prey* by Rita Thievon Mullin, *Horseshoe Crabs and Shorebirds: The Story of a Food Web* by Victoria Crenson, *Bats: Mammals That Fly* by Marlene Sway, *Bats! Strange and Wonderful* by Laurence Pringle, *Zipping, Zapping, Zooming Bats* by Ann Earle, and *Bat's Night Out* by Buffy Silverman.

Purpose: *Sometimes authors build informational text around a point of view. Sometimes a point of view represents a personal memory sparked by connections made to the photographs and actual events. Sometimes the pictures and text provide the ideas for writing a poem about something in the real world. Today I will show you how to build a poem around a point of view. I will use a picture book about sharks, so I will examine both the photos and the text to create my poem. In addition, I am going to use a simple scaffold to help me structure my thinking as I move through pictures and text.*

Brainstorm: Choose a picture from *Sharks* by Seymour Simon and display it on an overhead projector, visualizer, or document imager. Ask students to think about the text that was shared earlier that day or week. Elicit as many ideas related to the picture as possible and make a web on a chart or whiteboard. This brainstorming can be repeated for several photos from the book. An alternative for older students is to place a picture of a shark on the center of a piece of chart paper (from magazines or Internet sources). Students can work with a partner or small group to brainstorm and write words related to the picture. Create several of these charts and display them around the room. Students can do a "carousel" (walk around the room looking at the pictures and word webs to jot down and add their thinking about sharks to everyone else's chart). As a whole class, create a list of topic and point statements about sharks and display it on the board or chart paper.

Model: Begin to create an informational poem about sharks, choosing from the list of brainstormed topic and point suggestions. Use thinking aloud to let your students in on how you chose the ideas and how those ideas are making you feel. Use the scaffold "Talking about . . ." (shown on the following page) every time your point of view changes. Use the scaffold to close your poem. Lynne's model for a third-grade class reading about ocean creatures follows.

Talking about sharks
Terrifies me:
Bloodthirsty and powerful,
Attracted by the smell of blood,
Razor-sharp teeth that
Crack bones between jaws of steel,
Clouding the water with scraps of food.

Talking about sharks
Fascinates me:
Built for speed,
Extremely flexible skeleton
Built of cartilage,
Unchanged for millions of years,
The perfect hunter.

Talking about sharks
Makes me sad:
Over 100 million killed each year,
Threatened by commercial fishing,
Threatened by human pollution,
An unloved animal,
An undeserved bad reputation,
Will they have a future?

Talking about sharks!

Guided Writing: As a whole group, create another poem about sharks from the webs or charts that are displayed. Invite students to share a feeling. Then ask students to add information that seems to go with that feeling or point of view. Display these examples in a writing center or on a bulletin board. Students can also work in pairs to create shark poems that can be posted.

Independent Writing: Ask students to begin a "Talking About . . ." poem in their notebooks. They can choose to write a poem using a topic that the class already outlined, or they may want to choose a new topic and begin to jot down a new set of possibilities.

Offering students several choices can help differentiate among those who may still need more guidance and those who are ready to try it on their own. It is a good idea to divide the class into groups with sets of books about bees, ants, butterflies, or anything else you have on hand in your classroom or school library. Students can read and use the information to create a group web. Then they can write individual poems in their notebooks.

This scaffold can be tied to many personal experiences such as "Talking About Sisters" or "Talking About Brothers" as well as sports (Talking About Soccer). Remind students to focus their thinking around a point of view or use the scaffold to signal the reader that the point of view has changed.

Reflection: Using pictures and text to create informational poems that demonstrate your point of view involves lots of thinking and decision making. It may also involve a good bit of reading before planning and drafting can occur. Your class may want or need to spend several days reading about a topic before doing this activity. Encourage your students to find picture books that spark ideas and different points of view. Remember to focus on the strategy by guiding discussion around the following points:

How did the pictures/photographs help you think of ideas for your poem?

What type of topics work best?

Did the sharing of ideas help? How?

Did the word webs spark ideas that led to revisions or new thinking?

Was the scaffold helpful? How so? How might you change it? (Or did you change it?)

When might you use this strategy again?

What have you learned about point of view?

Building Content

Without sufficient detail, my students tend to write paragraphs that may

have an impressively relaxed tone, but that lack force, or memorability,

because there's nothing to sink one's teeth into as a reader.

—Laura Robb, *Nonfiction Writing: From the Inside Out*

When we talk about content, what we're really talking about are quality ideas. Students of all ages can usually come up with an idea. As a matter of fact, they often can come up with many ideas. The problem that students have with their writing is in the *development* of a good idea. On many occasions we have found that students complete a piece of writing that is built around empty content. That is to say, the piece moves from one idea to the next at a fast and furious pace, much like the video games that kids play today.

In order to help students develop their ideas, we must show them how the authors of the books we love develop content. In the case of nonfiction writing, they do this with rich descriptions, specific examples, step-by-step explanations, and wonderful anecdotes. That's what pulls us in and makes these books memorable. Remember that nothing about nothing still equals nothing. It's that zero property of multiplication: $10 \times 0 = 0$, $1000 \times 0 = 0$. It's not about how many ideas a writer has, it's about how a writer develops well-chosen ideas to make the writing explicit for his or her readers. Content is what gives a piece shape and substance—it's the meat and potatoes of a piece of writing.

Building Content with Rich Description

A good way to teach students to build content is through the use of description. Students are used to creating scenes in narratives to help their readers visualize settings, characters, and objects. They can easily recognize good description in nonfiction writing that does the very same thing. We have found that there are two kinds of descriptive writing for nonfiction. One relies heavily on the senses—describing what something smells like, looks like, or tastes like, for example. Pam Muñoz Ryan's *Hello Ocean* is a great book to use to introduce the use of the five senses to describe a setting. It is important for students to understand that writers do not always include all five senses—that good writing only includes the senses that best apply.

Notice how Diane Swanson uses description in *The Wonder in Water*:

For millions of years, the blue duck has lived in New Zealand—and nowhere else. Its blue color helps it hide among wet river rocks. Its streamlined head and large webbed feet help it swim through swift water. And its claws grip boulders tightly while the duck eats insects under water.

In *Arctic Lights Arctic Nights*, Debbie S. Miller describes the first day of the summer solstice in Alaska in the following way:

Splash . . . drip. *A cow moose dunks her head and clips off some lily pads. Her calf splashes through the water behind her. Across the lake a pair of trumpeter swans dabble for food. In the evening, mosquitoes softy whine, and the songs of thrushes drift through the cooling air.*

In *Everglades*, Jean Craighead George uses sound, sight, and touch to talk about the saw grass:

> *The grass prospered. When the winds blew, the saw grass clattered like a trillion swords. Each sword was edged with cutting spines. Of the larger animals, only the leathery alligator could walk unharmed among the terrible spears of the saw grass.*

Do you feel like you are right there? Sights and sounds as used in these examples help the reader visualize the scene and are perhaps the easiest senses for our students to include in their writing.

Using Pictures to Inspire Rich Description

My River by Shari Halpern introduces the concept of ecology to young readers through a simple text and colorful illustrations. The book begins with the question, "Whose river is this?" On each successive spread, the reader is introduced to a different living thing that is part of a river environment. The book concludes with the message that the river belongs to everyone, and it includes an illustrated glossary of the plants and animals that we meet throughout the book. Young readers are usually surprised that so many different forms of life can be found in a river. It is an excellent text for visualizing details and can move right into the writer's workshop.

In one first-grade class, teacher Cindy Algier used *My River* to help her students add details to their writing through rich description. Cindy began by displaying a picture of a river scene. She asked the students to describe what they saw, encouraging them to expand their thinking and add as many details as possible.

As the students engaged in this rich oral discussion, Cindy recorded their ideas on the board. The next step was to return to *My River*, again having the students describe the animals and plants they saw. The additional ideas were added to the list of words and phrases on the board. Students were then given the opportunity to browse through books about rivers. *Where the River Begins* by Thomas Locker, *A River Ran Wild* by Lynne Cherry, and *River of Life* by Debbie S. Miller are just a few books about rivers that offer rich details in their illustrations. The students then had the opportunity to draw as detailed a picture as they could of a river scene. While the students worked, they listened to a recording of river sounds. By this time, as you might imagine, they were quite involved in the project.

After admiring all of their finished works of art, it was time to write. Cindy asked the students to write a description of their river picture using as many rich details about what they saw (and possibly heard!) as possible. (See Figure 3.1 for a student example.) After the writing was shared, the students compared the importance of details in drawings to details in writing. They were

FIGURE 3.1
Michael's rich
description

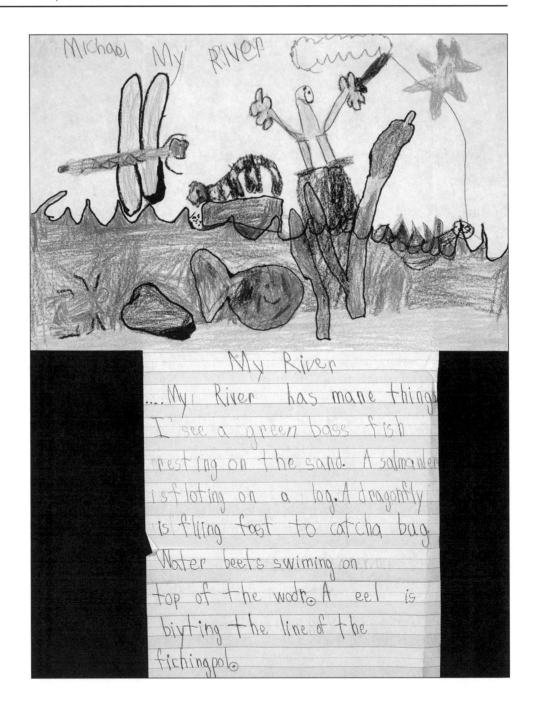

beginning to understand that rich descriptions in their writing adds the content
necessary to help the reader better visualize and comprehend.

Walking Readers Through Rich Description

In Steve Grant and Kate Tiedeken's fourth-grade classes, Lynne introduced writing vivid descriptions through *The Goodbye Walk* by Joanne Ryder. After reading the book aloud, Lynne asked the students to think of places where they

might have taken a "goodbye walk." Together with the classroom teachers, Lynne wrote a list of places they could potentially write about on the board. The students shared their own lists in small groups and then chose the one walk they wanted to write about to share with the whole group. Many children wrote about a favorite vacation spot, such as the mountains, the seashore, or Disney World, or leaving the old neighborhood on moving day.

Lynne suggested that students take a sheet of paper and divide it into six boxes. She asked them to make quick pencil sketches of the landmarks, secret or special places, and other objects, animals, or people that they might include in this piece. Not every child made six sketches. The idea of sketching was to get them to "see" the walk in their head.

The next day, Lynne reread the book and used a visualizer or document imager so the students could see the illustrations clearly. As she read, she stopped and asked students to give a name or heading to each part of the walk. The students came up with these sections: what it means to take a goodbye walk (define it as your introduction), landmarks, your secret or special place, what you notice for the first time, what or who you see today on your walk, where you pause to linger, and your summary or conclusion for this piece. These headings were written on chart paper so the students could refer to them as they wrote their own pieces.

Students chose to build content around the big ideas that fit their piece. Again, they did not have to use all of the ideas listed on the chart paper—they could choose. Lynne asked them to notice how Joanne Ryder told about the goodbye walk in the second person—using words like *you* and *your*. She asked the students to turn and talk about why the author did this. The students agreed that it helped the readers be there in the walk—like your readers went along with you. Although how a writer narrates a piece (first, second, or third person) is part of style (and is one of Joanne Ryder's fingerprints), it was important for the students to talk about it before they started drafting. Students talked about how they could develop content with rich description by appealing to the senses before they began to draft. Notice how Alyssa appeals to the senses and uses specificity to offer her descriptions:

> You remember when you were jumping up and down and yelling while the lifeguards just biked right by you.
>
> But today, this street is quiet and peaceful. Nothing runs by you, but the salty sea air which pulls you to the beach. No children laughing, just you and the cool fall breeze pushing summer's warm air and sunny skies away.
>
> As you walk home the small bush, short and plump, calls to you. You crouch down behind it and find a small doll made out of muddy sand with a leaf for a dress. You also find a teepee you had made out of three twigs and tied together with a piece of grass. You remember when you and your friend used to play with them all the time. You lightly put the doll down and leave.

Kendra's description appeals to the senses of taste, smell, and sound and adds emotional appeal as well:

> On a good-bye walk you are very busy watching everything around you. Now you stop to take in the sweet scent of the blackberry bushes beginning to ripen. You pick them one by one to taste their naturally sweetened seeds. You plop a giant berry into your mouth and press it under your tongue and allow the juice to slowly trickle down your throat.
>
> Today a branch hangs low in your path. You know this wonderful place so well that you can just make a simple turn and hear the caw-caw-caw of a crow. It's growing cold outside, and you're as jittery as the branches in the breeze.

Using Numbers and Comparisons in Descriptions

Descriptions that include factual information in the form of numbers or statistics can also help the reader to visualize. In Ben Hillman's *How Big Is It? A Big Book All About Bigness*, we find numbers to describe many of the objects included in the book. After all, it is a book about bigness, and what better way to describe size than to use numbers that measure size. Listen to Hillman's description of the Hindenburg:

> *Imagine an ocean liner floating through the air. That was the size of the German airship* Hindenburg—*the biggest thing that ever took to the skies. At 804 feet (245m), it was more than three times longer than a Boeing 747 and thirty-eight times longer than the Wright Brothers' first airplane.*

In *Soccer Counts!*, Barbieri McGrath and Alderman use numbers to help us visualize the goal:

> *The goal is eight feet high—about as high as a garage door. Netting at the back stops the ball when a team scores.*

Tim Knight describes the world's largest flower in *Fantastic Feeders*:

> *When rafflesia is ready to flower, lumps appear on the roots of the vine. These lumps are rafflesia flower buds, which are growing under the surface. When they finally burst out, each flower has five petals, the size of dinner plates. When fully open, the flowers are more than 3 feet (1 meter) across. The flower weighs up to 24 pounds (11 kilograms).*

Notice how in all of these examples the authors compare something we may not know to something we do know as a further aid to understanding through visualization.

Barbara Brenner also uses comparison in *Thinking About Ants*, although her description doesn't use specific number words:

> *First of all, think small, because the largest ant in the world is only about the size of a person's thumb. And some ants are small enough to hide inside an apple seed. So think tiny.*

Most of us will never have the opportunity to travel to Borneo to see the world's largest flower firsthand; however, children can wrap their minds around the concept of a flower with petals the size of plates. Here's a strategy that kids can easily try out. When describing something new, have them try to think of something familiar to their readers that is the same size, shape, or color. They could also offer a simple comparison, as Hillman did in *How Big Is It?* when he compared one transport of flight to another.

Victoria, a first grader, tried this strategy in her report about penguins when she helped her readers visualize the speed of the penguin walk:

> I learned about penguins in 1st grade. They toboggan to get around. They eat krill. They have a brood pouch to keep their eggs warm. They waddle as fast as people walk. They are very good swimmers. I love learning about penguins.

In searching through many of our books, we discovered that the compare/contrast organizational structure is a common strategy used by many authors to help build content. In *All About Frogs*, Jim Arnosky helps the reader understand the difference between frogs and toads by describing what makes them distinct. He uses the running text and features of nonfiction such as silhouettes, labels, and drawings to compare their size, shape, and jumps. It's important to note that Arnosky chose to compare frogs and toads in a book all about frogs because it is a common question readers have. So the savvy writer builds content by anticipating questions and answering them.

Notice how Seymour Simon does the same thing in *Spiders*:

> *Here's how to tell spiders apart from insects. All spiders have two body parts and eight legs. All insects have three body parts, six legs, and antennae. Some insects have wings. No spiders have wings or antennae . . . What do spiders and insects have in common? They have a hard outer skeleton and legs with jointed sections.*

Creating Content with Examples and Explanations

Young writers often engage in list writing. That is, they move from one idea to the next without offering any details to develop their thinking. Does this sample sound familiar?

Whales

Whales are the largest animals living in the sea. Did you know they are mammals? Whales are intelligent creatures. They are built for swimming. There are two main types of whales. I like learning about whales.

Most of the ideas in this piece could be developed further through examples and explanations. That's what authors do all the time. In nonfiction writing, it is important to explain processes, key vocabulary, and sometimes purposes. In *The Honey Makers*, Gail Gibbons explains the process of pollination:

> *At each flower the forager bee collects nectar with her* proboscis. *She stores the nectar in a special part of her body called the* crop, *or honey stomach . . . As she goes from flower to flower she comes in contact with a yellow powder called* pollen *. . . As the forager bee collects nectar, she carries pollen from flower to flower. This is part of a process called* pollination.

Jean Craighead George explains the process of cat communication in *How to Talk to Your Cat*. In this book, we learn how cats use their whiskers, tails, face, and legs in the process of communicating with humans. Keltie Thomas, in *How Baseball Works*, explains the process of pitching by breaking it down into steps. This author adds more content and explanation through the use of illustrations.

In *Colonial Times from A to Z*, Bobbie Kalman uses boldface print to highlight key vocabulary and offers an explanation in a simple sentence.

> *Q is for **quoits**. Quoits is a popular game among colonial children. It was played by tossing a rope or metal ring onto a stake called a **hob**.*

In another book, *Dolphins and Other Marine Mammals* by Kelley MacAulay and Bobbie Kalman, the authors use a comma after the boldface word to offer a definition within the same sentence:

> *Seals also stay on land while they **molt**, or shed their fur.*

In *Lacrosse in Action*, author John Crossingham also uses a comma to help define words:

*Begin by **cocking**, or bending back, your wrists. Even if your oppo-*
*nent gets to it first, you can check his or her stick and **dislodge**, or*
knock out, the ball.

Commas of apposition are often used by nonfiction authors to offer a definition or explanation within the running text so that the reader does not have
to stop to look up the word in a dictionary or the book's glossary. Students can
be encouraged to use this technique to offer an explanation through a simple
definition or sentence when they are doing research or writing process pieces.
In his piece, "How to Do a Freestyle Sprint," fourth grader Jeff offers this
explanation:

> Another thing you might want to consider is swim gear. One of those things
> would (of course) be a swimsuit. You could wear a **speedo** suit (which is
> what I prefer), or you could wear just a regular swimsuit. If you want to
> know the difference between the two, a **speedo** suit is snug and does not
> let any water in.

In nonfiction writing, authors often build content by explaining the purpose of a job, a piece of equipment, or a body part. In *Sky Boys: How They
Built the Empire State Building*, Deborah Hopkinson explains the job of each
member of the riveting gang:

> ***First man**, the Heater, gets the rivet red-hot in the forge and tosses it*
> *up quick. (A throw of fifty feet is nothing to him.)*

In *Burp! The Most Interesting Book You'll Ever Read About Eating*,
Diane Swanson discusses the job of your teeth and your saliva to describe how
digestion begins.

> *Saliva makes it easier for your tongue to move food around as you*
> *chew. It also contains enzymes that start the chemical breakdown of*
> *your meal by working on carbohydrates.*

Sometimes authors strengthen their explanations and build more content by
offering examples. Examples often help to define a concept or make it more
explicit to the reader. *Harvest Year* by Cris Peterson devotes a two-page spread to
each month and, through rich examples, gives readers a sample of the variety of
crops harvested in the United States. Consider the text for the month of August:

> *Sweet corn, eaten fresh from the cob, is ripe in August. Ohio veg-*
> *etable growers begin snapping the ears from the stalks in early morn-*
> *ing so they have fresh corn to sell each day. Blueberries from Maine*
> *are hand-picked with special rakes and packed in crates, but they're*

*especially delicious eaten right from the berry patch. In Iowa, oats
are harvested with a combine and trucked to grain elevators.*

The explanation for each month offers three examples. Clearly this author
understands the power of three to add the right amount of rhythm and detail
to the writing.

In *Stars Beneath Your Bed: The Surprising Story of Dust*, author April
Pulley Sayre makes a statement about dust on each two-page spread, then follows it with a list of examples to deepen understanding.

*Dust can be bits of unexpected things—A crumbling leaf, the eyelash
of a seal, the scales of a snake, the smoke of burning toast, ash from
an erupting volcano.*

It is interesting to note that the examples in the book lead to a final explanation of the role dust plays in creating the colors in sunrises and sunsets.

Tim Knight, in *Fantastic Feeders*, gives examples to show how animals
feed on nectar:

*Many animals have special body parts to help them get nectar. The
South American sword-billed hummingbird has a beak longer than
its own body. The beak lets it reach deep inside flowers. The
Australian honey possum has become so used to sipping nectar that
its teeth have almost disappeared.*

After students are given the opportunity to study the ways authors might
use these strategies to build content, they are better able to apply the strategies
to their own writing. In the example about whales, which we gave previously,
the student has the potential of developing five big ideas: size, type, characteristics of mammals (compared to fish), intelligence, and adaptations. For the
younger writer, you might ask him or her to choose the best idea or best two
ideas. Students can go back to the books they are using for research or the notes
they have taken to see which ideas they have the most information about. These
are probably the ones they should choose, unless there is time for more reading
and research. Older students could take each idea and develop a paragraph
around each one using examples, explanations, or key vocabulary definitions.
(See Your Turn Lesson 4 at the end of this chapter.)

Sometimes students have built some content, but it is still not specific
enough. The teacher can offer an effective revision lesson by asking students to
return to their writing to examine each paragraph for places where they might
be able to add an example. Using small colored dots, students could take a red
dot and place it at the end of a sentence where an example could be added. If
an example does not automatically come to mind, they can refer to their notes
and books. This process could be repeated using different colored dots to add

a definition for a key vocabulary word or an explanation if appropriate. Each time a student goes back to revise, he or she has a clear purpose to reread his or her writing.

Quotes and Dialogue Create Interesting Content

Writing about historical events or figures lends itself to the use of quotes or dialogue as another way to build interesting content. Writers use a splash of dialogue or intersperse quotes to liven up the writing as well as to offer a firsthand perspective. Peter Golenbock describes through dialogue a famous meeting between Branch Rickey and Jackie Robinson in *Teammates*:

> *Jackie rode the train to Brooklyn to meet Mr. Rickey. When Mr. Rickey told him, "I want a man with the courage not to fight back," Jackie Robinson replied, "If you take this gamble, I will do my best to perform." They shook hands.*

In describing another important moment in sports, David Adler uses dialogue in *Joe Louis: America's Fighter* to record the boxer's feelings after his famous fight against Max Schmeling. He adds further detail to emphasize the importance of this event at this moment in time (June 22, 1938) with the words of a newspaper reporter:

> *In just 124 seconds, Joe Louis had beaten Max Schmeling. "Now I feel like a champion," Joe Louis said after the fight . . .*
> *"The decline of Nazi prestige," one reporter wrote, "began with a left hook.*

Sometimes authors turn to a person's own journal, letters, or diary for snippets of dialogue. Don Brown does this in *Dolley Madison Saves George Washington*. Using Dolley's own words gives authenticity to the writing—it helps the reader view the author as a believable expert. In this excerpt, Britain had invaded America and many people had fled Washington; Dolley had remained.

> *August 22 found her with spyglass in hand at the top window of the President's Mansion, "watching with unwearied anxiety" for the president, her dear husband, in the field with his army.*
> *She later wrote that she saw only "groups of military wandering in all directions, as if there was lack of arms, or the spirit to fight!"*

Don Brown also uses authentic dialogue in *Uncommon Traveler: Mary Kingsley in Africa*.

In the book *John Muir: America's Naturalist* by Thomas Locker, a quote from Muir's nature journals is included on every page that has running text. Additionally, Locker includes a page at the very end of the book that is filled with selections of Muir's entries.

Throughout the book *Light Shining Through the Mist: A Photobiography of Dian Fossey*, we are inspired by the excerpts from her own journals and letters that author Tom Matthews includes on almost every page of text. These quotes add emotional appeal to the reader, who shares Fossey's roller coaster of emotions from joy to despair. The quotes bring her story to life and help the reader know who Dian Fossey was and why she should be remembered. They are an important part of the content of the book.

This use of authentic text in the form of letters and journal entries is a great opportunity to introduce the use of primary documents (diaries, newspaper accounts, letters, interviews, etc.) as sources of information that can help a writer obtain dialogue for building content. (For a more detailed explanation of how to use primary source documents, see Chapter 6.) It may be a good thing to caution your students that adding made-up dialogue, a technique used by writers of historical fiction, may change a piece from nonfiction status to fiction status.

Anecdotes Are a Breath of Fresh Air

Lucy Calkins (1991) shares an anecdote about Jane Yolen to illustrate how important a writer's notebook can be to a writer:

> *Jane Yolen pulled off the highway in a snowstorm to scrawl down a phrase she'd heard on the car radio. The announcer, trying to sell a fence, described it as "horse-high, hog-tight, and bull-strong." Yolen thought the words were too good to lose. Months later, they led to the first paragraph of* The Inway Investigators. *(45)*

An anecdote is a tiny story that is often used to illustrate a point about someone. It can be very funny or simply intriguing. Anecdotes are always based on real life. They do not have to be about famous people, but they often are. An anecdote is powerful when it is used to build content about a person by revealing some insight to that person's character.

We all know the story about George Washington and the cherry tree, used to highlight George's honesty. In the author's note for *George Washington: A Picture Book Biography* by James Cross Giblin, we learn that the popular cherry tree story was most likely fabricated. It was common practice in the 1800s for writers to make up anecdotes about famous people to illustrate their point. The fact that the cherry tree story has survived for so long just goes to show how powerful anecdotes can be.

A better anecdote to demonstrate George Washington's integrity and sense of fairness is told by author Frank Murphy in *George Washington and the General's Dog.* The anecdote involves an incident in which a dog belonging to the British General Howe followed soldiers back to Washington's camp. Instead of keeping the dog, Washington called a truce and returned Howe's dog to him with a note. News of this exchange even reached England, influencing many people's opinions about Washington. Mr. Murphy's book is based on extensive research with primary documents. In fact, a photograph of the actual note is included in the back of the book.

Why use anecdotes? Authors use anecdotes for many reasons. Besides illustrating a point or illuminating a character trait, an anecdote provides a breath of fresh air. Nonfiction text can become heavy and complex. We know that we slow down as readers when we read informational writing. The anecdote provides a break for the reader. Sometimes the writer will even change from third person writing to first person writing, as is the case in *Avalanche* by Stephen Kramer. Notice the shift in the following text:

> *People who have been swept away by an avalanche usually have clear memories of the moving snow's power. Paul Baugher was skiing in Washington state when he was caught in a snowslide. The snow carried him down through trees and over a cliff . . .*
>
> *I tried to ski to safety, but the snow caught me. It buried me and swept me downhill. I felt like I was shooting along in a fast-moving stream. I curled my body into a tight ball. The snow bounced me off a tree, and I lost my skis and poles. The next thing I remember was a feeling of floating as the snow carried me over the cliff.*

What reader would not want to read on? The firsthand account provides an anecdote that will help students visualize what it would be like to be carried off in an avalanche. The use of this anecdote provides a breath of fresh air in the context of a serious topic. Kramer also uses this strategy in *Lightning.* He includes the firsthand account of a lightning strike by photographer Warren Faidley, who snapped the pictures for the book:

> *The strike was so close and so bright I was blinded for a moment. The thunder was immediate—like a million drums going off in my head. I lost my balance . . . When I got to my feet and closed my eyes, I could still see the outline of the lightning bolt.*

Sometimes an anecdote appears in a sidebar, as in *The Brooklyn Bridge* by Elizabeth Mann. After talking about all the excitement that the construction project created, describing it as "the biggest show in town," the author highlights this point with an anecdote about master mechanic Frank Farrington, who made the first trip across the Brooklyn Bridge on a tiny swing attached to the first wire, a thick wire rope that was strung between the towers, while thousands of people cheered below. The use of the sidebar is a feature of nonfiction that offers our students who are more graphically oriented an option for displaying their research in an attractive format. You can find the same anecdote in the running text of Lynn Curlee's book *Brooklyn Bridge*.

David Adler's *Joe Louis: America's Fighter* includes an interesting anecdote that uses a quote from Joe Louis. Adler used many sources, including two Louis autobiographies and several other biographies about the prize fighter. The anecdote Adler chose to include was a milestone moment for the young Joe Louis:

> *One day, when Joseph was seventeen, his friend Thurston McKinney took him to Brewster's East Side Gymnasium, to see some real boxers.*
> *At Brewster's, Joseph fought Thurston and knocked him down. "It was like power pumping through me," Joseph said. He knew then that he wanted to be a boxer.*

A book for elementary school students that relies on the vehicle of anecdote is *My Brother Martin* by Christine King Farris. In this unique biography about Dr. Martin Luther King Jr., Farris reveals a side of Martin that most people don't know. In the following anecdote, Farris reveals the mischievous side of her brother:

> *Our best prank involved a furpiece that belonged to our grandmother. It looked almost alive, with its tiny feet and little head and gleaming glass eyes. So, every once in a while, in the waning light of evening, we'd tie that fur piece to a stick, and hiding behind the hedge in front of the house, we would dangle it in front of unsuspecting passersby. Boy! You could hear the screams of fright all across the neighborhood!*

These anecdotes make the author's family members very real to her young readers. They provide a good model for students who are writing informational narratives about their own family members.

In several fifth-grade classrooms, Lynne was helping the students write hero essays as gifts for family members and friends. She asked the students to think about the heroes in their lives—those people they were close to that had a special place in their hearts. After sharing several mentor texts containing anecdotes, such as *Mother to Tigers* by George Ella Lyon, *Talkin' About Bessie* by Nikki Grimes, and *My Brother Martin*, Lynne asked the students to consider what each story revealed about that person's character. She then shared a list of character traits about her grandmother from her writer's notebook. As she shared each trait, she tried to recall an anecdote to illustrate that particular quality. Sometimes she could and sometimes she couldn't. She settled on honest and fair and wrote the following anecdote on the board:

Grandma always tells me that "honesty is the best policy." She also tells us that it is important to try to be fair. Last summer, the boy who lived next door hit a softball through her kitchen window. When he came over to tell her, she thanked him for being honest. She made him pay for her window by doing odd jobs for her such as mowing the lawn and taking out the trash, but she gave him lemonade and homemade chocolate chip cookies (his favorite kind) while he worked. By the end of the summer, they were good friends. I could tell so many stories like this. All of them show that because Grandma is honest and fair, people like and respect her. Isn't that what everybody wants?

Lynne then encouraged her students to take a favorite person and make a list of character traits. After making the list, students took the time to consider each characteristic and think of an anecdote to illustrate one or several of them. Students orally shared their anecdote in small groups before writing them. Lynne encouraged students who were stuck to first think of a funny or powerful story about their person and then consider the character trait that the anecdote illuminated. While clipboard cruising, and later in one-on-one conferences, the fifth-grade teachers and Lynne noticed that some students struggled to keep the anecdote centered on their favorite person instead of on themselves. Some anecdotes ended up sounding like they were focused on the student author rather than the hero he or she was writing about. With some gentle nudging, students were able to revise their anecdotes to highlight a character trait about the close family member or friend instead. Malcolm wrote the following about his dad:

It was frustrating to play basketball. The other guys had great moves. They seemed to be natural at it. I was sort of embarrassed every time it was my turn to play. I kept fumbling the ball, and sometimes it even got away from me. Then one day last fall my dad took me to the park, and we practiced. I did not know how to dribble because I would always dribble with my palm. So my dad told me to "dribble with my fingertips."

He showed me how to do it, bouncing the ball up and down the blacktop with me running beside him. Then we changed places and he trotted beside me, chanting, "Just with your fingertips, Malcolm." When I did all that, I was amazed that I could play that well. I had confidence and felt much more relaxed on the court. My dad's a great teacher.

Later, when students created hero essays, they used an anecdote to build a paragraph in the body of their piece. Students noticed that anecdotes seemed to add a bit of pizzazz to their writing and helped them build content in a new way.

Hero
by Roy B., Grade 5

What is a hero? The answer is obvious for me. A hero is someone like my dad who is kind and hardworking and helps me with a lot of things. My dad will always be there for me.

My dad is my role model. I love and respect him. I want to be just like him when I grow up. One day I was at the park riding my bike. When I came around a curb . . . BAM! I flew right off my bike onto the concrete. I had blood all over my face and thought I had broken my face. All of a sudden, there came my dad. He asked me if I was alright and I said yes. He helped me up and cleaned me up. I felt much better. That is one of the reasons my dad is my hero.

Another time I remember playing baseball. I hit the ball with the bat so hard, the bat came back at me and whacked me in the eye. I started screaming so loud the whole city of Hatboro heard me. Again, my dad came to my rescue. He took me inside and fixed me up in no time at all. I felt better just because he was there.

My third reason has to do with another accident. I was running through the house and didn't see my cat. I tripped over him and the cat bit my foot (With a name like Killer, you'd expect something like that!). I started screaming and my dad raced to the rescue. He took Killer into another room and came back. He asked me if I was okay and I said yes. He washed my foot and put a band-aid on the spot where teeth marks were showing. Of course I felt much better.

I know that some people have super heros and athletes as role models, but my dad is my hero. He will always be there for me. I wish everyone had a dad like mine.

Cartoon Drawings Help Readers Visualize Text

Barry Lane (2003) cautions us that numbers and statistics are often empty ways to build content unless they are accompanied by a picture. We believe that the content of a text can be greatly enhanced by the use of cartoon drawings to help readers anchor a key concept in their mind.

For students who love to draw, Mike Venezia's books can be studied as mentor texts. Venezia uses anecdotes extended by his cartoon drawings throughout his books. The text included in speech bubbles adds humor to the content built through anecdotes in the running text. In *Leonard Bernstein*, the author tells the story of Leonard's Aunt Clara, who asked to store her piano at the Bernstein house when she moved. "The moment Leonard saw the piano and played his first note, he found himself hooked on music forever." The drawing shows Leonard as a little boy curled up on the piano keyboard sound asleep grasping a piece of music. His parents and sister are in their pajamas observing him, and in a speech bubble his father says, "I know Lennie loves that piano, but this is ridiculous!" Students might like to use Venezia as a mentor and extend their content in an informational piece with comic strip drawings and speech bubbles when it is appropriate to add humor or a more light-hearted view of a person, event, or problem. Venezia has written over three hundred informational texts about famous artists, composers, and United States presidents. His style of embedding anecdotes with comic drawings is a great example of a unique way to build content for upper-elementary through secondary classrooms.

In Sheri Young's fifth-grade classroom, Lynne and Sheri offered Mike Venezia's books to students to help them add to the content of the books they were creating about an American president. Each student chose a president to research, and read widely about him. After sharing some of Venezia's drawings, Lynne modeled with her own example. The art teacher, Katrina Nuss, got the students started with a plan to draw their cartoons and create their captions or speech bubbles. The students understood that humor usually played a large part in Venezia's work. Lynne and Sheri told the students that this work would offer a break from reporting about a heavy topic, while also helping to anchor key ideas in their readers' mind. Nicole, Paige, and Channelle had fun creating their cartoons accompanied with speech bubbles and captions (see Figures 3.2, 3.3, and 3.4). Your Turn Lesson 3 at the end of this chapter offers additional suggestions for building content with comics.

FIGURE 3.2
Nicole builds content with cartoon drawings.

**FIGURES 3.3
AND 3.4**
Paige and Channelle
build content with
cartoon drawings.

Features Fit the Facts

No discussion of informational writing would be complete without including the features of nonfiction as a way for students to build content. Although there are many opportunities to investigate the use of access features such as a table of contents, index, or glossary with students, sometimes we miss opportunities to instruct our students in ways to build content through visual features. These include illustrations and/or photos with captions, diagrams with labels, time lines, calendars, charts, tables, and maps.

Captions

Captions are an excellent way to extend content by providing additional specific examples. Mike Venezia does this in many of his books. In *Faith Ringgold*, we learn from captions that this artist was influenced by live jazz performances that she felt were art. Accompanying photos give specific examples of two of the artists she was fortunate enough to see perform live—Duke Ellington and Ella Fitzgerald.

Sometimes a caption provides a more detailed description including a wow fact. For example, in *Harvest Year* by Cris Peterson, the page dedicated to the July harvest talks about watermelons from Mississippi. The caption provides this wow fact: "These melons usually weigh between five and forty pounds, but can be as big as one hundred pounds." Other captions in this book help the reader to identify the objects in the photographs, such as combines, grain elevators, and conveyor belts.

Sometimes captions add emotional appeal through detailed descriptions. In the following caption that accompanies both a photo and an illustration from *The Brooklyn Bridge*, Elizabeth Mann helps us feel what it would be like to "walk across the footbridge."

> *A wooden footbridge was built for the workers to use. Word of the fantastic views from it spread quickly, and tourists came from all over to walk out on it. Standing hundreds of feet above a deep, fast moving river on a swaying, narrow, footbridge was a thrilling adventure for some. For others, it was a little too exciting. People panicked, fainted, and had to be carried back down. The footbridge had to be closed to the public.*

Diagrams and Labels

Many authors help their readers better visualize their topic through the use of diagrams and labels. For some authors, such as Gail Gibbons, the use of diagrams and labels are a fingerprint (a characteristic of the author's craft). In *The Honey Makers*, Gibbons provides diagrams for the parts of a honeybee, the

FIGURE 3.5
Andrew's diagram with labels

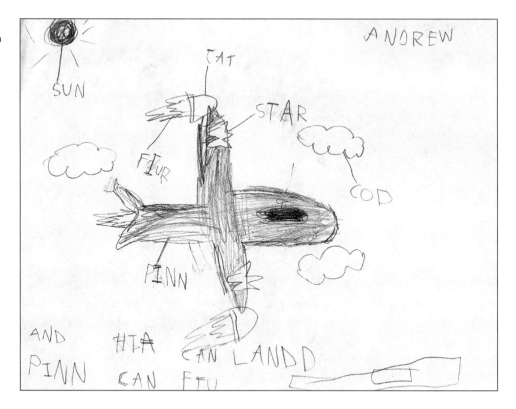

parts of a hive, the stages of the life cycle, the inside of a flower, a modern bee hive, and the special equipment used by a beekeeper.

Young writers can be easily nudged into using diagrams and labels in their work. They love to draw, and if you point out how authors use drawings and labels, you will soon find that your students will imitate this technique in a very natural way. In one kindergarten class, Rose was working with some students on responding to the nonfiction books they were reading. After exploring the books, she asked them to record the most important information they learned. Of course the students all included a drawing with their work, but Rose noticed that Andrew also labeled his drawing (see Figure 3.5). She pointed this out as something many authors of nonfiction do to help their readers deepen understanding, and she found some examples in books in the classroom for the students to explore. Soon all of the young readers and writers in the group were labeling their drawings, adding content to the ideas they recorded.

Time Lines

Time lines help readers understand things such as growth processes, the importance of seasons and weather to particular events, and the place of historical figures and events within a particular era. In *How Baseball Works*, Keltie Thomas creates a time line on a two-page spread that explains how the materials that baseballs are made of has changed over time. Gail Gibbons uses a time line to highlight inventions and people important to astronomy in *Stargazers*. Pamela Duncan Edwards and illustrator Henry Cole help us see the events leading up to the Revolutionary War and the Treaty of Paris with a time line included in the final pages of *The Boston Tea Party*. They use this technique again on the front and back end pages of *The Wright Brothers* to give a history of key events in the lives of these men, their accomplishments as pioneers of flight, and several historical events concerning flight after their death. In *Sky Boys* by Deborah Hopkinson, illustrator James E. Ransome uses a two-page spread to give a time line of the construction of the Empire State Building from June to November of 1930.

Your Turn Lessons 1 and 2 at the end of this chapter offer suggestions to teachers for how they can help students add content to their writing by including diagrams with labels and time lines.

Bringing Nonfiction to Life

The use of mentor texts can help students understand how to build content through rich descriptions of people, places, and events. Students can begin to see that authors of nonfiction often use examples and explanations to develop their big ideas. Additionally, key vocabulary words are explained and/or defined in an effort to be considerate to readers. Nonfiction comes to life with photos and illustrations enhanced with information only provided in captions—information that is not found in the running text.

With enthusiasm for the graphic novel growing by leaps and bounds, the work of author/illustrators such as Mike Venezia can help students find renewed interest in writing research by allowing them to include comic-strip type drawings with speech bubbles to add humor or another dimension of thinking to their writing. Visual and access features of nonfiction can also help students pay attention to the overall layout of text, adding a new dimension to the planning and development of content. Hopefully, by understanding how content is developed in nonfiction writing, students will have more success with writing in this genre as well as with reading it!

An Author's Voice:
A Good Storyteller Doesn't Have to Be a Good Writer, but a Good Writer Must Be a Good Storyteller

Jane Kirkland
Author of *Take a Backyard Bird Walk* and *Take a Beach Walk*

At first glance, writing nonfiction might seem straightforward and easy. It appears to be a two-step process: research and reporting. But nonfiction involves three processes: First you research, then you report, then you add your own personal style. It is style that brings facts to life and makes a topic interesting and exciting. What is style? It is the way in which a writer tells a story. Over time, writers develop their own unique styles and become good storytellers. A good storyteller doesn't have to be a good writer, but a good writer must be a good storyteller. Here are some tips to help you become a good storyteller of nonfiction:

Search for interesting content. Include a few little-known, unusual, revealing, or fun facts about your topic that you discover in your research.

Make content interesting. Some "boring" facts can be made more interesting if you use comparisons. For example, in a report on Monarch butterflies, you might include a photo or illustration of a Monarch and one of a Viceroy (which is a different species that mimics the Monarch). Or you might compare a Monarch's orange wings with black stripes to a Bengal Tiger's hide. Humor can help to make content more interesting. You could say that Monarchs have scales like fish, but they don't (thank goodness) smell like fish.

Tell a story. Write in a narrative voice. This is your chance to develop your own style. Style is often so overlooked in nonfiction that essays, reports, and school papers are simply lists of facts in sentence form that have no life and are, well, b-o-o-o-o-ring!

Make it personal. When you can, write from experience. If your topic is the White House and you've visited the White House, write about that experience and how you felt when you were there. If you think that the White House is a really cool place, tell the readers so, and tell them why.

Involve your reader. Ask questions and suggest actions. For example, in your White House report, ask if the readers have ever been to the White House. Or suggest that they visit the White House. You might suggest a good book about the White House or a website where there are more photographs of the White House. These things help to place your readers in your story and make your writing more interesting, exciting, and personal!

Read it aloud. Because you are the writer, your mind's voice will read your words back to you with the emphasis and inflection you intended. But when someone else reads your work, they might not interpret your work in the same way. When you are finished writing, ask a family member, friend, or teacher to read your work aloud to you. If they have difficulty with some sentences or words, rewrite those sentences or use other words. If they have a lot of questions during or after reading aloud, decide whether those questions should have been answered in your text and, if so, edit your work. I learn the most about my writing and make the best improvements when I hear how other people interpret my words when they read them aloud.

Incorporating these practices into your nonfiction writing will help improve your writing. Remember, a good storyteller doesn't have to be a good writer, but a good writer *must* be a good storyteller.

Your Turn Lesson 1

Building Content with Diagrams and Labels

Visual information, in the form of boldface words and headings, diagrams, labels, captions, illustrations, charts, and photographs, is an important part of many nonfiction texts. In her book *Make It Real: Strategies for Success with Informational Texts* (2002), Linda Hoyt describes investigations as a powerful tool for "synthesizing learning and teaching the craft of informational writing" (289). And investigations is a brief exploration into a topic displayed visually in a double-page layout. They are appropriate for any grade level but will vary in complexity. This Your Turn lesson was inspired by Hoyt's work. While it describes how to help students build content with diagrams and labels, it can be used to teach any form of visual information.

Hook: Return to some nonfiction books the students are familiar with and discuss with them how the author used diagrams and labels to build content by further explaining the information in the text. Good choices would be books by Gail Gibbons, such as *The Honey Makers* or *Stargazers*, *Surprising Sharks* by Nicola Davies, *All About Frogs* by Jim Arnosky, or *From Seed to Sunflower* by Dr. Gerald Legg.

Purpose: *In nonfiction writing, sometimes authors include special features such as diagrams and labels to help them explain their topic and build content. Today I'll show you how you can do this in your writing, too.*

Brainstorm: Together with the students, create a list of topics that they know a lot about (topics that they might consider themselves to be mini-experts on). This is known as an expert list or authority list and is a wonderful tool to have posted in the classroom for writing ideas. Make sure to include your own topics. Students can also keep their own expert list in their writer's notebooks. Entries might include such things as football, karate, babysitting, or horses, to name a few.

Model: Choose one of your expert topics and think out loud about how a diagram with labels might help explain something about it. For example, Rose has played the violin since she was a little girl, so her thinking might sound like this:

> *Since I know a lot about the violin, I think I'll explain something about that to you today. I could draw a diagram of a violin and label the parts, or I could use a diagram to show how to hold the violin, or I could draw and label the parts of the bow. I think the first thing someone would want to know are the parts of the violin, so I'll start with that.*

Divide a sheet of paper in half and demonstrate to the students how you would write the explanation or description on one side and sketch a diagram with labels on the other side as an extension of that thinking. Rose's example would look something like Figure 3.6.

Shared/Guided Writing: You could try this out with your class in a couple of ways. One possibility is to pick a topic that the class has shared knowledge about—the school, the classroom, a class pet, or maybe a topic you are studying in science or social studies. Together you can cre-

FIGURE 3.6
Rose's diagram of a violin with description

A violin has many parts. The main part is the belly that is most often made of spruce. On the belly are the f-holes, important to the sound made by the violin. The tailpiece, chin rest, and fingerboard are also found on the belly. These parts are usually made out of ebony. At the top of the violin are the scroll and the peg box. The pegs that are used to tune the four strings are housed in the peg box. The strings are attached at the tailpiece and are supported by the bridge.

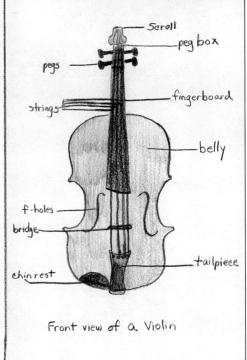

Front view of a Violin

ate a mini-report that would include a diagram with labels. Alternatively, you could read a short text from a nonfiction book that describes something without an added diagram. Then use the information from the book to create a report with a diagram. Most books by Seymour Simon are good choices for this activity.

Independent Writing: Individual students can return to their expert lists to do a mini-report explaining or describing some aspect of their topic; then they can add a diagram with labels. They might also choose to do some further exploration on a topic of interest and report on that. Display these in the classroom to give all students the opportunity to see the work of their classmates and have their own work honored. As students learn about building content through other forms of visual information, they can eventually include a combination of visual features in their mini-reports.

Reflection: Ask students to reflect on how this strategy worked.

How did the use of the diagrams and labels contribute to your report?

Were you able to build more content through the use of the diagram? If so, how?

What other forms of visual information would add to your report?

When might you use this technique again?

Your Turn Lesson 2

Creating a Time Line

There are many different ways that authors use time lines to organize their thinking and explain and extend content. Time lines can take on many different forms. They can be linear—a simple listing with dates and a concise statement or phrase, as Tom Matthews did in *Light Shining Through the Mist: A Photobiography of Dian Fossey*. Time lines can also proceed in the same linear fashion but use drawings or photos to accompany a date or a label. An example of this type of time line can be found in *Capital! Washington D.C. from A to Z* by Laura Krauss Melmed.

Time lines can be organized around years, months, or even days—anything that is used to measure time. Sometimes time lines are used to place an important person or event in the context of what is happening in the world at that time. The end pages of *The Boston Tea Party* by Pamela Duncan Edwards places that historical event in a time line to show the events leading up to the Revolutionary War.

Time lines can also be used to explain a process, such as how an animal or a plant becomes a fossil. Students enjoy being able to represent information visually.

Hook: Gather some books that have examples of time lines. In addition to those mentioned above, other good choices are *Vote!* by Eileen Christelow (the time line of voting rights extends her style of writing with speech bubbles and cartoon characters), *The Life and Times of the Honeybee* by Charles Micucci, *The Honey Makers* by Gail Gibbons, *Madam President: The Extraordinary, True (and Evolving) Story of Women in Politics* by Catherine Thimmesh, *Joe Louis: America's Fighter* by David Adler, *They Lived with the Dinosaurs* by Russell Freedman, and *From Seed to Sunflower* by Dr. Gerald Legg. Allow students to explore these books to discover the different looks and various purposes that time lines can have.

Purpose: *In nonfiction writing, authors sometimes include time lines to help them provide readers with a sense of order or chronology. Often this helps readers make sense out of events or processes. It can also help us as we write by highlighting for us those ideas that we want to develop in our running text. Today I will show you how you can use a time line in your writing.*

Brainstorm: Ask students to brainstorm key events in their lives and record them in their writer's notebooks. Have them write ideas as they occur to them, not necessarily in any particular order.

Model: On chart paper, quickly write key events from your own life in a random order. Read them aloud to the students. Make sure you have placed childhood events in various places in the list so that your students can see that an order is lacking. Think out loud as you organize your list by using a time line to make it more meaningful for you and a reader of your autobiography. One option could be placing positive events above the time line and negative events below the time line.

Shared/Guided Writing: Return to a picture book biography or a book that explains a process that your students are familiar with from a read-aloud, content area unit, literature circle, or guided reading group. Together, brainstorm key events and dates or time periods that may be included. Discuss possible time line formats—students may actually suggest the mentor text that might fit best as a model for the work you are doing. Ask students to evaluate the events or descriptions. Are they all needed? Which ones could be omitted? Which ones are still needed? Students can be placed into groups and assigned a description or event to record on a sentence strip. If the students are going to draw, they can use a square of construction paper. Triangles could also be cut out to flag the dates. When everyone is finished, assemble the time line as a class.

Independent Writing: Students can return to their brainstormed list of events to create their own time lines for an autobiographical sketch they may be working on at present or at some future time. If you are doing mini-research reports, encourage students to look for a place where they might include a time line. For a real-world event, such as hosting an Alex's Lemonade Stand at your school to benefit pediatric cancer research (see Chapter 6), students could create a time line of important things to do to get ready for the event or to keep people posted about what progress has been made. Older students can create a time line to serve as a checklist that will move them along to complete a long-range project and meet a deadline.

Reflection: After students have a chance to create their own time lines, gather them together to reflect on how the strategy worked. If possible, display their time lines in the classroom and encourage a critique.

How did you choose what information to include or not include on your time line?

How did it help your reader?

How did creating the time line help you as a writer?

Was making the time line worth the effort? Why?

What book have you read that could have included a time line to help you understand something?

When will you use the time line strategy again?

Your Turn Lesson 3

Using Comics to Add Humor and Build Content

Today students are becoming very interested in the graphic novel. We know that many of our students love to draw. Introducing comic strip drawings with speech bubbles may be a way to hook reluctant or struggling writers to continue to learn about a topic and build content while adding humor and having some fun, too.

Hook: Gather some books by author/illustrator Mike Venezia. There are over three hundred books to choose from in this series featuring famous artists, famous composers, and the U.S. presidents. Allow students to examine the pages for the cartoon drawings, encouraging them also to read the running text on the same page. Discuss how the cartoons extend the reader's thinking and help to build content in a humorous, playful way. Other options include *The Magic School Bus Inside a Beehive* by Joanna Cole (or any other book in this series), or *Vote!* by Eileen Christelow.

Purpose: *Students, today we took a look at the work of author/illustrator Mike Venezia and talked about how he used cartoons with speech bubbles to anchor big ideas in the reader's mind through humor. This might be something you would like to try in your own writing about yourself, your family members, your friends, or even a historical figure or event. Today I will show you how you can use an event in a person's life to add humorous content to a biographical piece. Then you can try it out in the biography you are writing.*

Brainstorm: If the class is familiar with a famous person because you've read about him or her in a read-aloud or studied him or her in a social studies or science unit, it would be good to continue to use that person. Have students brainstorm key events in that person's life and list them on chart paper or on the board. Brainstorm again for key character traits and list them as well. For this lesson, we are using Benjamin Franklin and Jean Fritz's book *What's the Big Idea, Ben Franklin?* Events could include his kite-flying experiment, his trip to England as ambassador, or his publication of witty sayings in *Poor Richard's Almanac.* Character traits might be determined, curious, inventive.

Model: Decide on an event and/or characteristic as the focus of a cartoon with speech bubbles to add humor and/or make a point. Begin by writing a paragraph to explain the historical context of the event. You could link it with a particular character trait as well. Here is an example for Ben Franklin's kite flying:

> Ben believed that lightning and electricity were the same thing. He wrote to European scientists to urge them to experiment with long iron rods fixed to high structures. Franklin's curiosity would not allow him to leave the experimentation up to others. He decided to test it out on a stormy night using a kite with a long wire extending to a key. Franklin felt the shock in his hand, thus proving that electricity and lightning were one and the same.

Sketch a cartoon showing Franklin in a workshop designing the kite with the long wire and key attached. Add a colonial person next to Franklin. In the speech bubble above Franklin, include this statement: "I find it shocking that scientists have not yet concluded that electricity and lightning are the same thing." Above the colonial figure, include this speech bubble statement: "Do you think you have found the key, Mr. Franklin?"

Shared/Guided Writing: Distribute one or two books about the person you are researching (in this case, Franklin) to groups of three or four students. Also, give them a copy of a book by Mike Venezia to provide a model of cartoon drawings and speech bubbles. You can pair writers and illustrators. It's good to have a classroom expert list to pull from. (Early on in the year, students brainstorm expert or authority lists, which are posted in a writing center to identify good spellers, handwriters, artists, or problem solvers, to name a few.) Circulate around the room to offer suggestions, resources, and encouragement. As students complete their cartoons, post them around the room. Direct students to carousel with their group, pausing for a few minutes in front of each cartoon to reflect on the humor and how it added to the content.

Independent Writing: Students can return to their own biography to list events and traits in their writer's notebooks. After choosing an event or trait, students can create their cartoons. The use of a response group or peer is helpful for students who may struggle either with drawing or the concept of a speech bubble to produce humorous dialogue. Remember, in real-world writing, authors have editors. Suggestions from peers or gentle nudges from the teacher may be all a student needs to take a risk with this new form.

Reflection: Ask students to reflect on how this strategy worked for them and when they might be able to use it.

Do you believe that cartoons can strengthen the content of your informational writing? How so?

What was the hardest part of this strategy?

What helped you to be successful?

In what other ways or in what other places can you see yourself using this technique?

Your Turn Lesson 4

Adding Details to Avoid Listing

Return to books that have been used in a content-area unit, such as science or social studies, or in a literature discovery circle (a literature circle with nonfiction books). If you are using an anthology, you can also use a nonfiction piece or the supplementary trade books that complement it. Explore your nonfiction guided reading selections as well. For this particular lesson, we are using books about whales, such as *The Best Book of Whales and Dolphins* by Christiane Gunzi, *Super Swimmers: Whales, Dolphins, and Other Mammals of the Sea* by Caroline Arnold, *Whales and Dolphins* by Susanna Davidson, and *Whales and Dolphins* by Anton Ericson.

Hook: It's good to start with what the students are already familiar with. Books with headings work well. Choose one and write or display the heading on the board. Ask students to think about what information they expect to learn from reading about this particular big idea. Display and read aloud the text the author created to go with the heading. Discuss with students whether the information is similar to what they expected to find. Call attention to how the author builds content through examples, explanations, or description. Note if the author explains a key vocabulary term within the running text.

Purpose: *When writing nonfiction, it's easy to go from one big idea to another without fully developing the content for each main idea you are presenting to the reader. We often refer to this type of writing as listing, or creating a piece with empty content. Today we will practice using our strategies for developing content through examples, explanations, and descriptions.*

Brainstorm: Ask the students to brainstorm the big ideas they would probably use in a report about whales (or the topic you have chosen). It works better if the students have read something about the topic to establish the appropriate background knowledge. For whales, some examples of big ideas might include whales are mammals, whales are intelligent, and whales are built for swimming.

Model: Take some of the key ideas the students have shared during brainstorming and write one paragraph that is simply composed of big ideas. Here is our example:

Whales

Whales are the largest animals living in the sea. Did you know they are mammals? Whales are intelligent creatures. They are built for swimming. There are two main types of whales. I like learning about whales.

Have the students count the big ideas in the paragraph. Take one of the big ideas and model how to build content with an explanation, description, and/or example.

Whales are built for swimming. Shaped like torpedoes, whales are stream-lined to cut through the water with ease. They have little or no hair on their skin just like competitive swimmers who shave the hair on their bodies to reduce the pull of the water. This pull against the swimmer's push is referred to as the **body's drag**. All whales use their tails to push them through the water, but unlike fish that move their flukes (the strong wings on their tails) from side to side, whales move them up and down. The **dorsal fin**, the stiff fin on their back, varies in size and is used to help whales stay on course while swimming.

Have the students find the places where you built content through an explanation of key vocabulary. Return to the model to find examples and descriptions. These sentences could be underlined in different colored makers to code each content-building strategy used.

Shared/Guided Writing: Choose another big idea and have the students work in partnerships or small groups to extend the content through explanations, examples, and descriptions. For the first time through, it works best if everyone is working to develop the same big idea. Make sure students read and discuss before writing to avoid plagiarism. After they create their paragraph, have them return to their books to check for accuracy. They should also discuss where they used examples, an explanation, a description, or a definition of a key vocabulary word.

When students are satisfied the big idea has been fully explained, the paragraphs can be written on chart paper and displayed in the room. Allow students to carousel around the room to read the paragraphs and to notice similarities and differences. At this point, there should be some reflection on what was noticed and how the information improved the original paragraph that was merely a list of ideas.

Independent Writing: Students can return to the brainstormed list of big ideas to work on extending the content of another idea on their own. Or, they can return to a report they might be working on and look for a place to develop a key concept or big idea through examples, explanations, and/or descriptions.

Reflection: Share these paragraphs or revisions in writing workshop over the course of the next several days. Ask students to think about the specific strategies they used and how it strengthened their piece of writing.

Introductions
and Conclusions

When I introduce leads to young writers, I ask them to think about

fishing, to imagine the writer as an angler and the reader as a fish.

Writers cast out their first line of words in hopes of hooking the reader

and reeling him into the text.

—Stephanie Harvey, *Nonfiction Matters: Reading, Writing, and Research in Grades 3–8*

When you purchase a beautiful print or an original drawing, it's not ready to hang on your wall until you choose the perfect matting and frame to bring out the best in the picture—the colors, lines, shapes, and textures. That's exactly what effective introductions and conclusions do for a nonfiction piece: They "frame" the information an author has chosen to present to readers, helping to highlight and reinforce key concepts and the author's purpose in an attractive, interesting, and often original way.

Discovering the Possibilities for Introductions

Does this opening sound familiar?

> Hi. I'm Susan and I'm here to tell you all about honeybees. Listen carefully and you will hear lots of interesting facts about honeybees.

Or how about this one?

> Hello. My name is Bobby Jones, and this is my report about Abraham Lincoln. He lived in a log cabin and liked to read. He grew up to be the sixteenth president of the United States. A lot of important things happened while he was president. Here are some of them.

You are only a few sentences in, and already you are dreading reading these reports. Students often struggle to introduce informational topics in ways that will grab their readers' attention and motivate them to read on. Because we live in an information age, we are constantly bombarded with nonfiction on the Internet, radio, TV, newspapers, and magazines as well as best-selling books. Readers are forced to make choices about what they can read. It often comes down to choosing between information that is written to hook the reader before he or she even finishes the first paragraph, or material that has no voice or craft.

Sometimes, part of the problem is author engagement. Student authors are not passionate about their topics, and therefore they struggle to find an appropriate place to begin. Often, the real problem is that young authors try to write a good beginning for an informational piece before studying it and becoming a mini-expert. It is through wide reading—one topic across many different books—that our students will find an appropriate and enticing way to introduce their topic. In nonfiction writing, the writer must do a good deal of thinking, reading, and planning before a lead paragraph is written. In fact, he or she may have many false starts, returning to rewrite the lead after completing the body of the text.

Learning from Authors

Let's return to Susan's report about honeybees. Perhaps she would have crafted a better introduction if she had first set aside time to do some wide reading, not only to gather information but also to explore the way other authors introduce their topics. In *Honeybees*, Deborah Heiligman begins:

> *When you see a bee on a warm summer day, do you think, "OW! That bee is going to sting me"? Don't worry. If that bee is a honeybee, she is after something sweeter than you.*

Notice how Heiligman connects with her readers who look at bees and are immediately afraid. She speaks to them in a friendly way and quickly puts their minds at ease. Charles Micucci begins with a snapshot of the honeybee as a valuable insect in his book *The Life and Times of the Honeybee*:

> *For thousands of years the honeybee has been one of our most valuable insects. It has supplied people with honey for sweetening foods, and with beeswax for candles and many other useful items. In addition, the honeybee has helped farmers all over the world to increase their fruit and vegetable harvests.*

Perhaps one of the more interesting ways to lead into a nonfiction piece is to create a scene, again helping readers to visualize and bring them into the moment. Gail Gibbons's lead begins before her title page and ends with the title *The Honey Makers*:

> *It is springtime. Two beekeepers have placed a beehive on a hill. Activity begins around the hive. The honeybees and the beekeepers are . . .* The Honey Makers.

In contrast to our student author, Bobby, let's look at the way Kay Winters began her book *Abe Lincoln: The Boy Who Loved Books*:

> *In the wilds of Kentucky, 1809, a boy was born. His mother called him Abraham, his last name Lincoln. His bed was made from corn husks, his covers, skins from bears. His cabin built with logs from towering trees.*

Notice how Kay Winters establishes her expertise right from the start by giving us little details about Abe's bed and home. She continues to help us visualize a log cabin, sharing interesting features such as a door that opens and shuts on leather hinges.

Neither of our student authors included any information that most of their readers didn't already know. It is important to keep in mind that nonfiction writing should target what your audience doesn't already know, not simply restate already known facts. A good way for writers to evaluate if they have written an interesting introduction is to ask themselves, "Could I have written this introduction without reading anything about my topic first?" If the answer is yes, chances are the introduction will not serve to hook the reader.

While it is true children should research across many books and other resources, from a writer's perspective, the crafting of a good introduction may be accomplished by reading books on varying topics across the genre the author is trying to imitate. For example, Bobby is writing a report about a famous person. He doesn't only need to read books about Abe Lincoln in order to find the right hook for his readers. Instead, he could immerse himself in the craft of picture book biographies or short chapter book biographies. Consider the lead of Jean Fritz's *Bully for You, Teddy Roosevelt!* Fritz begins:

> *What did Theodore Roosevelt want to do? Everything. And all at once if possible. Plunging headlong into life, he refused to waste a single moment. Among other things, he studied birds, shot lions, roped steer, fought a war, wrote books, and discovered the source of a mystery river in South America. In addition, he became governor of New York, vice president of the United States, then president. This was a big order for one man, but Theodore Roosevelt was not an everyday kind of man.*

Using a question as a lead is not a stretch for most students. However, answering it with a summary list may be something new.

Widening the Range of Possibilities: Sharing a Secret

What are other possibilities for nonfiction leads? You are probably familiar with some of the more commonly used leads for informational text, because they are also used to compose narratives—questions, snapshots of setting, snapshots of character, dialogue, and action. Figures 4.1 and 4.2 offer examples from first graders who are beginning to experiment with some familiar leads.

When you start to examine informational text more closely, you might find interesting mentor texts that can help your students imagine a wider range of possibilities for a nonfiction lead.

Consider the lead paragraph from Frank Murphy's *George Washington and the General's Dog*:

> *George Washington is one of America's greatest heroes. Most people know that George was honest and brave. But there is something about George that people don't always know. George Washington loved animals.*

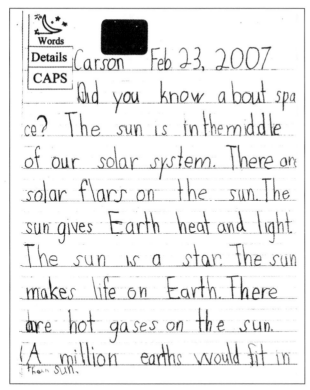

FIGURE 4.1
Carson begins with a question.

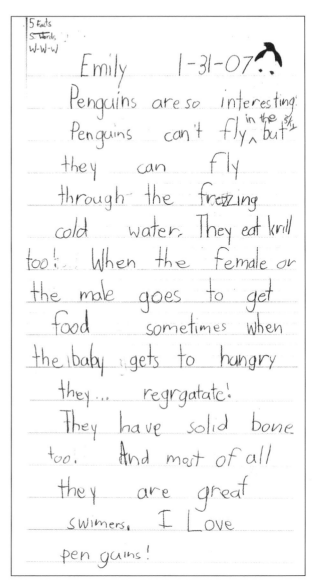

FIGURE 4.2
Emily begins with an interesting fact.

If we study Murphy's lead, we notice that he begins by telling us the familiar things that everybody knows about George Washington. The strength of this beginning is the sharing of a simple truth about Washington that most people don't know. We call this type of lead "sharing a secret." Murphy repeats this type of introduction in his book *Babe Ruth Saves Baseball!* For students, whose audience is often other students, this type of lead is very tempting. Kids love secrets. You can find other examples of this type of lead in books such as *Thank You, Sarah: The Woman Who Saved Thanksgiving* by Laurie Halse Anderson and *Amelia and Eleanor Go for a Ride* by Pam Muñoz Ryan. Anderson starts with a rhetorical question, one she knows her audience will answer "yes" to:

You think you know everything about Thanksgiving, don't you?

She elaborates with the information all students hold in their memories about Thanksgiving and ends by telling her readers that she has something different to share that is something they probably don't know (the secret) but is newsworthy:

Well, listen up. I have a news flash. . . . WE ALMOST LOST . . .
THANKSGIVING! Didn't know that, did you? It's true.

This type of lead is effective because the true purpose of informational writing is not to tell people what they already know, but to tell them what they don't know. An effective lead that shares a secret lets the reader know that it is worth it to invest the time to read on.

Although *Amelia and Eleanor Go for a Ride* is a fictionalized account, we learn in the author's note that the incident described was an actual event but was something that most people didn't know really happened. The true stories about these two women usually are not placed together in the same text. Muñoz Ryan's book shares the secret of a flying adventure the night Amelia and her husband were invited to dinner at the White House. Don't miss the author's note that thoroughly explains the research behind this book and the photograph from that evening, which illustrator Brian Selznick found.

Lynne and colleague Bruce Bloome experimented with the sharing-a-secret lead with Bruce's fourth graders, who had been reading biographies. Instead of asking the students to write the traditional book report, Lynne and Bruce wanted the students to write a more focused piece that could also serve as a book talk. They felt that using the sharing-a-secret lead would provide an interesting hook to reel in readers. For many of the fourth graders, it would be a risk, but without risk taking, one cannot grow as a writer. After Lynne and Bruce shared some mentor texts as well as their own examples, the students were able to reread parts of their texts to hunt for a secret—something interesting and little known about their famous person. A few of the resulting introductions follow.

You probably know Neil Armstrong was the first man on the moon, landing in a vehicle named the Eagle. (". . . one small step for a man, one giant leap for mankind.") But I bet you don't know that he was an Eagle Scout.

Dylan

You probably know that Beethoven wrote music and that he became deaf. But I bet you don't know that Beethoven was a very odd man who couldn't be bothered with clean and stylish clothes in a time when people dressed in fancy clothes and the most fashionable style was pigtails.

Alisa

In 1929, a little hero was born. His name was Martin Luther King, Jr. But he wasn't a hero when he was born . . . not yet. I bet you didn't know that Martin Luther King was a great piano player. When he started to play, everyone thought he would grow up to be a great musician.

Michelle

Finding a secret to share wasn't always easy. Some students ran into difficulty because their books were about sports figures, and the students kept sharing statistics as secrets until Bruce pointed out that statistics are something that can easily be found in a record book. One solution would be to read about one person across many texts to find the secret. Students should understand that some leads for both fiction and nonfiction do not work well with every piece of writing. However, it is important to stretch writers with choice and give them the opportunity to reflect on which strategy works best for a piece.

In final reflections, Bruce commented that perhaps the students would have been more comfortable if they had first started sharing a secret about themselves. Lynne used this advice when she started working with Kathy Randolph and Tina Madison's fourth graders. It worked! Students more easily transitioned into sharing secrets about their famous person when they had already shared a secret about themselves. In the following example, Jordin had no trouble writing with enthusiasm:

> Most people know Jordin loves dogs and loves to play hockey. But most people don't know that at the age of eight he knocked his front grown-up teeth out.
>
> Jordin was playing with his friend Jason in his backyard. And after he was done drinking a plastic water bottle, he thought they should squash the bottle with the cap on. Jordin and Jason hit the bottle with a metal baseball bat, a three-foot log, and about a 52 pound rock. None of those things worked. They thought and thought of everything, until they thought of something awesome.
>
> They decided to put the plastic bottle under a metal chair and jump off of the roof which was about twelve feet off the ground. Jordin leaped into the air and right when his feet hit the chair the metal part flew up and . . . WHAM! His teeth were shattered into little pieces.
>
> Jason called for Jordin's mom and dad. They raced him to the emergency ward at Abington Hospital. He had to wait for what seemed like a small eternity before he could get help. His parents were pretty scared, but most of all it was Jordin who was terrified! Eventually, the dentist had to build him two fake front teeth.
>
> Now you know Jordin's secret. His two front teeth are not his own, and it didn't even happen while he was playing hockey. SHHHH! Keep this secret to yourself.

Another Possibility: Creating a Scene

Once students have researched a topic and are ready to begin to write, they can use some of the facts they know to create a scene. Creating a scene combines snapshots of character and setting and describes something that is happening. This technique helps writers synthesize the information they are researching and serves to draw the reader in for a closer look. It is similar to the flash draft writing that JoAnn Portalupi and Ralph Fletcher suggest in *Nonfiction Craft Lessons: Teaching Information Writing K–8* (2001). Gail Gibbons creates a scene in *Beacons of Light: Lighthouses*, as she did in her book *The Honey Makers*:

> *Waves thrash and winds swirl, tossing a ship about in the darkness. Then, in the distance, a light appears. It flashes three times, disappears, then flashes again. On board, the ship's crew recognizes that this is a lighthouse signal. It is telling them to veer away from something hidden beneath the water. The captain locates a rocky ledge on his chart and uses the light signal to plot their position.*

Gary Lopez opens his book, *Sharks*, with a scene that is bound to create interest, hook readers, and reel them in! It could be used to introduce an informational or persuasive piece, depending on the focus and direction a young researcher would take. Notice how the author builds suspense and doesn't reveal his subject until the final word in the opening paragraph:

> *The ocean water is clear and blue in the bright sunshine. Under the surface, schools of colorful fish swim through the water. Among them swims a sleek animal with a long tail and very sharp teeth. This animal is cruising through the water looking for its next meal. People all over the world fear this creature. What is it? It's a shark!*

The opening of *Lightning* by Stephen Kramer paints a picture of a thunderstorm that brings readers into the scene, helping them make connections with everything they know about thunderstorms.

> *Late in the evening, a cloud hangs in the sky. The air is calm. The birds are quiet. Even the blades of dry grass are still. Everything is hushed, waiting. Suddenly a giant spark leaps through the air, connecting earth and sky. The spark flickers for an instant and disappears. There is a moment of silence. Then a tremendous CRACK rips through the quiet. Booming echoes follow, rolling across the land. A thunderstorm drifts across the summer sky.*

Creating a scene is a way students can open a persuasive piece without a traditional format that includes stating the purpose and point in the opening sentence. It is effective because students can create a rhetorical question from this scene that will help them solidify their position with readers, breaking down possible barriers. In Lynne's class, the fourth graders had brainstormed topics for persuasive writing for target audiences. One student, Shane, had read a lot of books about skateboarding and skateboarding parks. He wasn't happy with his lead paragraph. He said it would put the township commissioners (his target audience) to sleep. He said it almost put him to sleep writing it! Lynne directed him to a familiar nonfiction author for fourth graders, Stephen Kramer. After reading the opening to *Lightning* several times, Lynne asked Shane what he noticed. Shane could see that Kramer created a vivid snapshot of setting and there was action—things happened. Lynne asked Shane to imagine an everyday skateboarding scene that he could recreate for his readers. She asked him to envision what he sees now that would help his readers understand what he wanted for the future. Shane revised his introduction in this way:

> Shane and his best friend Ryan have just started their summer vacation. They get an early start and head for Kyle's house. The smooth road rolls beneath their boards and they pick up some speed. Riding in the streets is the only good place for skateboards. With the wind whistling in their ears, they go even faster as the road starts down a steep hill. Suddenly, a car pulls around the corner and misses Shane by inches. He loses his balance and falls onto the curb. Ryan loses his nerve and ends up colliding with a parked car. The boys aren't really hurt. But what about the next time? We need a skating park in our community.

Give students the option of combining creating a scene with the more traditional format for an introductory paragraph as in the following student sample:

> Everything is put away and in its place. The bed and chest of drawers are shining—so new and clean. The desk has many drawers to put pencils, paper, and other school folders inside. I don't have to worry about finding anything anymore because my new room is so neat and clean. Mom and Dad, can you picture it? Getting some new bedroom furniture would be so cool. It will help me be more responsible and will serve as a reward for doing chores and getting good grades in school. Don't you think I deserve it?
>
> Chris, Grade 5

Some authors extend the scene to create more of a story around the information to be delivered. In *Everglades*, Jean Craighead George creates a storyteller who is poling a boat through the Everglades with a group of children. The story scaffold is always written in italics, making it easy for readers to separate the story from the facts. Illustrator Wendell Minor adds to the authenticity of the book by depicting the storyteller as a Native American.

In *Penny: The Forgotten Coin*, Denise Brennan-Nelson interrupts her story about two boys who help a penny discover her value and presents the reader with facts about pennies in the form of a time line. Students can try to write a narrative about their topic choice after researching, and they can embed the story in an informational or persuasive piece to frame the beginning and end, or within the body of their writing. Nicola Davies often chooses the story structure to write her books, as she does in *Bat Loves the Night* and *One Tiny Turtle*. Davies chooses to place additional information, separate from the narrative-informational text, in a different font on some of the pages. Another book that illustrates this concept is *All in Just One Cookie* by Susan E. Goodman.

Developing Setting: Creating a Sense of Era

Often students have trouble developing a sense of setting. They just don't see it as important, as evidenced in their narratives when setting is sometimes summed up in one sentence, such as "We went to the park." In informational writing, description of setting can not only be inviting to the reader, it can be crucial information to the understanding of the text that follows. For example, in *The Emperor's Egg*, Martin Jenkins begins:

> *Down at the very bottom of the world, there's a huge island that's almost completely covered in snow and ice. It's called Antarctica, and it's the coldest, windiest place on earth. The weather's bad enough there in summer, but in winter it's really terrible. It's hard to imagine anything actually living there.*

This beginning helps us appreciate the information we will learn about Emperor penguins who live in this harsh environment.

But sometimes students need more than a setting that gives a description of *where*. They need to focus in on the *when* as well. We call this creating a sense of era. Notice how Peter Golenbock creates a sense of era in *Teammates*, a story about Jackie Robinson and Pee Wee Reese:

> *Once upon a time in America, when automobiles were black and looked like tanks and laundry was white and hung on clotheslines to dry, there were two wonderful baseball leagues that no longer exist. They were called the Negro Leagues.*

Before starting his story, Golenbock goes on to describe how hard things were in the Negro Leagues, giving his readers a sense of era. He mentions details such as "Towns had no restaurants that would serve them, so they often had to eat meals that they could buy and carry with them." The reader is also drawn to the clever way Golenbock uses colors (black and white) in his lead sentence to emphasize the differences between blacks and whites at that time.

Kathleen Krull gives us another look at the 1940s in her book *Wilma Unlimited: How Wilma Rudolph Became the World's Fastest Woman.*

> *No one expected such a tiny girl to have a first birthday. In Clarksville, Tennessee, in 1940, life for a baby who weighed just over four pounds at birth was sure to be limited.*

In a conversation with Frank Murphy about his lead in *The Legend of the Teddy Bear*, the author revealed to us that his revisions to recreate a new beginning were based on his editor's suggestion. Frank created this nostalgic opening by developing a sense of era:

> *In the days when America was a younger country and much of the land was filled with dense green forests, animals roamed freely through the great American wilderness. In the cities, the clip-clop of horses' feet could be heard as they pulled black buggies through the bustling streets. Smoking black trains rolled across the countryside connecting cities and towns to prairies and forests, moving travelers across the wild territories of America.*

Let's look at how Robert Burleigh uses proper nouns and describes the sights and sounds of a New York City neighborhood in his opening to *Edna*:

> *From my apartment I can see the far-off tall buildings, the laundry flapping on nearby roofs, and down below, the hurdy-gurdy man playing his organ and kids zipping by on roller skates . . . The Great War is ending, women are getting the vote, and it's a new America.*

Maira Kalman also relies on the use of proper nouns to create a sense of era in her opening to *Fireboat: The Heroic Adventures of the John J. Harvey*. She lists important facts that serve to take readers back to a time they would not have experienced firsthand.

> *New York City. 1931. Amazing things were happening big and small. The Empire State Building went up, up, up. Babe Ruth hit his 611th home run in Yankee Stadium. The tasty candy treat Snickers hit the stores. The George Washington Bridge was suspended elegantly across the mighty Hudson River. Champion Pendley Calling of Blarney won Best in Show at the Westminster Kennel Club.*

With practice, students can imitate this same strategy, using the facts they have gathered during their research to create a sense-of-era lead. Here are two examples from a fourth-grade classroom:

> The time of poor. The time of nothing. That's the time Elvis Presley was born. The world was struck by the Great Depression, and it was as if the world's hope was drained. Almost every person was poor—no shoes, no food, no job—and no one liked it.
>
> Patrick

It was a time when people had no cars and rode on horses and donkeys. Men wore poofy pants and hats with feathers. People performed in plays for William Shakespeare, but only men could do the plays. If the plays needed a girl in them, the young men dressed up as women!

Melanie

Your Turn Lesson 3 at the end of the chapter offers suggestions for how you might present this strategy to the students in your classroom.

Compare/Contrast Leads

It works well to introduce the compare/contrast lead after doing some work in reading workshop comparing and contrasting characters, settings, problems, or events of stories and informational articles. Most students are familiar with a Venn diagram and understand how to use it. Creating an introduction with a comparison format is a fresh way to begin a piece of writing. Although this structure is often found within the body of texts as an organizational scaffold, it is not often found in introductions. A good place to begin experimenting with this type of lead is in the context of a biography or when writing about animals, planets, or foods.

In *Always Inventing: The True Story of Thomas Alva Edison*, author Frank Murphy uses a combination of a snapshot of setting and a compare/contrast lead:

> *The year was 1847. The winter was cold and snowy. The place was a little town in Ohio. Inside a snow-covered, redbrick house, a baby boy was born. His parents named him Thomas Alva Edison.*
>
> *Most babies cry a lot, but Thomas hardly ever cried. Instead, he cooed and laughed a lot. Baby Thomas was different in another way. He looked like he had questions to ask.*

Ken McNamara also uses a comparison lead in *It's True! We Came From Slime* to talk about the different kinds of creatures that inhabited our earth in different time periods:

> *Life on earth is always changing. A hundred million years ago, dinosaurs tramped through the forest. But long before that, an amazing number of animals wandered and slithered over the land, or swam and crawled in the seas. And if we went right back in time, we'd find that the very first creatures, thousands of millions of years ago, were so small that you couldn't see them. All you'd see is just a bit of slime.*

It is important to point out to students that Murphy begins his introduction with a snapshot of setting to segue into his comparison lead. His introduction is important since it shows how Edison's quality of curiosity about his world, even at an early age, led to his experimentation and discoveries. Murphy shows us that authors often use a combination of strategies to develop an interesting introduction.

In McNamara's comparison lead, at first the reader recognizes a time-order relationship. On closer examination, we can see how McNamara is also comparing sizes of creatures, starting with the enormous dinosaurs and ending with living creatures so small you wouldn't even recognize them as living creatures. Other examples of the compare/contrast lead can be found in Gail Gibbons's *Spiders* and Martin Jenkins's *Chameleons Are Cool*.

What If . . . ?

Sometimes authors put the readers in a situation where they have to imagine a different world, a different place, a different life, or a different point of view. We call this the "What if . . .?" lead. In *Almost Gone: The World's Rarest Animals*, Steve Jenkins starts with a snapshot of a familiar bird and then poses a "What if . . .?" situation:

> *There is a bird perched outside your window, a small bird with a black head, a white throat and a gray body. It is a chickadee. Suppose this bird and all the other chickadees in the world died out—became extinct. Would it matter? Well, you'd never again see a chickadee sitting outside your window or flying or feeding its young or building a nest. You'd never again hear a chickadee chirping. And that would be sad. And there is much more to it than that.*

Jenkins continues to imagine this "What if . . .?" scenario, informing the reader of the larger effects the loss of this bird would have on our planet. He provides the reader with a larger lens to view the world and his text about endangered animals.

Books like *Are You a Spider?* by Judy Allen (and other titles in the Backyard Books series) and *The Snail's Spell* by Joanne Ryder use a "What if. . .?" lead by asking the reader to become something else and imagine a different life. Often this type of "What if . . .?" text uses the second person point of view. *The Snail's Spell* begins:

> *Imagine you are soft and have no bones inside you. Imagine you are grey, the color of smoke.*

Not all "What if . . .?" leads are found in books about animals. Tanya Lee Stone uses this type of lead in *Elizabeth Leads the Way*, a book about suffragette Elizabeth Cady Stanton:

What would you do if someone told you you can't be what you want to be because you are a girl? What would you do if someone told you your vote doesn't count, doesn't matter because you are a girl? Would you ask why? Would you fight . . . for your rights? Elizabeth did.

In Eileen Christelow's *Vote!* the reader must imagine a "What if . . .?" concerning a town about to choose a new mayor. The author then takes you through the ins and outs of the voting process as candidates run for the mayor of an imagined town.

Students can try out a "What if . . .?" lead in writing about topics such as the effects of drought, flood, or other natural disasters. Common topics generally studied in elementary classrooms such as pollution, rainforests, or community workers like firefighters or police officers also lend themselves to the "What if . . .?" lead. In one third-grade classroom, students had an opportunity to research ants to gather material for a contest. Many of the students felt right at home with this new lead and were eager to try it out.

What if you had millions of brothers and sisters and only one mother? How would you all survive? If you are an ant, you survive because you depend on each other.

Daniel

What if you were an ant? You would have a family just like us and a queen ant who is the mother of all the ants.

Maria

Imagine you are growing smaller. You are shrinking. You have six legs, a head, a thorax, and an abdomen. You have antennae and incredible eyes. You don't look anything like a human and yet you are just like us in so many ways.

Timyla

What if one day you woke up and you found you were in the time of the dinosaurs? The dinosaurs can't see you because you are so small.

Nick

The Definition Lead

Many nonfiction authors rely on a definition lead to begin their text. A definition lead can help clear up misunderstandings and allow the reader to categorize information, assimilating the new knowledge with their schema. It can also introduce key vocabulary—one or two essential words that will reappear throughout the text or that will help provide the author's take on the subject matter. In *Owls* by Sandra Markle, owls are defined as predators:

> *The animal world is full of predators. Predators are the hunters who find, catch, and eat other animals—their prey—in order to survive. Every environment has its chain of hunters. The smaller, slower, less able predators become prey for the bigger, faster, more cunning hunters. And everywhere, there are just a few kinds of predators at the top of the food chain. In nearly every habitat, this group of predators includes one or more kinds of owls.*

April Pulley Sayre combines a snapshot of setting with a definition based on examples in her lead for *Stars Beneath Your Bed: The Surprising Story of Dust*:

> *At sunrise, the sun, low in the sky, peeks through dusty air. Dust from us and dirt and dinosaurs scatters light, painting the sky like fire. Dust is made everywhere, every day. A flower drops pollen. A dog shakes dirt from its fur. A butterfly flutters, and scales fall off its wings. That's dust. Dust is little bits of things.*

This book has additional information about dust and sunsets on the final pages, separate from the main text. A shared writing experience could be created using information from these pages and imitating the author's syntax found on her first two pages.

Collecting Strategies for Leads

As we discussed in *Mentor Texts: Teaching Writing Through Children's Literature* (2007), when students begin to explore possibilities, they need a permanent place to record their ideas. This can be accomplished by creating a classroom chart or through the use of a writer's notebook. Charts and notebook lists are ongoing as students continue to discover and categorize their findings. It is important to note that a lead paragraph may involve the use of several strategies, and, therefore, may be placed appropriately in more than one category. Encourage students to come up with their own headings for nonfiction leads that don't seem to have a home in any of the categories already named. Figure 4.3 offers some possibilities for nonfiction leads.

Discovering the Possibilities for Conclusions

Just as one of the hardest things to teach students in narrative writing is how to develop an effective ending, it is difficult to teach them how to write a powerful conclusion in nonfiction writing. One of the problems a teacher of writing encounters is the lack of a true conclusion or summary at the end of many nonfiction picture books, text books, and informational articles. It is important to find mentor texts that offer choices for our students beyond a restatement of

Questions
Wonderful Nature, Wonderful You by Karin Ireland
All About Owls by Jim Arnosky
Surprising Sharks by Nicola Davies

Anecdote
My Brother Martin by Christine King Farris
Women of Hope: African Americans Who Made a Difference by Joyce Hansen
Bully for You, Teddy Roosevelt by Jean Fritz

Setting (Where)
Abe Lincoln: The Boy Who Loved Books by Kay Winters
Welcome to the Sea of Sand by Jane Yolen
Uncommon Traveler: Mary Kingsley in Africa by Don Brown
Always Inventing: The True Story of Thomas Alva Edison by Frank Murphy

Definition Lead
Behold . . . the Unicorns! by Gail Gibbons
Sea Turtles by Gail Gibbons
Stars by Seymour Simon

Creating a Scene or Story
Everglades by Jean Craighead George
Beacons of Light: Lighthouses by Gail Gibbons
Penny: The Forgotten Coin by Denise Brennan-Nelson
The Honey Makers by Gail Gibbons

Quotes/What People Say
Flight: The Journey of Charles Lindbergh by Robert Burleigh
The Story of Ruby Bridges by Robert Coles

Comparison/The Other Side
Weird Friends by Jose Aruego and Ariane Dewey
Chameleons Are Cool by Martin Jenkins
Amelia and Eleanor Go for a Ride by Pam Muñoz Ryan
Spiders by Gail Gibbons
Always Inventing: The True Story of Thomas Alva Edison by Frank Murphy

Setting—Sense of Era (When)
Edna by Robert Burleigh
The Legend of the Teddy Bear by Frank Murphy
Fireboat: The Heroic Adventures of the John J. Harvey by Maira Kalman
Teammates by Peter Golenbock

Amazing Facts
The Man Who Walked Between the Towers by Mordicai Gerstein
Henry's Freedom Box by Ellen Levine
Cactus Hotel by Brenda Z. Guiberson

Action
Bat Loves the Night by Nicola Davies
Sun Up, Sun Down by Gail Gibbons
From Slave Ship to Freedom Road by Julius Lester

FIGURE 4.3
Leads for nonfiction writing

the main ideas introduced in the lead paragraph. We have discovered several interesting possibilities that can work for students of all ages.

Concluding Characteristics: Connecting with the Reader

Authors like to conclude with a set of characteristics when talking about animals or people. It is a positive way to end a book, often making the reader connect in a personal way. In Charles Micucci's book *The Life and Times of the Ant*, the reader is reminded that ants are enduring creatures whose habits and traits are worthy of study:

> *Ants evolved from wasps more than a hundred million years ago. They have been dodging footsteps ever since. As dinosaurs thundered above ground, ants dug out a home below. The mighty dinosaurs are long gone, but the little ant has survived . . .*

> *The tunnel of time continues for the ants. Their hard work inspires people today, as it has for many centuries.*

Gail Gibbons uses this technique in *Behold . . . The Unicorns!*:

> *The unicorn still represents the qualities most people value. They are seen as being gentle, brave, strong, kind, and noble creatures. They live around the edges of our imaginations and in our legends. Behold . . . the Unicorns!*

Frank Murphy does the same thing in *The Legend of the Teddy Bear*. His closing sentence talks about a teddy bear as a "trusted, faithful, and timeless friend whose dedication is always ready and never-ending."

The Way We Are Known

When writing about important people, the focus on qualities can shift to a major accomplishment—what the person is most known for. For example, in *When Marian Sang* by Pam Muñoz Ryan, the final paragraphs describe Marian Anderson's accomplishments and end with the one thing that had eluded her for so many years—singing with the metropolitan opera.

> *Tonight was her debut with the metropolitan opera.*
> *At long last, she had reached the sun and the moon. The curtains parted . . . and Marian sang.*

In *The Great Houdini: World-Famous Magician and Escape Artist* by Monica Kulling, the conclusion is built around the essence of who Houdini was in life—a magician. Kulling takes the most important thing about a magician (performing tricks) and uses it as the scaffold to describe Houdini's entire life. She recaps points made throughout the book that demonstrate how he achieved greatness:

> *Perhaps Houdini's greatest trick was becoming who he was. He was born into a poor family. He was uneducated. But through hard work and determination, he became the world's most famous magician and escape artist. Houdini wrote books, starred in movies, and was the president of the Society of American Magicians. Once, reporters asked Bess if she knew the secret of Houdini's success. She replied: "It is Houdini himself. That is the secret."*

Lynne talked to her fifth-grade students about their work with bio poems and how the last line could be a sentence or phrase representing the essence of the person, event, or concept. For example, in a bio poem about the rain forest, the last line could be "lifeline for our planet." For Abe Lincoln, it could be "emancipator." Using their knowledge of bio poems, the students turned their attention to the biographies they had just finished reading and tried to come up with a word or phrase that would capture the person, his or her work, and/or his or her career and use it to create a final paragraph. (See Your Turn Lesson 2 at the end of this chapter.)

The Recap

Recapping major events is a popular way to conclude a nonfiction piece of writing. Authors do it in different ways. Sometimes important facts are written in individual sentences. Other times, authors create a list introduced by colons or set aside with dashes. And sometimes, authors use a list as a way to lead to a final statement that uses the title, or part of the title, as a closing. As you can see from some of the examples already given, ending with the title is a powerful way to conclude.

Anderson's *Thank You, Sarah: The Woman Who Saved Thanksgiving* is a book that uses both listing and repetition of the title to form a solid ending. It's interesting to note that the author pulls together perhaps the most important character traits that Sarah Hale exemplified.

> *It took Sarah Hale thirty-eight years, thousands of letters, and countless bottles of ink, but she did it. Nothing stopped Sarah. That bold, brave, stubborn, and smart lady saved Thanksgiving . . . for all of us. THANK YOU, SARAH!*

Kay Winters also uses a list of facts to conclude her book *Abe Lincoln: The Boy Who Loved Books*. By using dashes, she creates an effective list in one sentence. Then she restates the idea created from the list in her final sentence:

> *Abraham Lincoln—born in a log cabin, child of the frontier, head in a book—elected our sixteenth president! From the wilderness to the White House. He learned the power of words and used them well.*

Lingering Questions

One pervasive idea we want our students to come away with after researching and writing about informational topics is the notion that the true learner is always left with more questions. As we mentioned earlier in this chapter, questions can be used in an introduction to stimulate interest and whet a reader's appetite in a subject. Questions can also be an effective way to conclude an informational piece, especially when they point to those wonderings that remain unanswered. Stephen Kramer uses this strategy in *Lightning*:

*Each year, scientists learn more about lightning. But there are still
many unanswered questions. Exactly what happens during each part
of a lightning flash? Can we predict when and where lightning will
strike? What is ball lightning, and how does it form?*

In *Out of Sight: Pictures of Hidden Worlds*, author Seymour Simon concludes
by asking questions that scientists are still trying to answer:

*What are the secrets of matter? Does life exist on other planets?
Where did life itself come from? . . . Who can tell what strange and
fantastic hidden worlds remain to be explored?*

Using Quotes and Primary Documents

As students conduct research on their topics, they will be doing more than just
gathering facts. They may come across interesting quotes or primary documents
that might be used effectively in their introductions or conclusions. This strategy serves to inspire readers and gives them something to think about long after
the reading has been completed. *Teammates* by Peter Golenbock ends with a
quote by Pee Wee Reese about his teammate Jackie Robinson. Notice also how
the author links the ending to the title:

*"I am standing by him," Pee Wee Reese said to the world. "This man
is my teammate."*

The final page of *Sky Pioneer: A Photobiography of Amelia Earhart* by Corinne
Szabo is a quote that captures the essence of who Amelia Earhart was and her
foresight about women's changing roles:

*Please know I am quite aware of the hazards. I want to do it because
I want to do it. Women must try to do things as men have tried.
When they fail, failure must be but a challenge to others.*

Jeannine Atkins takes a slightly different twist to the idea of quotes in her book
Mary Anning and the Sea Dragon. Throughout the book, Mary Anning hears
the voice of her father as an inspiration. His words are repeated in several
places throughout the story. The book concludes with the sentiments of
Anning's father:

*And she'd return to the shore to look for fossils, to hear the wind and
her father's voice: Don't ever stop looking, Mary.*

Besides quotations, other forms of primary documents can help a reader bring
closure to a nonfiction text. Robert Burleigh uses a poem by Edna St. Vincent

Millay to conclude his picture book biography *Edna*. In *Days of Jubilee: The End of Slavery in the United States*, Patricia and Frederick McKissack choose the thirteenth amendment to the constitution to be the last thing their audience reads. Frank Murphy includes a letter from Teddy Roosevelt as part of his conclusion to *The Legend of the Teddy Bear*. The use of primary documents in a conclusion gives the author the look of the expert, the voice of an authority, and leaves the reader with the impression that this is an author who can be trusted.

Framing Your Work: Finding the Right Introduction and Conclusion

In your classroom, begin by looking at the introductions and conclusions of the nonfiction books in your classroom library. That's what we did. Talk to your colleagues and share examples of openings and closings you feel your students can imitate. Remember, if you display the cumulative work you do in the classroom by charting examples, your students will always have a visual reminder of the possibilities for their work. Get them to help you by examining sets of books and taking notes about the craft of nonfiction introductions and conclusions in their writer's notebooks. Owning this process frees them to make their own discoveries, name them, and try them out in their own writing.

In the following piece, Diana, a fourth grader in Kathy Randolph's class, used a sharing-a-secret introduction and conclusion scaffold in her biography piece:

> Most people know that many courageous men and women risked their own lives to hide Jewish people during World War II. However, most people don't know that Luba Tryszynska was a Jewish woman who saved fifty-four children. Do you want to know a secret?
>
> Most people don't know that before the war Luba lived in Poland with her son and husband. They had few things, but they were so happy until Luba's son and husband were taken away from her. Everyone on the train was whispering that they were headed to a death camp at Auschwitz. As soon as the train pulled into the station, her son Isaac was torn from her arms. Two years later she could still hear him calling for her.
>
> Luba was lucky that the Nazi's believed she was a nurse. She knew that her beloved son and husband were probably killed. This all happened just because they were Jewish. Luba had to be brave and do what she could do to help others. She took fifty-four Dutch children from the concentration camp at Bergen-Belsen. The Dutch nicknamed her "The Angel of Bergen-Belsen."
>
> This is such a terribly horrifying part of history. I can't believe it but it's true! Don't keep this news a secret. Spread the word about Luba and her act of courage. Everyone needs heroes in their lives and hope for a better tomorrow.

An Author's Voice:
Unforgettable Introductions and Conclusions—Made to Stick

Frank Murphy
Author of *The Legend of the Teddy Bear* and *George Washington and the General's Dog*

Most people know that a story should have a great beginning. And most people know that a story should have a great ending, too. But do you know why these two parts of a story are so important? Let me fill in you in!

Blanche McCrary said, "You can't wait . . . for even one line in to gain the reader's attention. You've got to grab them by the lapels in the first paragraph, and by the end of the first page if you don't throw them across the room you'll lose them." So, you must capture the attention of a reader and not let go. Likewise, you have to try to get your reader to walk away from the last lines saying: "Wow!"

Your ending should be made to stick! Etched in their minds and hearts. Unforgettable. Sometimes writing an ending that echoes the way you wrote your beginning is a way to accomplish this.

My book *Babe Ruth Saves Baseball* starts with what people already know about the Babe and ends the first page with a question: "But do you know the best thing about Babe Ruth?" It connects with the book's ending: "But now you know the best thing about Babe Ruth—how he saved baseball."

There are lots of ways to begin a story: flashback, onomatopoeia, a famous quote, starting in the middle of the action, or as Lynne and Rose discovered in some of my books, sharing a secret. Now you know the secret: You should write a beginning that grabs a hold of the reader (and never lets go!) and write an ending that sticks to their minds and hearts (forever!).

Your Turn Lesson 1

Creating a Scene

Hook: Return to some nonfiction mentor texts that open with a scene to help the reader visualize the place, the characters, and the action. Some good choices are *Lightning* by Stephen Kramer, *The Honey Makers* and *Beacons of Light: Lighthouses* by Gail Gibbons, and *Cactus Hotel* by Brenda Z. Guiberson. After reading the passages aloud, ask your students what they notice.

Purpose: *Some authors choose to introduce their topic by creating a scene. It pulls readers in and helps them visualize what they are reading about. Today I will show you how to use some of the facts you are collecting from your research to create a scene that can be used as an introduction.*

Brainstorm: If the class is studying a topic together, have them brainstorm some of the facts they have learned and record them on the board or chart paper. Students who are researching individual topics can brainstorm a list of facts in their writer's notebooks.

Model: The use of short texts or passages is excellent for modeling in front of students. A wonderful resource for this lesson is *Frogs* by Ann Heinrichs. This is part of the Nature's Friends series published by Compass Point Books. For this lesson, Rose chose the section "How Frogs Eat." After reading it aloud, she listed some of the facts she had learned:

- Frogs have sticky tongues that unfold from the front of their mouths.
- Frogs swallow insects whole.
- Frogs' eyes sink in and push the food down.

Then she created a scene that served to illustrate the facts:

> It is quiet near the pond. Frog sits on the edge of the pond hidden among the wet leaves and twigs. If you listen carefully, you can hear the drone of passing dragonflies. Quick as a wink, frog's tongue darts out of his mouth like a party horn. The dragonfly is trapped on the sticky surface and swallowed whole. Frog's eyes sink into his head. Ahhh—lunch!

Shared/Guided Writing: Share another short passage from the book you used to model, then list some important facts and use shared writing to create a scene. If the class is studying a topic together, do a shared writing based on one category of the research. For instance, if the class is studying penguins, you could focus on the facts associated with how penguins move to create a scene in a shared writing situation.

Independent Writing: When you think students are ready, have them return to the list of facts they brainstormed about the topic they are researching individually or to the list of facts about the class topic. You may want to have students create a quick sketch of their scene before they write it. This is especially useful for younger students, but older students like it also. Have students form partnerships for sharing. Partners can give feedback as to how well the writing helped them visualize what they were reading about.

Reflection: Ask students to reflect on how this strategy worked for them.

How is creating a scene effective as an introduction to a report?

Your Turn Lesson 2

Creating a Summary: The Way We Are Known

Many writers will write informational pieces about people in their family, their coaches, their teachers, and their friends. They will also write about famous people—their heroes. Authors use the very essence of who a person is—what he or she is remembered for or known for—to summarize their writing about the person in a way that will be most memorable, lingering in the readers' minds long after they stop reading. Students can use this strategy first about themselves and then about a family member to internalize this strategy and make it part of their schema.

Hook: Use a nonfiction mentor text that captures the essence of what a person is best known for to create an effective summary for the piece the students are writing, such as a biography report. A favorite choice is *The Great Houdini: World-Famous Magician and Escape Artist* by Monica Kulling. Other options include: *When Marian Sang* by Pam Muñoz Ryan, *Teammates* by Peter Golenbock, and *Jackie's Nine: Jackie Robinson's Values to Live By* by Sharon Robinson.

Purpose: *Some authors choose to conclude their story of someone's life by capturing the way that person is best known. Sometimes this is accomplished by describing an action, and sometimes it is a characteristic or something that is associated with the person's career. It is an effective way of summing up what you want your reader to remember. Today I will show you how you can use an action or trait that a person is known for to create a powerful ending for a biographical or autobiographical piece.*

Brainstorm: If the class is studying a genre such as biography, have each student give you a characteristic or action that would represent the person he or she is studying. Record the names of the people and the corresponding actions or traits on chart paper. You can do the same thing for people in their families, friends, or even themselves.

Model: After reading Robert Burleigh's *Stealing Home: Jackie Robinson: Against the Odds*, return to other books about Jackie Robinson, such as *Teammates* by Peter Golenbock and *First in the Field: Baseball Hero Jackie Robinson* by Derek Dingle. Decide on an action or characteristic that would best describe Jackie Robinson and write a conclusion that uses that action or characteristic as a focus. Here is an example from Lynne's notebook:

> Jackie Robinson stole the hearts of baseball fans across our country. He stole the spot of the first African American to play for a major-league baseball club. He stole the heart of his teammate, Pee Wee Reese, who publicly declared his support for Jackie at a game against the Cincinnati Reds. He stole the pennant for the Dodgers two years in a row with home runs, incredible fielding, and yes, stolen bases! His greatest achievement, however, was stealing places for other African American ball players right alongside of white players. And in 1962, he stole a spot in the National Baseball Hall of Fame.
>
> Jackie Robinson continues to steal the hearts of young athletes who aspire to be like their larger-than-life hero who often stole home, beating the odds. I guess you could say he spent a lifetime doing just that!

Shared/Guided Writing: Share another the-way-we-are-known ending from a book like *When Marian Sang* by Pam Muñoz Ryan. If the class has read a biography from a guided reader, a trade book for literature circles, or the literature anthology, use that common experience to create this nutshell summary. A good place to start might be with a well-known figure like Abraham Lincoln—the Great Emancipator. The action could be "He freed . . ." Or use someone like Martin Luther King Jr. and "I have a dream." Use the phrase "He dreamed of . . ." to create a the-way-we-are-known summary/conclusion for the shared writing experience.

Independent Practice: Students can return to the chart they originally created through brainstorming about individual biographies or people in their families, or they can continue to research and read more about a person mentioned in their social studies or science text. Once they find the action or character trait, allow time to turn and talk with a partner or response group. A few students may need to check in with you in an individual conference. Use sharing time just for the summary/conclusion, not the entire piece of writing.

Reflection: Ask students to reflect on how this strategy worked for them.

> *How did creating a summary with the technique of the way we are known strengthen your piece of writing?*
>
> *What was the most difficult part of crafting this kind of ending?*
>
> *What helped you to be successful and work through the difficulties?*
>
> *Can you see yourself using this kind of summary again? When would you use it?*
>
> *What will this type of summary/ending do for your reader? Why do you think so?*

Options: Create a bio poem as an alternative form to summarize the way we are known or a where-I'm-from poem. (Find examples in *Roots in the Sawdust: Writing to Learn Across the Disciplines*, edited by Anne Ruggles Gere, or the bio poem format mentioned in this chapter.)

Your Turn Lesson 3

Writing an Introduction by Creating a Sense of Era

Many young writers are still developing their understanding of a good beginning for an informational piece. Authors use the setting—the where and the when—to bring their readers to a place and time that may be very different than what they are familiar with. Students can play around with different techniques to create a sense of era as they internalize this strategy.

Hook: The opening paragraphs of *The Legend of the Teddy Bear* by Frank Murphy or *Teammates* by Peter Golenbock provide excellent models of beginnings that describe the setting by developing a sense of era. Other books with openings that work well with this type of lead include *Wilma Unlimited: How Wilma Rudolph Became the World's Fastest Runner* by Kathleen Krull; *Edna* by Robert Burleigh; *First in the Field: Baseball Hero Jackie Robinson* by Derek Dingle; and *Fireboat: The Heroic Adventures of the John J. Harvey* by Maira Kalman.

Purpose: *Writers, today I'm going to show you how you can create a sense of era by developing the when as well as the where in your opening paragraph. We've already talked about a few different ways that authors begin informational writing (such as starting with a question, creating a scene, using a comparison structure, or sharing a secret). Today we're going to practice writing an introduction that helps the reader understand the time in which an event happened or someone lived.*

Brainstorm: Read the opening to *Teammates.* Continue to read the first four paragraphs. Make a list of the things that Golenbock includes to help his readers understand the time in which Jackie Robinson lived (the Negro League existed, blacks and whites didn't go to the same schools and had to use different drinking fountains, many hotels would not rent rooms to the Negro League players, etc.).

Make a list of ways we might help a reader get a sense of era. This list might include some of the following items: the name of the U.S. president, games children are playing, best sellers, popular movies, well-known actors and rock stars or bands, wars, major events in history, TV programs, inventions, modes of communication (cell phones, text messaging, letters, telegrams, e-mail), candies.

Model: Use some of the ideas from the list to create an example about your own life (your childhood might work best for elementary and middle school children). After you write, students turn and talk about what they notice. Ask: How did I create a sense of era? Here is an example from Lynne's notebook:

> The long driveway between the row houses on Sydney and Durham Streets teemed with children of all ages. Basketballs bounced, hula hoops twirled, and baseballs flew to first base, a torn piece of cardboard. Girls chanted, "Cinderella dressed in yella . . ." while the slap, slap, slap, slap of the jump rope smacked the ground. When it was dark, the driveway emptied. Families sat in front of the one television they owned and watched "The Ed Sullivan Show." Sometimes the girls gathered on stoops to exchange "boy

stories." Boys guzzled coke from ice-cold, pale mint-green colored bottles to cool off after a game. It was the sixties. Doors weren't locked. The Beatles were the rage. People believed they could change the world.

Guided Writing: Invite students to try creating a sense of era just like you did. You may want to start with a shared experience. A good place to start would be to create an introduction to an imagined autobiographical piece about themselves. What kinds of things tell us about living in this new millennium? List some ideas and create a piece that could apply to everyone in your class.

Independent Practice: Ask students to return to a notebook entry or a piece they already wrote that could be revised to begin with a lead paragraph creating a sense of era. Students could also be given the option of using this lead to write a biography report or a research paper around a particular event.

Reflection: After students share their revisions or new beginnings, ask them to reflect on what they did.

> *How did using this introduction technique help you begin?*
>
> *How did your piece improve by beginning with a description of era?*
>
> *How did the words you used help the reader to visualize the setting and understand a time in history?*
>
> *Is the setting (in this case, the* when*) important to what you are writing about?*
>
> *When could you use this again? Would you change anything?*

Options: Ask students to add to the sense of era by using a simile that is linked with a time period. See the revision for the model above, which strengthens the era piece by adding a simile about an Elvis Presley tune.

> The long driveway between the row houses on Sydney and Durham Streets teemed with children of all ages. Basketballs bounced, hula hoops twirled, and baseballs flew to first base, a torn piece of cardboard. Girls chanted, "Cinderella dressed in yella . . ." while the slap, slap, slap, slap of the jump rope smacked the ground. When night as velvety soft as a "Love Me Tender" Elvis tune covered the neighborhood, the driveway emptied. Families sat in front of the one television they owned and watched "The Ed Sullivan Show." Sometimes the girls gathered on stoops to exchange "boy stories." Boys guzzled coke from ice-cold, pale mint-green colored bottles to cool off after a game. It was the sixties. Doors weren't locked. The Beatles were the rage. People believed they could change the world.

Other options include having your students create a collection of introductions for famous people and events using a sense of era, which you can then gather in a binder to keep in the writing center or post on a bulletin board. Students can use the writer's notebook to copy other examples of creating a sense of era from literature as they find them.

Your Turn Lesson 4

Writing a Definition Lead

Hook: Sometimes the easiest way to get students to write an effective introduction is to use the definition lead. Examples can be found in Belinda Weber's *Animal Disguises*, Rod Theodorou and Carole Telford's *Lizards and Snakes*, *Rain Forest* by Angela Wilkes, and *Discovering Dolphins* by Stephanie and Douglas Nowacek. You may also discover your own examples in books your class has used. Return to these books and help your students discover or name the definition lead.

Purpose: *Sometimes the hardest part about writing is getting started. One of the easiest ways to begin a nonfiction piece is to define for your audience what it is you are writing about. Today we will have the opportunity to try out a definition lead and see how it works.*

Brainstorm: Together with the students, create a list of their heroes. Give students some time to turn and talk about these people in small groups before writing their personal definition of *hero* in their writer's notebooks. Let them share these definitions in a small group and then reach consensus on a good definition to share with the whole group. Post these definitions and allow students to offer their opinions about what it means to be a hero. Compare the students' definitions with the dictionary definition. Since students may now have a broader definition of what it means to be a hero, return to the list that you brainstormed and allow students to offer additional responses.

Model: Choose a person from the brainstormed list who you can write about. Perhaps begin with the dictionary definition of *hero* and extend the introduction to include your own thinking. Lynne chose to write about her grandfather.

> The word *hero* means many things to people. Webster's dictionary defines a hero as a person who is admired for his or her qualities. This definition speaks to my feelings about my grandfather. He is generous, fair, and hardworking. They are the reasons why my grandfather is my hero.

She then gave the students another option. Instead of defining a hero, she could begin by defining *grandfather*.

> According to Webster's dictionary, a grandfather is the father of your mother or your father. For me, *grandfather* means so much more.
>   My grandfather is my hero—the person I want to be like when I grow up. He is my role model for generosity, fairness, and work ethic. Everybody should have a hero like my grandpa.

Shared/Guided Writing: Choose a person who could be considered a hero and who the class is familiar with through social studies, science, or reading units. Another option is to choose a familiar book character from a read-aloud or anthology selection. In a shared writing experience, write a short paragraph about the person or character beginning with a definition lead of what it means to be a hero.

Independent Writing: Invite students to choose a hero to write about from the brainstormed list. They might also choose to return to a piece they have been working on to revise their introduction with a definition lead. For example, they might be writing about karate, pollution, or leader dogs for the blind. It is important to note that students do not have to use a dictionary definition. Rather, they can begin by creating a definition that they believe is the way most people define a subject or concept. They can follow this explanation with their unique definition. Rosa, a fifth grader, began her hero essay about her mother this way.

> What is a hero? Spiderman? Superman? Batman or Underdog? No way! Those heroes are definitely not for me. My hero doesn't fight criminals or fly through the air. My hero certainly doesn't have a catch phrase like, "No need to fear! Underdog is here!" though she can easily save my day. My hero is my mom. Mom is the type of hero that is loving, helpful, and loyal to her commitments. That's my definition of *hero*.

Brittany, another fifth grader, wrote:

> What is a hero? A hero to me is someone who you can look up to and someone who cares for you and loves you a whole lot. Not some cartoon hero. Heros should be as wonderful as my parents.

Ryan chose to return to his piece about pyramids.

> To a mathematician a pyramid is a geometric shape. To the people of ancient Egypt a pyramid was a monument built to honor a pharaoh. Today the Great Pyramid of Giza is one of the seven wonders of the ancient world.

Reflection: In whole group, ask students to share their examples of definition leads or revisions of lead paragraphs using this new strategy. Use these questions to guide their thinking about how the strategy worked:

Was it easy or difficult to write a definition lead? How so?

Did you make use of the dictionary?

What other sources could you use to help you write a definition lead? (For example, if students are writing about soccer, they might get a definition from a coach or a book about soccer.)

When might you use this strategy again?

Writing to Persuade

We want students to have opinions, to be passionate about these

opinions, and to defend them with strong, well thought out and

elaborated arguments.

—Barry Lane and Gretchen Bernabei, *Why We Must Run With Scissors:*
Voice Lessons in Persuasive Writing 3–12

Persuasion is all around us. Drive in the car and notice the billboards and neon signs in the cities. Turn on the television or pick up a magazine or newspaper and you will be bombarded with messages urging the use of products and services to help you look better and feel better. It's almost a matter of survival to understand deeply the extent to which persuasion affects our lives. The best way to give students the strategies they need to navigate a world of persuasion is to give them the opportunity to try it out themselves, beginning with our youngest writers.

The Power of the Written Word

Our students probably come to us knowing more about the art of persuasion than we realize. Children everywhere have most likely used a variety of techniques to get parents to give them what they want. They might argue, plead, whine, or demand with varying results, but have they ever thought about writing as a persuasive tool? In Doreen Cronin's classic book *Click, Clack, Moo: Cows That Type*, a group of very educated animals makes Farmer Brown aware of their demands through writing. Their letters are simple yet effective in convincing Farmer Brown that a compromise could be reached. This book illustrates the power of the written word—the heart of persuasion.

Working with second graders in Pat Cleveland's class, Rose began teaching about persuasive writing first by helping them define what it means to persuade. Together they returned to some familiar books, such as *Dear Mr. Blueberry* by Simon James and *Earrings!* by Judith Viorst. Rose also introduced them to *Thank You, Sarah: The Woman Who Saved Thanksgiving* by Laurie Halse Anderson. These books helped the children come to the understanding that to persuade means to convince someone to think or act in a certain way. Rose also wanted the students to realize the power of the written word—that oftentimes discovering your arguments and writing them down in a convincing way is more persuasive than just talking. That's how Mr. Blueberry tried to convince Emily that she really couldn't have a whale in her pond and how Sarah Hale was able to finally persuade President Lincoln to make Thanksgiving a national holiday. In *Thank You, Sarah* we read:

> *And Sarah Hale had a secret weapon . . . a pen. When Sarah saw something she didn't like, she picked up her pen and wrote about it. She wrote letters. She wrote articles. She wrote and wrote and wrote until she persuaded people to make the world a better place.*

The next step was to show the students the importance of having sound reasons, or arguments, to make your case. Rose told them that one way to make sure you thought of good reasons was to create a for/against or pro/con chart. She told them that she needed their help in deciding on a book to read aloud in a first-grade class. One of the parents was going to be a guest reader, and she had

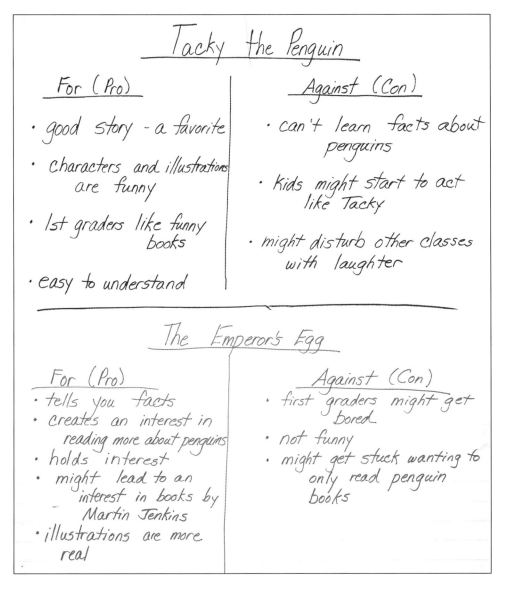

FIGURE 5.1
Pro/con chart

asked Rose which book the first graders might like better—*Tacky the Penguin* by Helen Lester, or *The Emperor's Egg* by Martin Jenkins. Rose knew the students were familiar with both of these books from studying about penguins as first graders. Together they made a pro/con chart for both books (see Figure 5.1). Rose told them that even if they knew which book they would recommend, they needed to think of arguments for and against both books. This thinking would help them form their arguments and explore all possible reasons.

It was a tough decision, but the students felt that *Tacky the Penguin* would make a better read-aloud. Through shared writing, they wrote the following paragraph that Rose said she would include in a letter to the parent who had asked for the advice:

If you want a book about penguins that will be a big hit with first graders, then *Tacky the Penguin* by Helen Lester is the book you should read. First, most first graders enjoy funny characters, and Tacky is hilarious. He wears ridiculous clothes and he always does the wrong thing which gets him in a lot of trouble. Second, even though you can't learn facts about penguins from this book, it would be an easy story for first graders to understand. For those reasons you should read Tacky the Penguin to the first graders. But be careful because they might start laughing too loud!

The next day, Rose asked the students if they would like to try writing a persuasive paragraph for something they might want for the classroom or the school. She reminded them that since they would need sound arguments, it would have to be something realistic. Together they brainstormed a list that included a field trip to the Museum of Natural History, having more time on the computers, a longer recess, an extra story time, and having an additional gym period. The students did get a little carried away when one suggested turning the soccer field into a one-hole golf course and another suggested that the school buses be replaced with coach buses. But these ideas turned out to be very popular, and the students assured Rose and their teacher that they could come up with good arguments. After reviewing the elements of a good persuasive piece from the shared writing they did the day before (a strong introduction that states the topic, an explanation of two or three good reasons or arguments, and a concluding sentence), the students were ready to try it out. They began by creating a pro/con chart in their notebooks, then they wrote. Although the paragraphs were eventually turned into letters (the letter format was a whole other lesson), these examples from the second graders in their own words (grammar and spelling were not edited) will give you some idea of how well they were able to internalize the power of persuasion:

I think we should have more story time because reading storys to us is very important so that we can get lots more ideas for our weekend news by making good beginnings, good endings, and good confentions. Second of all, if you start reading more we will want to read the other books if it has a series. And Mrs. Cleveland, everyone in your class loves when you read. Because you read very fluently and you have very good expreshion. Like when you read that book with the Grandma in it George where's my medicine.

Maddie, Grade 2

Can Room 6 go on the computer more often? First of all, if we go on the computer more we could lern more and go on web sights. We could lern about animals, read a lot, and lern different langijes. The second reason is we could have lots of fun and play lots of cool games. That's why I want to go on the computer more often.

Amy, Grade 2

Can we please change the soccer field into a golf course? First of all we would see how far we can hit and we could learn the game. Second of all someone could get hit but we could put a sign that says "keep out danger". And it might cost much but we could have a bake sale and get money. So can we please get a golf course?

Reid, Grade 2

After the students wrote and shared, Rose asked them to reflect on what they had learned about persuasive writing and when they thought they could use it again. Maddie shared that she had been asking her parents to get her a portable electronic game so that she would have something to do on long car rides. "Now I know that begging isn't going to work," she explained. "I'm going to write down all the reasons I should have one [a portable electronic game] and send them a letter, just like Sarah Hale!"

Using Fiction to Help Students Understand Point of View

In order to understand what it means to write good persuasion, students must develop a keen awareness of their audience's point of view. They must understand that any persuasive issue can be seen through different lenses, and these lenses are often colored with perceptions that are gender based, age based, peer based, and culture based. When writers offer a persuasive argument, they need to understand why their readers may have trouble with their arguments. As Atticus explained to Scout in *To Kill a Mockingbird* by Harper Lee: "You never really understand a person until you consider things from his point of view . . . until you climb into his skin and walk around in it."

One of the best ways to introduce students to the concept of point of view is through fiction. A classic book for point of view is *William's Doll* by Charlotte Zolotow. William's father, brother, and next-door neighbor all have reasons why they feel William should not have a doll. His grandmother, however, is of a different mind and buys William the doll he wants so badly. Her persuasive argument, offered to William's father as her point of view, is hard to refute:

"He needs it . . . to hug and to cradle and to take to the park so that when he's a father like you, he'll know how to take care of his baby and feed him and love him and bring him the things he wants, like a doll so that he can practice being a father."

The young girl in *Earrings!* by Judith Viorst has a different point of view from her parents regarding the age at which pierced ears are appropriate:

They say I'm too young. I'm not too young. I'm actually very mature for my age.

In *I Miss Franklin P. Shuckles* by Ulana Snihura, Molly's point of view shifts due to peer pressure, and she rejects Franklin's friendship.

At school everyone makes fun of his skinny legs and funny glasses. I can't be friends with him anymore. Everyone will laugh at me too.

Fortunately, she comes to her senses by the end of the story and saves a friendship by returning to her original point of view.

Yoko by Rosemary Wells demonstrates how people can arrive at a point of view without really knowing or understanding why. Yoko's friends are familiar with traditional lunch fare such as peanut butter and jelly sandwiches. When Yoko brings in sushi, her friends comment:

"Ick! It's green! It's seaweed!"
"Oh, no!" said the other Frank. "Don't tell me that's raw fish!"
"Watch out! It's moving," said Doris.
"Yuck-o-rama!" said Tulip and Fritz.

Recognizing that all writing, regardless of mode, is generated from the author's point of view is important. Especially in today's age when young readers have access to so much print from so many sources, the critical reader must recognize that not all opinion is valid or profound. Young writers must become mini-experts on their topics to be able to support their points of view and sustain them throughout a piece of writing with clear, concise arguments.

Developing the Argument

In addition to supporting understanding of point of view, fiction is also a friendly vehicle to explore how arguments are developed and to reflect on the effectiveness of those arguments. There are many mentor texts to use with students of all ages to help you do just that. Young writers will appreciate the humor involved in the correspondence between Emily and Mr. Blueberry in *Dear Mr. Blueberry* by Simon James. The book also helps children understand that good persuasive writing will not always change someone's thinking. As Mr. Blueberry tries to convince Emily that a blue whale could not possibly be found in her pond, students can conduct research to support Mr. Blueberry's arguments with specific details. This research will help them come to the understanding that any argument should be based on fact. A T-chart can be created to make the relationship between arguments and supporting details explicit to students:

Arguments	Supporting Details
A blue whale is too big for a pond.	Whales are the biggest animals on Earth. Whales can be 100 feet long. Whales weigh up to 190 tons.
Whales are migratory.	Whales travel, or migrate, between cold waters in summer and warm waters in winter. Food is plentiful in cold summer seas, and babies are born in warm winter seas.
Whales eat shrimp-like creatures.	Blue whales are baleen whales. They use the baleen as a food filter and eat krill. Krill are small, orange sea creatures that look like shrimp and measure about two inches in length. Blue whales eat nine tons of krill each day.

Another way to use a T-chart is to ask students to come up with better arguments than a character suggests in a story. Good choices for this activity would be *Earrings!*, *The Good-Bye Book*, and *Alexander, Who's Not (Do You Hear Me? I Mean It!) Going to Move* by Judith Viorst. Students can evaluate the strength of the arguments that are already presented and rule out the ones that sound like pleading, begging, or whining. They can also rule out arguments that are not sensible or justifiable, such as the argument from the young girl in *Earrings!* who says:

> *I tell them I'm the only girl*
> *In my class*
> *In my school*
> *In the world*
> *In the solar system*
> *Whose mom and dad won't let her have*
> *Pierced ears.*

Knowing Your Audience

In *Arthur's Thanksgiving* by Marc Brown, young readers learn that it's important to recognize the different ways people will view things. It's a great book to introduce how a writer should always think about his or her audience before writing. Arthur has the job of directing the Thanksgiving play and assigning the role of the turkey. In trying to convince each of his friends to take the role of the turkey, he uses good persuasion by appealing to a quality that each friend is known for. He varies his arguments to target Muffy's sense of fashion, Brain's intelligence, and Binky's strength.

In a fourth-grade class that Lynne visited, the students were studying Pennsylvania. To help students visualize and make connections to what it would be like to live in the Pennsylvania colony in the time of William Penn, Lynne asked them to write a letter to a friend or relative in the voice of a colonist. They used books that included *The Pennsylvania Reader* by Trinka Hakes Noble, for examples of letter writing, and *Pennsylvania* by Gwenyth Swain, for details about living in the Pennsylvania colony, to write a letter that would convince someone else to make the trip across the Atlantic. John wrote to a "friend" in Scotland who was a farmer like himself. He knew the importance of writing to a target audience and wrote about the advantage of farming in Pennsylvania:

March 10, 1751

Dear Spencer,

We're missing you here in Pennsylvania. The hunting is excellent. You can fish and trap every day. Pennsylvania is a beautiful place in the New World. You can even have your own piece of land, and it is fairly cheap. It is very easy to grow crops here since the soil is so rich, and you won't have to give the extra crops to the lord of the manor in order to stay and farm the land. In Scotland, the land is stony, but not so here. There are trees for shade and firewood. There are many people here from Scotland. They have settled in the western part of the colony where I live. You will not be alone. Come soon.

Yours,
John

Andrew wrote to "Richard" and targeted his friend's business sense, desire for a better life for his family, and love of reading.

October 13, 1737

Dear Richard,

I am having a great time in Pennsylvania. It is a great life. That is why I am writing to you. It would be a great life for you and your family. Richard, you would have a fantastic business here as a cloth merchant and would earn yourself lots of money. Land is also sold at a fair price.

If you bring your wife and children, your wife would have a better life here. Your children would have plenty of opportunities like being able to use the lending library established by Ben Franklin or could go on to the university. Philadelphia is the biggest and richest city of the colonies, so they will all find good jobs.

I know you like to read. You should know that we have a newspaper, a published magazine, and an almanac. You are free to travel where you want, and you can say what you want. You would love to be able to offer opinions about what you are reading and thinking. I suggest you come to Pennsylvania. You won't be sorry.

Your friend,
Andrew

This particular writing is an example of a RAFT assignment, which is so effective to help students learn how to persuade with vivid arguments by always focusing on a target audience. The information presented is always developed with that audience in mind. So much of what we write today in school is written for a grade, with no real audience (except the teacher) to channel the thinking. This writing is often voiceless—without the passion and fire to move anyone, especially the writer. RAFT stands for role, audience, form, and topic. In the previous examples, the students took the roles of colonists who settled in Pennsylvania, wrote to a target audience—a friend or relative in Europe—in the form of a friendly letter, and the topic was coming to live in Pennsylvania. Sometimes this assignment is referred to as RAFTS, the final letter standing for a specific verb such as convince, design, invent, or compose. A RAFT lesson plan can be found in *Teaching Content Reading and Writing* by Martha Rapp Ruddell (2008).

The Counterargument

An excellent mentor text to illustrate the counterargument is *I Wanna Iguana* by Karen Kaufman Orloff. The book is a series of letters that the character Alex writes to his mother to try to persuade her to let him have a pet iguana. She responds to each letter with a letter of her own, offering a counterargument. For each counterargument, Alex must reevaluate his thinking and consider the situation through the eyes of his mother, or, as Harper Lee suggests, he must walk around in her skin. Other sources for the counterargument include *The Perfect Pet* by Margie Palatini and *Can I Keep Him?* by Steven Kellogg. In Kellogg's book, Arnold keeps bringing home pets, real and imaginary, and asks to keep them as a pet. His mother provides a counterargument for each one:

> *"I found a lost kitten wandering in the street. Can I keep him?"*
> *"No, Arnold. Your grandma is allergic to cat fur. If we kept it, she couldn't visit anymore. Take him back where you found him, and please don't bring any more cats and dogs into the house."*

Arnold doesn't try to consider a rebuttal, he just brings home a different animal each time. Here's an opportunity to ask students if there are any arguments Arnold could present to change his mother's thinking. Some third graders suggested vacuuming the house before Grandma comes over, keeping the cat in one bedroom in a carrier until Grandma leaves, or taking the cat to a kennel when Grandma visits. By third grade, students are able to consider the possibility of the counterargument, anticipating problems their readers could have with their persuasive argument and responding accordingly.

A pro/con chart (see Your Turn Lesson 2 at the end of this chapter) or any graphic organizer that will allow students to spill out their thinking about an issue—both for and against—is a good way to begin. Most of the time students have already chosen on which side of the issue they stand, but sometimes the thinking recorded on the graphic organizer is surprising and causes them to change their position before they start to draft. Lynne was working with some fifth-grade classes that were reading and discussing a news article about the use of uniforms in school. Carly was sure she would not like to wear uniforms in school and was ready to write a persuasive piece against school uniforms. But after thinking about it and recording both sides of the issue, she changed her mind. "What caused you to change your thinking?" asked Lynne. Carly said that she felt the stronger arguments supported school uniforms—arguments such as school spirit, easily recognizing strangers, and not making anyone feel out of place. However, she still had a strong sense of what arguments her peers would have against uniforms.

A dichotomous checklist (yes or no) with a few main criteria is helpful to students as a tool for self-evaluation as they prewrite, draft, and revise their work. The following points could be included in such a checklist:

1. What the author wants the reader(s) to do or think is clear.
2. There are logical reasons given to support each argument.
3. There are statements that show the author has anticipated arguments and answered problems the reader may have.
4. The argument is believable—it is written in a sincere and honest way.
5. The author has stayed on target.

This same checklist can be used as a tool for peers and/or a target audience to offer feedback about the effectiveness of the persuasion. If it is given to a target audience, you can provide a place for arguments and allow time for sharing and reflection.

In Figure 5.2, Kristin, a third grader, understands how her mother feels about guinea pigs and is able to counter what she believes her mother's thinking would be.

Amie, another third grader, anticipates her mother's counterarguments to having a slumber party in Figure 5.3.

The Importance of Reflection

In teaching persuasive writing it's important to give students the opportunity to collect feedback from their target audience in the form of checklists or written comments. Students can use this information to revise even a published piece or set goals during writing conferences for future work in this mode of writing. Additionally, the praise that is received for a job well done will spur them on and give them the confidence they need to continue to be successful. In the example previously given, after Amie presented her mother with her arguments for having a slumber party, her mother gave the following feedback:

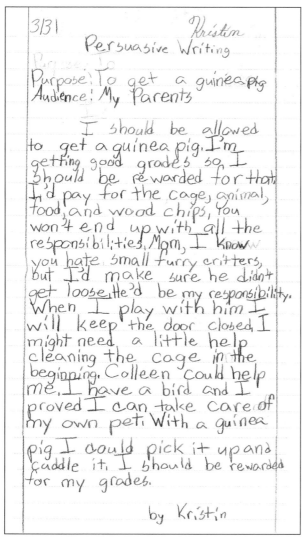

FIGURE 5.2
Kristin's persuasive writing

FIGURE 5.3
Amie's persuasive writing

I have to tell you, Miss Dorfman, Amie read her rough draft of this persuasive speech to me before her birthday. It was so convincing then and filled me with such a feeling of guilt that I did break down and give her a sleep over party. Now after hearing the finished product I can hold my head high and know that I did the right thing. There were many different things going on at one time around her birthday, and I wasn't sure I could pull together a party. I am certainly glad that I made that extra effort. Amie's reasoning and her caring heart are hard things to argue against.

Reflective questions about the work students do around a genre or mode will help cement their learning and make experiences repeatable. These questions also can be used to focus writing workshop discussions during share time or during conference time. Here are some possible questions to ask your students to help them internalize the process of self-evaluation:

1. How did you grow/change as a writer from doing this persuasive writing assignment?
2. What did you learn about persuasive writing?
3. If you could do this assignment again, would you change anything? Why or why not?
4. Tell me about the strengths of your piece. Why is this a good piece of writing?
5. What was the hardest part of this assignment? Explain.

Persuasive Responses to Literature

Older students can write a letter, journal entry, or even an editorial as a response to chapter books to practice a persuasive argument around a particular point of view. After reading *Tuck Everlasting* by Natalie Babbitt, students can develop a pro/con chart to help them make a decision about their perspective on drinking from a spring that would give them the gift of eternal life. Lynne often has her students ponder this question, create a chart, and discuss with a partner or a small group before writing. She also asks them to respond before they finish the book and know what the character (Winnie) decided to do.

Another book that lends itself to debating an issue is *Shiloh* by Phyllis Reynolds Naylor. Students can choose Marty or Judd's point of view and write an argument to convince readers that Shiloh should or should not be returned to his rightful owner. In Lynne's own fourth-grade classroom, students worked in pairs or small groups to write a convincing argument to support or refute Marty's case. Individually they took on the persona of Doc Murphy, Marty's parents, Marty, Judd, and even the dog himself. They revised their arguments in small groups and presented them orally to another fourth-grade class, which served as the jury. Lynne's student teacher (dressed in the graduation gown that he would be wearing within the next several weeks) played the judge. The students had to assume a voice that was both honest and sincere and that targeted arguments that would convince their peers. Ricky wrote a persona piece, becoming the dog:

> I'm Shiloh and I would like to live with Marty. I think Judd is abusive because all he bought me for is to hunt and chain me up. I never get to sleep inside where it is warm. Judd chains me up until we go hunting. One day Judd kicked me so hard that my side was hurting, and I could hardly breathe! Now with Marty, it is a whole different story. When I'm with Marty and his family, I never get kicked around. I never feel hungry, and they never chain me to the house. Marty knows I won't run away because we love and trust each other. When I'm with Marty we take long runs together and play on

the hill. His whole family pets and plays with me. I feel like I'm really part of the family. I think I should belong to Marty. That is my decision. I hope it is yours, too.

Mary Ellen took the side of Judd:

Hi, my name is Judd and I want my dog back! I think Shiloh should be returned to his rightful owner, me. Shiloh was with Marty for one week and he was almost killed. The other dog ripped Shiloh's ear and Shiloh had to be stitched up.

Shiloh would get lonely during the school year if he stays with Marty. Marty doesn't have anyone home to be with Shiloh. I have other dogs for Shiloh to play with. I've said some mean things to Shiloh, but sometimes I say things I don't mean. Everybody does! If Marty keeps Shiloh, he won't hunt, and he IS a hunting dog.

The Preston family doesn't have any spare food or money, and can't even afford a telephone. What'll happen if Shiloh gets hurt? I have all the stuff Shiloh needs. I bought him, took care of him, and fed him since he was a puppy. I think this shows Shiloh should belong and stay with me.

The jury convened and did not reach a decision until the following day. This drove the students crazy! But the other class took their job seriously. They had taken notes, and when they did present the verdict, they offered an explanation as to how they arrived at their decision. No one felt like a loser, because the strengths of arguments presented for both sides were highlighted. (By the way, Marty got to keep his dog!) A further extension of this fictionalized persuasive activity can turn real-world. Students can write letters to family, friends, and community members asking them to support organizations that protect animals.

Many students have experienced what it's like to move to a new home. Using both *Tales of a Fourth Grade Nothing* and *Superfudge* by Judy Blume, students can decide whether the Hatcher family should return to their Manhattan apartment in busy New York City or stay in Princeton, a suburban New Jersey community. Writing in the voice of the oldest sibling, Peter Hatcher, students can write to "their parents" to convince them to stay or move back. Again, a pro/con chart here is very helpful to determine the most effective arguments that could be used. In her third-grade classroom, Lynne reminded students to think about their target audience, Mr. and Mrs. Hatcher, and what would be appealing arguments for each one. Since Lynne was fairly certain that her students (living in a suburb of Philadelphia) would choose arguments to stay in Princeton, she chose to model with arguments to return to New York. The third graders had to consider each facet of this decision-making process, not just how it would affect them (or in this case, Peter Hatcher). Lynne made a quick list on the board noting the family members and the arguments that would be convincing for each one. For example, for Dad, she listed opportunities for advertising jobs and that he wouldn't need a car. For mom, she listed opportunities to visit museums and a smaller house to clean. She encouraged the students to do the same before they began to draft. In the following examples, the students' arguments target the welfare of the entire family:

Dear Mom and Dad,

Don't you think it would be nice to stay in Princeton? Face it! There is cleaner air so it would keep us healthier. And it is so quiet here everybody can take a snoozer! Just think about it. There is less traffic so we can ride bikes in the street and on bike paths! Isn't that great! It would be safer to stay in Princeton because you wouldn't get mugged like Jimmy or Dad. What could be better? What about when Tootsie grows up . . . we will need more room. Don't you think it will be wonderful?

Your son,
Peter (Matthew)

Dear Mom and Dad,

It would be a lot better if we stay in Princeton. First of all, clean air would be good for our health. A larger house would give us more space and we could have a yard of our own. Dad, you could take naps after a hard day because it would be quieter. It would be safer, too because of less criminals. We could ride in the streets with very few cars. And Mom, you could garden in our own yard. We could have our own rooms (I don't think Tootsie would like to sleep in a room full of boys). Best of all, I don't have to put up with Sheila! It would be healthier, safer, and we would be happier if we stayed in Princeton.

Your son,
Peter (Mary Ellen)

Sometimes fiction deals with important real-world topics. Many students have to deal with moving, so writing in response to *Tales of a Fourth Grade Nothing* and *Superfudge* helps them explore this issue and the points of view involved in a little more depth. A good companion book or alternative for younger students is Eileen Spinelli's *Where I Live*. In this book, the main character, Diana, does not want to move. As the book progresses, her feelings change. In addition, written response to *Shiloh* in the voice of the many characters can lead to exploration of current issues that appear every day in the news—issues such as animal abuse, animal abandonment, and the rights of pet owners.

For developing writers, the story format is a friendly and familiar vehicle to learn about the world. Fiction offers a certain comfort level with a topic and establishes the background that students need to continue to explore nonfiction material around that same topic.

Developing the Argument with Nonfiction

Nonfiction books can be paired with fiction to help students discover the importance of developing clear arguments. Jean Davies Okimoto's *Winston of Churchill: One Bear's Battle Against Global Warming* presents arguments in the form of banners and posters used by polar bears in a friendly protest. In order to have students write persuasively about global warming in different formats, they need solid facts to support their arguments and help them speak with the voice of authority. Books such as *Why Are the Ice Caps Melting? The Dangers of Global Warming* by Anne Rockwell, and *A Clean Sky: The Global Warming Story* by Robyn Friend can offer the facts students need to develop their thinking. In *The World That Jack Built* by Ruth Brown, a familiar scaffold is used to show how pollution has changed the landscape and endangered both plants and animals. This book can be paired with *A River Ran Wild* by Lynne Cherry to gather facts about pollution.

Hey, Little Ant by Phillip and Hannah Hoose is a work of fiction written in play format that is perfect for a persuasive writing unit. In this book a boy is about to squish an ant when the ant speaks to him to plead for his life. Two points of view are presented, and arguments (the ant's and the boy's) can easily be charted. Last spring we used this book in both a first-grade and a third-grade class to give students the opportunity to write persuasively. A real-world purpose presented itself to us in the form of a contest sponsored by the authors. Students were invited to answer the open-ended question posed at the end of the book, "What do you think the kid should do?"

We began by charting the arguments presented by the boy and by the ant. After charting, students were asked to talk with a partner and decide which character had the stronger arguments. Even first graders recognized that some of the kids' arguments weren't valid. One particularly weak argument was built around peer pressure. First grader Quinn shared, "Doing something just because your friend does it is never a good idea." The third graders thought the most convincing argument was the one given by the ant about changing roles— if you could put yourself in the ant's place, would you still think it was a good idea to squish ants for fun? Although the students in both classes felt that the ant had the stronger arguments, they couldn't develop them with supporting details. To help them with this, the next step was to bring in nonfiction books about ants and have them read widely and chart the facts. Books such as *Thinking About Ants* by Barbara Brenner, *The Life and Times of the Ant* by Charles Micucci, and *Are You an Ant?* by Judy Allen were good sources. We read aloud, read together from pages shared on a visualizer or document imager, and read in pairs and individually. As students shared interesting facts they learned about ants, we charted them for future reference. Rose was surprised at how much background knowledge the first graders already had about ants. They had studied insects in the fall, so they had a basis from which to add to their knowledge.

Lynne and third-grade teacher Jon DeMinico referred to the arguments the ant had given in *Hey, Little Ant* and asked the students to use those arguments and what they had read to come up with a topic statement that also made a point. Students shared these in whole group and Lynne listed them on the board. The third graders came up with several topic statements:

Ants are a lot like people.
Ants help the farmers.
Ants are important to their habitat.
Ants are amazing and interesting creatures.

After the students considered which topic statement appealed to them, they returned to the chart of facts and their books to see if they could come up with an explanation, description, or example that would support their topic sentence. Lynne and Jon modeled how to do this before the students got started. These supporting facts were recorded in their writer's notebooks. As they worked, Lynne and Jon conducted roving conferences to make sure the students' information matched their topic statement. Sometimes they encouraged the students to dig deeper or even change their topic statement if they seemed to be going in a different direction.

After the students had finished a draft of their essay, Lynne asked them to return to their introduction and think about an interesting lead or attention grabber that they could use before their opening topic sentence. She used the book *Almost Gone: The World's Rarest Animals* by Steve Jenkins, *Imagine a Day* by Sarah Thomson, and *Somewhere Today* by Bert Kitchen as mentor texts to create a "What if . . .?" or imagine-a-world lead. Lynne modeled with the following example:

Imagine having the strength to lift a car high above your head. "Impossible!" you might say. But if you are an ant, you are able to lift fifty times your own weight. Ants are truly amazing creatures.

The students returned to their drafts and tried it out. If it didn't work for them, they used other familiar leads, including questions, a snapshot of a character (an ant), and a quote from a text. The next day, students looked at their concluding remarks and realized they had not returned to the original question they were trying to answer: "Should the kid step on the ant?" Jon and Lynne asked the students to make sure their conclusion answered this question, wrapping around to their introductory statements if possible.

Michael imitated Bert Kitchen's lead and made it work for him:

Somewhere today an ant is building—digging dirt and making rooms everywhere. Ants are just like us. They do amazing things! It's fascinating to learn about them.

Ants milk insects called aphids like farmers milk cows. Aphids are like pets to the ant. Nurse ants lick the larva to keep them from drying out. Nurses help us if we get hurt. Ants have brothers and sisters in their family just like our family. They have rooms in their colony like nurseries, hallways, and even storage rooms. It's hard to believe it, but they have a special room to bury dead ants.

As you can see, ants are more like humans than you would think. They do amazing things! Tell that kid with the raised up shoe not to step on that ant. If he knew more about ants, he'd never do it!

Danielle chose a "What if . . .?" lead and created hers in the form of a question.

What if you woke up one morning and you were the size of an ant? You could get stepped on by a human. You could get eaten by an animal, too! You would be carrying stuff all day, in and out of the ant nest. You would also have to feed your whole colony. Thank goodness you would be one of many!

Even a blade of grass would look like a tree to you. An ant's work is never done. If you were an ant you would have to help feed the larva or dig some more tunnels or rooms. Ants need all their nest mates to keep the colony from starving. One ant is definitely missed! If the boy steps on that ant, things might not get done. Who will dig rooms? Who will take the garbage out? Who will carry dead ants back to the nest to be placed in a special burial room? Who will lick the larva to keep them from drying out? Don't step on that ant!

Shanice chose a question lead to begin, but ended with the "What if . . .?" scaffold:

Do you love your family? Did you know ants have a mother, brothers, and sisters? Ants are a lot like humans. Their family works like our mom and dad work. They feed their family. They have homes like us. Ants dig a nursery, bedrooms, corridors, and even storage rooms. Sounds like a fancy mansion, right? Did you know nurse ants make the little ants feel better? They lick them to keep them from drying out.

Today ants live almost everywhere in the world—just like us. Each ant has at least one job. Ants cannot speak, but they can touch each other and give each other messages. They are smart. They leave trails so the other ants can follow.

Ants are splendid creatures. Ants and people are alike in many ways. What if you were an ant? Would you want to be stepped on? Consider that before you squish that ant!

Rose did something similar with Mary Jane Corabi's first-grade class. Her goal was to make sure the facts they used to support their argument matched

FIGURE 5.4
Brendan writes in the voice of the ant.

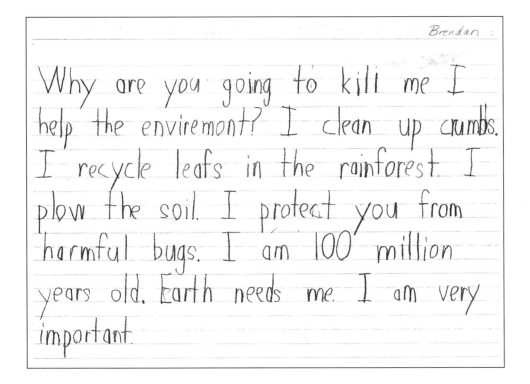

> Brendan :
>
> Why are you going to kill me I help the enviremont? I clean up crumbs. I recycle leafs in the rainforest. I plow the soil. I protect you from harmful bugs. I am 100 million years old. Earth needs me. I am very important.

the big idea, or topic statement, they chose to present. After the class decided together and charted what they felt were the big ideas, Rose returned to the list of facts. Using different colored sticky notes, she helped the students code which facts matched which big idea. She then suggested different ways they might choose to begin their piece. "You could begin by simply stating why you think the boy should not kill the ant. Or, you could pretend you are talking directly to the kid," she explained. The students then suggested different things they might say to him.

Brendan asked, "Can we pretend to be the ant?" Rose, thinking that writing in the persona of the ant might be difficult for these first graders, was not going to suggest it. But since the question came directly from them, she realized she might have underestimated their abilities. (See Figure 5.4 for Brendan's piece.)

Using oral writing (talking through the piece without actually writing it down), Rose modeled how she might choose which big idea or argument she felt she could best support with facts, and how she might state that in the opening of her piece. She then went on to support the argument with facts. The students then decided on arguments and supporting facts of their own and discussed them with a partner. Rose asked a few students to share in front of the class and used questions to guide their thinking. When she was satisfied that everyone was ready, the students got started with their writing. (See Figures 5.5 and 5.6 for examples of students' arguments.)

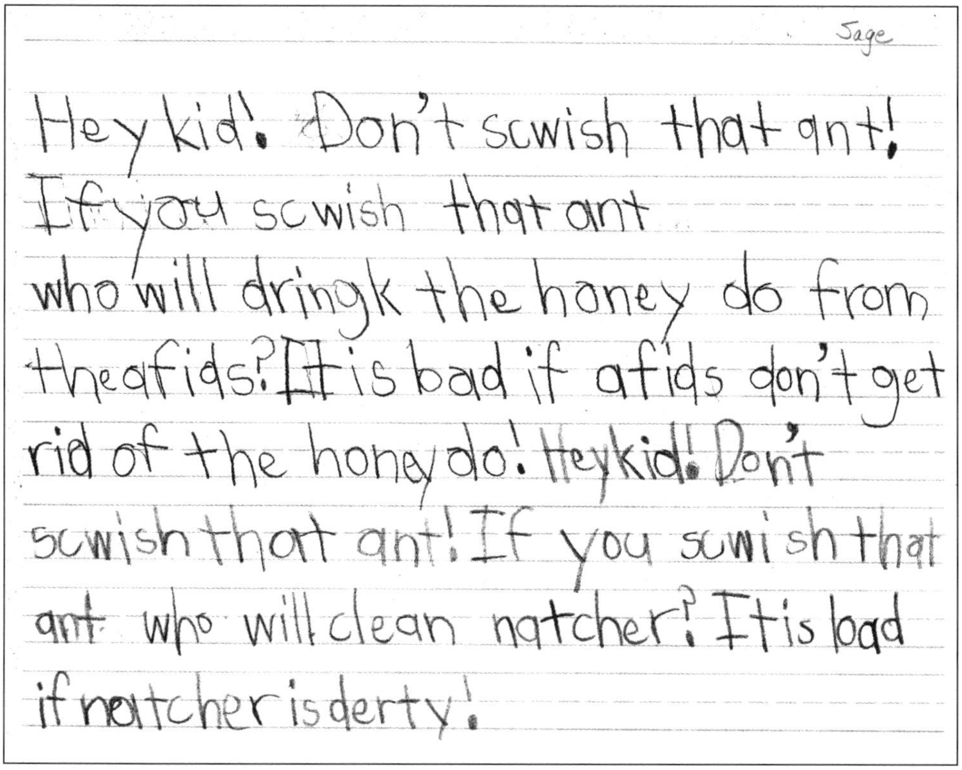

> Sage
>
> Hey kid! Don't scwish that ant! If you scwish that ant who will dringk the honey do from the afids? It is bad if afids don't get rid of the honey do! Hey kid! Don't scwish that ant! If you scwish that ant who will clean natcher? It is bad if natcher is derty!

FIGURE 5.5
Sage directs her argument to her target audience (the kid).

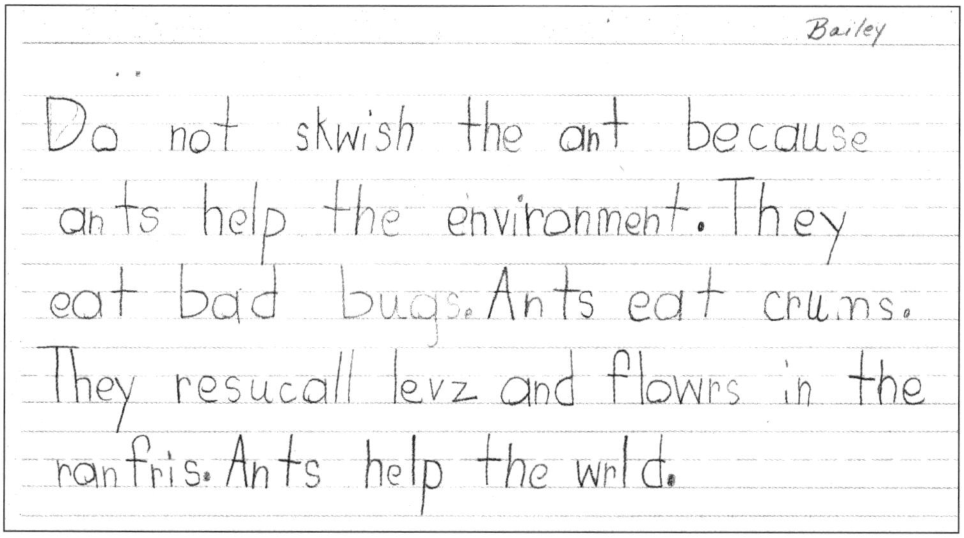

> Bailey
>
> Do not skwish the ant because ants help the environment. They eat bad bugs. Ants eat crums. They resucall levz and flowrs in the ranfris. Ants help the wrld.

FIGURE 5.6
Bailey argues that ants are helpful.

The next day, the students shared their pieces in whole group and Rose asked them to think about what they had learned. "What you just did," she explained, "was use writing to persuade, or convince, someone that he or she should act in a certain way. What helped you do that?" The students told her they learned that convincing arguments must be strong, and that they must have facts to support what they said.

"Sometimes you have to do research and know what you are talking about. You can't just make it up," offered Nick.

We received notification that more than two thousand entries were submitted to the *Hey, Little Ant* writing contest. Three students from Jon's third-grade class won honorable mentions and received autographed copies of the book. On a very hot day, Lynne and Jon treated the students to popsicles. They decided to go outside to eat them and share their sticky sweetness with the ants (drip . . . drip . . . drip!).

Book Reviews and Book Talks

One of our personal mentors, Regie Routman, provides a solid rationale for spending time teaching students how to give effective book talks.

> *Most of the books I read have been recommended by friends. It makes sense, then, to give students that same opportunity. A friend's enthusiasm about a book often "sells" it. It is not unusual for a whole class of students to read books by an author one of their classmates has recommended.* (2000, 58)

Writing a book review or giving a book talk lends itself to persuasive language and offers students the opportunity to learn more about writing in this genre.

At Rose's school, the students were preparing for an evening program for Read Across America, a celebration of Dr. Seuss's birthday and an opportunity to encourage students to read independently. The whole school was working on book reviews to showcase their favorites and to offer new titles to the parents and students who would be attending the program and reading the reviews. In Heather Lovelace's first-grade class, Rose modeled a book review with one of her favorites, *Crab Moon* by Ruth Horowitz.

> Have you ever gotten up in the middle of the night to do something special? That's just what happens in the book *Crab Moon* by Ruth Horowitz. Daniel gets up in the dark to watch hundreds of horseshoe crabs come to the beach to lay their eggs. Later that morning, he has to be very brave to save one of the crabs. I loved the part where the horseshoe crab looks like a queen as she pulls her shell through the sand. If you like the beach and stories about animals, you will love this book. It might even make you want to learn more about horseshoe crabs!

After sharing her model, Rose asked the students to tell her what they noticed about what kinds of things were included in her book review. In whole group, Rose charted their findings. The students told her that she had a good opening sentence. They also noticed that she told a little bit about the book without giving the whole thing away. She included her favorite part and also what type of reader would enjoy this book. Of course, the title of the book and author must be included, as well as a good ending sentence.

The first graders brainstormed and charted the titles of many of their favorite books. Rose started by asking the class which books they had enjoyed as read-alouds. This way she could create a shared writing experience. Together they wrote a review for *Never Spit on Your Shoes* by Denys Cazet, a favorite read-aloud from the beginning of the year. As the students included the aspects of the sample book review that they had identified (good opening sentence, favorite part, and so on), Rose checked them off on the chart. If things were missing, they could easily see it and revise the book review to include the missing ingredient. Their completed book review follows.

> *Never Spit on Your Shoes* by Denys Cazet is a great story about the first day of first grade. Arnie tells his mom all the things he learned, like what the classroom rules are, how to spell "boys," and how to count. The illustrations with the speech bubbles make it even funnier. Our favorite part was when the first graders all lined up at the window to watch the kindergarten bus going home. We think they were wishing they were on it. We recommend this book for anyone who remembers what the first day of school is like. It will make you laugh out loud!

The students' overnight assignment was to think about a book they would recommend to someone. The next day, they wrote and illustrated their book reviews, which were displayed on the wall outside their classroom. As they wrote, they referred to the chart that listed the key components they had identified for a book review.

Ellie wrote:

> Have you ever wanted to stay up late? Then *Don't Let the Pigeon Stay Up Late* by Mo Willems is a good book for you. The book is about a pigeon that wants to stay up. When he argues with you he says it's the middle of the day in China. My favorite part is when the pigeon goes crazy and when he gets frustrated. I recommend this book to anybody that likes funny books. I hope you enjoy.

Michael wrote:

> Did your town ever get toppled by pasta? Then you should read *Strega Nona* by Tomie dePaola. Strega Nona helped a lot of people. Strega Nona asked Big Anthony to do some of the work. One day when Big Anthony was milking the goat he heard Strega Nona singing. Big Anthony peeked in the window. He saw her using the magic pasta pot. My favorite part was when the town got toppled by pasta. I recommend this book to people who like funny books. This book will make you laugh.

Book reviews can easily become book talks. In Lynne's school district, Upper Moreland, students from kindergarten through twelfth grade write book talks to be used in videos for reading incentive assemblies and to be aired on the school's television channel. The purpose is twofold: to create lifelong, independent readers, and to help students and their parents choose wonderful books. At the Upper Moreland Intermediate School, Lynne and classroom teachers model how to create a book talk. Lynne offers the following advice:

1. Begin with an attention grabber or interesting lead.
2. Mention the title of the book and its author early on and again toward the end of your talk.
3. Share enough of the book to get the reader's interest—often the problem or goal the main character has.
4. If possible, include the genre and/or tell who would like to read this book.
5. Be able to talk—not read—your book talk for videotaping purposes or class shares.

Third-grade teacher Joanne Costello created a book talk for the reading incentive assembly. Notice how she used parentheses in her written book talk to give her stage directions for performance purposes and followed the stage directions with a short phrase for effect:

(Snap fingers) In an instant! That's how quickly your life can change, and that's exactly what author Peg Kehret discovers and then later goes on to describe in an autobiographical piece *Small Steps: The Year I Got Polio*. The year is 1949 and a vaccine to prevent this devastating disease has yet to be discovered. Peg is a normal teenage girl who goes from one day worrying about things about the Homecoming Parade to the next day fighting for her life.

One afternoon while singing in her school's chorus, Peg feels a slight twitching in her leg. The next thing she knows, she is collapsed onto the floor. Upon arriving home, her mom realizes Peg has a high fever. What at first seems like a case of the flu is quickly diagnosed as polio. Immediately, Peg is taken to the hospital and is no longer permitted to see family or friends. Scared and alone, Peg must find the strength within her to fight the greatest battle of her life. How does she succeed? To find out you'll have to read this powerful and inspirational book, *Small Steps: The Year I Got Polio* by Peg Kehret.

Nicole, one of Joanne's third-grade students, decided to use a snippet of dialogue to grab her reader's attention. She posed several questions throughout her book talk to keep the reader thinking and to tempt the reader to read the book. This question format is often used by nonfiction author Jim Arnosky, an author familiar to Joanne's students. Notice, too, how Nicole modeled her book talk after her teacher's.

> (Whisper) "Wake up! Wake up!" That's what Annie whispers to her older brother Jack in the Magic Tree House book, *Afternoon on the Amazon* by Mary Pope Osborne. Why is she in such a hurry to wake him up? Annie is excited to begin her journey to the Amazon River. You see, Annie and Jack have a secret tree house that magically takes them wherever they want to go. All they have to do is point to a picture of a place to travel and poof—they are there. What happens when they meet up with some dangerous crocodiles and poisonous snakes? What amazing adventure do they get into? Well, you just have to take a magical trip with the book *Afternoon on the Amazon* to find out the answers to these questions.

In Gretchen Elfreth and Barbara Hollish's fourth-grade classes, the students worked collaboratively to write book talks for the videotaping as well. However, they had another real-world purpose for their book talks. The students were also inviting the entire community to visit the Alex's Lemonade Stand at two events to raise money for pediatric cancer research. (Read more about this project in Chapter 6.) Marissa and Donna provided the background knowledge they felt the audience would need to understand the importance of their support for the project. They incorporated their knowledge of a play or reader's theater format to write and deliver this very persuasive book talk:

Marissa: If life hands you lemons, make lemonade. This is what a brave young girl named Alex Scott would say. Even though she was ill with cancer herself, she was a hero for many children.

Donna: Our class read an inspiring book called *Alex and the Amazing Lemonade Stand* by Liz and Jay Scott. This story uses a fun rhyming pattern to tell about Alex's plan to make a lemonade stand with lemonade extra sweet and icy cold. As days passed, Alex's lemonade stand was a huge success. Quickly, Alex's lemonade stand grew and soon there were stands in all kinds of locations. Every year the lines grew longer as kids all over the world were inspired to help out to raise money to find a cure for cancer. After years of selling lemonade, Alex's Lemonade Stands have raised millions of dollars for pediatric cancer research.

Marissa: Now you know the story about Alex Scott. It is your turn to buy or donate to the Alex's Lemonade Stand at the Curriculum Fair on April 24 and Family Fun Night on May 16. Not only will you have fun at these events and support a great cause, you will have a chance to win this book!

Donna: Yes. This inspiring story can be yours! We will be holding a raffle. Simply purchase a ticket, and if you are the lucky winner you will be the owner of . . .

Together: *Alex and the Amazing Lemonade Stand.*

Marissa: Together we can make a difference!
Donna: Buy lemonade and help fight cancer!

In Teresa Lombardi's fifth-grade class, students also created book talks as advertisements for the reading incentive assembly program. Zach wrote about one of Lynne's favorite picture books.

> Have you ever wanted to do something really badly but you just couldn't do it? In their book *Painting the Wind* by Patricia and Emily MacLachlan the young boy wants to paint the wind but he never can. During summer he follows all different kinds of painters around his island, trying to imitate what they do. His favorite painter is the landscape painter, who paints his dog Meatball running in from a wave. He has captured the wind. Can the young boy paint the wind? Read this book about mentors, *Painting the Wind* by Patricia and Emily MacLachlan to find out. The beautiful illustrations and inspiring story may give you the courage to try something new!

David wrote about a book the entire class had read during literature circles and was using to help make reading/writing connections.

> Have you ever heard of the Underground Railroad? In *Freedom Crossing* by Margaret Goff Clark a girl named Laura and a boy named Bert have a stop on the underground railroad. When their parents are in Buffalo at the Saturday market, a slave named Martin comes to their house. Bert is worried about hiding Martin. He's not sure his new stepmother will approve. What happens next is a great adventure, secretive and dangerous. Will Martin cross the border to Canada or will he be caught by the slave catchers? If you like historical fiction, read *Freedom Crossing* by Margaret Goff Clark to find out.

The Importance of a Road Map

A solid approach to persuasive writing instruction includes a plan for writing workshop that contains key elements presented in a logical order. In this chapter, we shared many ideas. To help you see the whole picture at a glance, we've created a road map with sign posts to guide you as you travel with your students to explore persuasive writing.

Road Map for Persuasive Writing
- Understanding Point of View
- Using Persuasive Writing for Real-World Purposes
- Persuasive Writing Topics
  Personal Issues
     Sample

Topic: getting a pet
Audience: parents
School Issues
Sample
Topic: wearing uniforms
Audience: principal and teachers
Community Issues
Sample
Topic: need a bus stop on our street
Audience: school board
World Issues
Sample
Topic: recycling
Audience: people who throw away recyclables
- Narrowing the Topic to a Manageable Size
- Graphic Organizers for Persuasion (Pro/Con List)
- Formats for Writing (travel guides, business letters, advertisements, etc.)
- Understanding the Rhetorical Question
- Writing an Introduction
Leads
Thesis Statement (topic and point)
Snapshots of Setting
Snapshots of People
Stating Your Arguments
Transitions Within and Between Paragraphs
- Writing the Body
Structures: compare/contrast, cause/effect, problem/solution
Using a Narrative to Persuade as the Body of the Piece
Arguments and Supporting Details
Anecdotes
Examples
Explanations
Statistics
Transition Words and Phrases
- Writing a Conclusion
Restate the Thesis Sentence or Point
Summary Statements
Rhetorical Questions
Transition Words or Phrases
Personalized Connection, Visualization, Food for Thought

After reading Ron Hirschi's books about the seasons with one fourth-grade class, Lynne created a shared persuasive writing experience. She paired students to create a list—one partner listed reasons why summer was the best season in Pennsylvania, and the other partner took the opposite point of view. After some writing time, students had one minute each to read their arguments to their partners, adding any they came up with orally. Partners had to simply listen, but they were required to share their partner's best argument in whole group. Lynne only charted the arguments against summer as the best season, which would be used in a shared writing piece. Lynne purposely chose arguments against summer because most students, if given a choice, would argue that summer was the best season of all. She wanted the fourth graders to work hard to develop solid arguments supporting a point of view that was different from their own. Good persuasion centers on a writer being able to recognize the other perspectives that their readers may entertain.

Using the arguments on the chart, the students were called on to identify any entries that seemed to go together and underline them in one color and to use another color for a different set of facts or opinions that belonged together. After they were finished, Lynne asked them to come up with the big ideas. There were three main arguments: the weather, boredom, and pesky plants and animals. Next, the students were introduced to the idea of the rhetorical question—something you ask but don't expect an answer to because you expect your audience to answer it only one way. The rhetorical question or statement is powerful because it helps you get your audience on your side in a subtle way. You get them to agree or disagree with something, and then they find that their thinking supports what your persuasion is about. In the shared writing experience sample that follows, you will notice that the fourth graders worked hard to include rhetorical questions and statements. Of course, they probably have overused this technique, but that is what writers do when they are trying something on for size.

It is important to note that Lynne's fourth graders had many opportunities to try out what they were learning through Your Turn lessons as part of a persuasive writing unit of study before they composed this piece. Learning how to write persuasively takes time. Although we can begin to teach our youngest students what persuasion means, their sophistication with it will develop as they mature and collect strategies in their writing toolbox.

Summer in Pennsylvania is NOT for Everyone!

Are you looking forward to beetles, flies, floods, and temperatures that could fry an egg on the sidewalk? Of course, not! That is why summer is not a favorite season of many people. Boredom, pesky plants and animals, and weather are three reasons why summer is not the best time of the year in Pennsylvania.

Boredom is one reason why summer is not the best season in the keystone state. When you are at home, your parents are still at work.

Television is boring after a while. Besides, who wants to watch reruns all day long? Most days, it is simply too hot to play outdoors. It can be ninety degrees well before noon. Even your dog doesn't want to play fetch with you! Also, a lot of your friends are away at summer camps or visiting relatives, and the unlucky ones are attending summer school. If you do go to summer camp, you still may be bored blue! Arts and crafts, eating snacks, and playing relay races really are not all that entertaining. How many key chains made out of gimp can you bring home to your parents? Summer is really boring!

Annoying pests can take the shape of plants or animals. Have you ever suffered from poison oak or poison ivy? Scratch, scratch, scratch! Additionally, bug bites surely leave marks on your skin. They may swell up and itch. That's what happens every time I get mosquito bites. Today, there is more cause for alarm. Mosquitoes carry West Nile Virus and can make human beings very ill. Some people get allergic reactions from bee stings. Once I broke out in hives after being stung by wasps and had to get to the drugstore immediately for allergy medicine. Horse flies and deer flies bite horses and people. Whenever you try to have a picnic, you'll be visited by flies and ants. Flies even land on your food. Who wants to dig into the potato salad after flies have been sitting in it? Yuck! Summer is the season for these wretched plants and insects.

The most important reason why summer is not the best season in my state is the weather. Sure, there are balmy beach days. However, summer weather brings on a host of problems. First of all, outdoor fun is outdoor sun. Too much sun can cause severe sunburn and even sun poisoning. In some cases, people have to visit their doctor or a hospital to be treated. Additionally, years of summer sun can cause life-threatening skin cancer if you don't protect yourself with sunscreen and limit your hours in the sun. Sometimes, it is so hot and humid that you feel you cannot breathe or that you will faint. Some people actually suffer from heat strokes. Furthermore, most people do not enjoy sweating and having their clothes stick to their skin. When you are playing or gardening, salty beads of sweat drip into your eyes. Car drivers are often blinded by the intense sun, and accidents can occur. And what about those dark leather car seats against the backs of your bare legs? Ouch! Even the steering wheel is hard to grip. No, summer weather is not ideal!

In conclusion, summer is not the best season of the year. Summer can be downright boring. In addition, we are constantly fighting a bug and plant problem. It's way too hot, with weather that brings a host of health problems. By now I'm sure you'll agree that summer will never win the Oscar for an award-winning performance. Summer is never going to get a standing ovation from the Pennsylvania crowd—not ever!

An Author's Voice: About Writing Nonfiction

Trinka Hakes Noble
Author of *The Scarlet Stockings Spy* and *The Pennsylvania Reader*

I've always loved stories. I love to hear them, read them, and most of all, I love to write them. So, writing nonfiction is a challenge for me. Sometimes nonfiction and informational writing can be boring and difficult to read, especially if it is bogged down with complex details and endless facts. I never want anything I write to be boring! So, when I write nonfiction, I make it sound like a story. This way the reader is interested right from the start.

One way I make nonfiction sound like a story is with my use of language. In *The Pennsylvania Reader* I wanted to write about how Pennsylvania got its name. So, I started with this sentence:

> *Long ago, in the year 1682, a ship named Welcome sailed up the Delaware River.*

It feels like the beginning of a story, like you are entering a time and place long, long ago, and you are, but you are also learning historical facts. This draws the reader in just like a story but it also gives the reader valuable information.

Another way I make sure my nonfiction writing is exciting and interesting is to start with the most amazing fact or bit of information about a subject. In *The New Jersey Reader*, I wanted to write about wildlife and migration patterns in the state, especially along the Cape May Peninsula. Did you know that the horseshoe crab is 350 million years old? And for every single one of those 350 million years, they have come ashore by the many thousands to the same Cape May and Delaware Bay beaches to lay their eggs. Isn't that amazing? To me, it's beyond amazing! Starting with an incredible fact makes the reader want to learn more. But this only works if you, the writer, are curious too.

So, when you are writing nonfiction, make sure the topic is something you are excited and curious about, something you want to learn more about, and then your reader will too.

Your Turn Lesson 1

Stand Up and Deliver Speeches

One way to prepare students to write more effective persuasive pieces is to give them a chance to practice presenting good arguments for or against a topic. This can be done through an oral presentation given from notes or brief points jotted down as a memory jog. As students gain more practice with this type of on-the-spot speech, they should be able to jot down ideas and be prepared to "stand up and deliver" within five minutes, making this activity one that can easily fit into different parts of the day.

Hook: Short, on-the-spot speeches can be introduced to students through mentor poems. You may have some favorite poems you use in your classroom to help students develop fluency. Examine these as sources for possible one-minute speeches. Some of our favorites for this activity include "Belinda Blue" by Jack Prelutsky, "Sarah Cynthia Sylvia Stout Would Not Take the Garbage Out" by Shel Silverstein, and "Summer Squash" by Donald Graves.

Purpose: *Writers, in order to write effective persuasive pieces, you first must be able to think of good arguments and be able to support your arguments with sound reasons. Today I am going to show you how to practice making good arguments, and Sarah Cynthia Sylvia Stout (or Belinda Blue, etc.) will help us.*

Brainstorm: Engage the students' interests by thinking of things they like or don't like to do or eat or places they like or don't like to go. You could also connect to topics across the curriculum. A list might include the following topics:

> Why Grades Should/Should Not Be Given
> Why It Is Important to Recycle Newspaper
> Why We Should Go to School
> Why Our Class Should Have a Field Trip to _____
> Why _____ Should Not Be Served in the Cafeteria
> Why We Should/Should Not Have a Class Pet
> Why Lincoln Was a Great President
> Why the Beach Is the Best (or Worst) Place to Vacation
> Why I Should/Should Not Go to Summer Camp

Together with the class, brainstorm some possible arguments on a variety of topics appropriate to your grade level that could be supported with reasons (we like to suggest that students can generate eight to ten reasons on a topic so they can expand their thinking and speak for a minute).

Model: Return to one of the poems you used at the beginning of the lesson and use it as a model for listing reasons for an argument. For example, if you were using "Sarah Cynthia Sylvia Stout," you would probably want to persuade her to take the garbage out. Using information from the poem and your own ideas, you might jot down the following reasons on the board or chart paper:

1. No one can walk in the house because there is so much garbage blocking the door.

2. The walls of the house are cracking because of the pressure from the garbage piles.
3. The roof of the house is being pushed off because of all the garbage.
4. The rancid smells are making everyone sick.
5. The neighbors have all moved.
6. No one will come over to play.
7. The garbage piles are attracting flies.
8. The garbage piles are attracting rats.

Using the reasons listed, model giving an on-the-spot speech using the reasons that Sarah should take out the garbage. You can expand on each point as you speak, but remember that you have only one minute.

Shared/Guided Writing: Choose an argument from the brainstormed list and ask the class to help list the reasons to support it. Try to do this in no more than three minutes. Have students work in small groups or pairs and practice presenting the reasons in no more than one minute. Each group can then choose a representative to present the arguments to the class.

Independent Writing: Students can return to the brainstormed list and choose a different topic or come up with one of their own. While writing good persuasive arguments might involve some research, this is an extemporaneous exercise designed to give students the feel of presenting an argument. They should list their arguments in a short amount of time and then be prepared to present them orally.

Reflection: As students deliver their speeches, the effectiveness of the arguments can be judged by their peers. Make sure students think not only about which arguments were most effective but also why they were effective. They might also think about how the arguments were delivered—were there any special words or phrases that helped to persuade the listener? Of course, they should also reflect on how the strategy might help them when they write a persuasive piece. The following questions can help guide the discussion:

How did doing an on-the-spot speech work for you?

How could you use this strategy as you prepare to write a persuasive piece?

What kinds of words are the most effective in helping you get your point across?

Your Turn Lesson 2

Writing from a Point of View Using a Pro/Con Chart

Hook: Lester Laminack's *Snow Day!* provides an excellent model to explore point of view and how it can be used in writing. Although this book is a work of fiction, it is readily adapted for student use, as it details a real-world event for many students, teachers, and parents. In order for this lesson to be effective, this book first should be used as a read-aloud. Return to it and show a few pages on chart paper or an overhead transparency and have students turn and talk about the thinking of either the adult or the child in the book. Examine the use of emotional impact that is tied closely with a point of view and the use of first-person narrative. By this time, students should be noticing that point of view can be the same for adults and children. Later on, they will explore how point of view can be the same or very different.

Options: *All About Frogs* by Jim Arnosky, *Baseball, Snakes, and Summer Squash* by Donald Graves, *Talkin' About Bessie: The Story of Aviator Elizabeth Coleman* by Nikki Grimes, *Hummingbirds: Tiny but Mighty* by Julianne Gehman, *Hiroshima* by Lawrence Yep, *Under the Blood-Red Sun* by Graham Salisbury.

Purpose: *Writing always is approached from a point of view, regardless of genre. Often, we use writing in the first person when we are explaining our point of view, or the first person collectively as in "We, the members of the fifth-grade class . . ." If we use a pro/con chart to help us see both sides of an issue, it can help us to establish our point.*

    Today I will show you how to create such a chart before you write. Considering questions such as how your audience will react to your topic and the information or arguments you present to them will guide your thinking about details you'll need to add to your writing so that it is clear to the reader. If an unusual adjective can add a strong feeling or a bit of humor to the writing, you might consider using one or two in your list. Phrases will always provide more help than one-word responses.

Brainstorm: Ask students to think about this statement: "It's snowing!" Imagine looking out the class-room windows in the morning hours and seeing the snow falling in thick sheets. Instruct the students to take a page in their notebook and fold it in half, labeling one side "Pro" and the other "Con." Divide the class in half. Ask half of the students to write ideas in their pro/con charts from the point of view of children—pros about the snow falling and cons about the snow falling. Ask the other half of the students to jot down some thoughts in their pro/con charts from the point of view of their parents and teachers. Have students share with partners first. One partner should represent the point of view of a child, and the other partner should represent the adult perspective. In whole group, ask students to share orally, and record some of their ideas on chart paper set up for the children's and adults's perspectives. Ask students to share a thought from their partner that is original or convincing.

Model: Share some of your ideas about snow (or whatever topic you choose to use, which could include people, events, or places that are important to you). Stretch any single-word thinking into a phrase using adjectives, adverbs, or verbs. For example, "fun in the snow" is not specific enough. Show students how you would ask yourself, "What kind of fun?" Change your chart response to "making snow angel sculptures in fluffy snow."

Begin to write a paragraph around the issue from one point of view, using the class pro/con chart as your guide. Revise by finding some places that could use an adjective or two or a specific detail, example, or explanation. Try to stretch your thinking by including some thinking that is not listed on your chart or the class chart. A variation is to take a piece from your writing portfolio or writer's notebook and revise for a different point of view. Here is Lynne's example:

> When I was in elementary school, I couldn't wait for the first wicked snowfall! It meant sledding down slippery hills, battling in never-ending snowball fights, and building a sturdy snow fort. Best of all, it meant staying home from school.
>
> Now, when I see snow I cringe. "What will the roads be like by the time we leave school?" I think. If the snow keeps falling outside, I wait for the phone call that will tell us we are going have an early dismissal. I pray that I have my scraper and brush in the car and that the snow is not too deep since I didn't wear boots (I always forget them!). I am wondering about my tires and if I should have invested in new ones before the winter got underway.
>
> Then I think about what is in my fridge, and I realize that I will have to make a quick stop at the convenience store for some milk, bread, greens, cheese, and cereal (but it won't be quick because everyone else will be making the same stop as well!).
>
> Even if we have a snow day tomorrow, my day will be spent shoveling snow from my sidewalk and driveway and clearing snow from my car roof, windshield, and windows. That could take hours! A day off from school? I'd rather be in my classroom with the kids!

Guided Writing: Ask students to take the kids' point of view to write a paragraph about their thoughts and feelings concerning snow. To get them started, write a lead sentence with the class. Next, ask them to write several sentences about snow in their notebooks, using their pro/con chart to help them. Ask students to revise for specific details. Invite one or two students to the front of the room for a guided conversation. Ask them to share their sentences. Write their examples on the board or chart paper. Continue to add to the list of examples as more children share and/or ask children to create more examples from their notebooks using the chart.

Tell students that when they are writing by themselves they can ask themselves questions to get ideas for examples, explanations, thoughtshots, or descriptions to add to their writing. These questions include: What would readers want to know? What would add humor? What would add another feeling? Examine the pro/con chart for more examples. Hold an open discussion using the following questions as guides: What does your writing do for the reader? Do any examples jump out at you? Why? Do you think adults would understand your point of view? Change their minds?

Independent Practice: Have students return to their seats and add some language until their writing becomes as clear as possible. They can then share again with their partner and receive feedback.

Reflection: Ask writers to reflect on how the strategy of using a pro/con chart worked for them. As a group, discuss how the writing became crisper as examples, explanations, and specific descriptive words were added. Ask them to think about how they could use this chart to scaffold their thinking during independent writing time or during partner share. Have them think about the way they could use this strategy in another piece such as a poem or informational/persuasive report they have already written. For their writer's notebook, encourage them to collect examples of pieces that are clearly written from one point of view. Use books, magazines, newspapers, and other sources, including the work of their teacher and fellow classmates.

Your Turn Lesson 3

Revising Persuasive Writing

There are many ways authors may revise a piece of writing. As we discussed in this chapter, persuasive pieces are built around strong arguments. For young writers, understanding that persuasive writing must target an audience and anticipate problems that may arise is an important first step. The writer can provide an answer or solution to the anticipated problem within the body of the text. This Your Turn lesson provides a revision plan to help young writers be more successful.

Hook: Choose some of the mentor texts you have been using in the classroom and examine the way a character tries to resolve problems he or she may have. Look for books where characters are trying to persuade someone to do something and reread them aloud. Ask students to chart the arguments and star or underline any arguments on the chart where anticipated problems are discussed in some way. The Treasure Chest of books for this chapter provides many good resources. If you write these out on chart paper, they can be posted in the classroom. Good options include *Tuck Everlasting* by Natalie Babbitt, *Dear Mr. Blueberry* by Simon James, *Hey, Little Ant* by Phillip and Hannah Hoose, *Earrings!* by Judith Viorst, *Charlotte's Web* by E.B. White, *Can I Keep Him?* by Stephen Kellogg, and *The Perfect Pet* by Margie Palatini.

Purpose: *As we have been discussing, revision is a very important part of any piece of writing. Revision can begin as early as the prewriting (planning) stage, but today we are going to focus on revision work after a final draft of persuasive writing has been completed. In persuasive writing, keen audience awareness is often key to the success of the piece. Today I will show you how you can revise your writing to produce that kind of persuasive argument—one that satisfies the reader by anticipating problems he or she may have with your persuasion.*

Brainstorm: In this lesson, brainstorming is closely tied to the use of literature in the hook. As students examine a piece of literature and discover different types of arguments (the writer's arguments solely based on his or her topic and point, and the arguments the author thinks of that his or her reader may have against that point), they are actually engaging in a type of brainstorming.

Model: Either read a previous persuasive piece of your own or use a piece of literature the students are familiar with. We'll use *Hey, Little Ant* by Phillip and Hannah Hoose as our example. Display a chart that lists the arguments of the ant on one side and the boy on the other. Now choose a character, such as the ant, and write a short persuasive piece from that perspective. (If you need to shorten the time, prepare this piece ahead of time.)

As you revise, use one color to underline your topic sentence and point. Then choose a different-colored marker to underline your main arguments with their supporting details. If you have three arguments, then you should use a different color for each one. Be sure you have some sentences that are not underlined. Think out loud. Find some sentences that are misplaced or off topic. Explain why and cross them out or move them.

Now go back and look for any sentences where you anticipated an argument the boy might have and answered it (be sure to refer to the posted chart displaying the arguments). Choose a new color and give those sentences a second underline. (Some of these sentences may already have been underlined as supporting details.) Finally, look at the chart again. Add a sentence or two that anticipates another of the boy's arguments and helps to refute or negate it.

Shared/Guided Writing: Students work in pairs or response groups to imitate the procedure you have modeled, using a piece of persuasive writing they have already drafted. Circulate the room with a clipboard to conduct quick conferences wherever additional help is needed. Basically, the students will use the following process:

1. Find the lead sentence. Check to see if it states your opinion in a positive way. Underline this sentence in red.
2. Find your main ideas/arguments. Check to see if they all have sentences that state the main ideas and supporting details. Underline these sentences in blue.
3. Find sentences that answer questions or respond to arguments your reader may have and underline these sentences in green.
4. Do you have any sentences left? Could they be misplaced? Are they on topic? Could they be changed or eliminated?

Students share their revision work with a partner or in small group. A scaffolded conversation with the whole group can follow, during which students share what they have learned from trying it out. You may want to share information gathered during your clipboard cruising.

Independent Writing: Ask students to continue revisions of previous persuasive pieces using their colored pencils. Students may also wish to start new pieces and concentrate on developing their audience awareness and anticipating problems their readers may have.

Reflection: After students have the opportunity to revise or write, ask them to share in whole group or small group. The following questions can help guide their thinking. Ask students to respond to one or several reflection questions in their writer's notebook.

How did you grow/change as a writer?

What did you learn about persuasive writing?

What revisions did you make based on the comments or suggestions from your response group? From the revision work with colored pencils?

What was the hardest part of the revision work? Explain.

Did this revision process improve your piece? How so?

Your Turn Lesson 4

Listing to Find Your Main Arguments

Many young writers are still developing their understanding of how to organize their thinking for a persuasive piece. They can use a listing technique—writing down all the ideas that pop into their head—to find both their main arguments and their supporting details. Students can play around with different techniques to create their lists as they make this strategy part of their schema.

Hook: Eileen Spinelli's *I Know It's Autumn* provides many wonderful reasons why autumn may be the best season in Pennsylvania (and other mid-Atlantic and New England regions). Options may include familiar books such as *In November* by Cynthia Rylant or *Fall* by Ron Hirschi. (We are using fall for this lesson, but any other topic could work.)

Purpose: *Writers, today I'm going to show you how you can create a list to develop your main arguments and supporting details for a piece of persuasive writing. We've already talked about a few different ways that authors begin to plan persuasive writing (such as starting with a pro/con list or creating a web). Today we're going to practice writing a list that helps the writer imagine the possibilities for arguments for any given topic and point.*

Brainstorm: Reread *I Know It's Autumn*. As you read the first four or five paragraphs, make a list of the things that Spinelli includes to help her readers understand the beauty of this season. Continue to add to the list as you read the book. Students can make personal connections and add their own thinking to describe the magic of fall.

Model: Use the ideas from the list and add some of your own to create a list of specific details, examples, and descriptions that show off autumn as the best season. Think out loud as you choose one idea and underline it with a red marker. Scan the list to find any other sentences or phrases that seem to go with the one you underlined. For example, you could underline sentences that have to do with Halloween and Thanksgiving. After underlining all the related sentences or phrases in red, develop an argument sentence to connect them all. For example, if you underlined the sentences and phrases about Halloween and Thanksgiving, you could say, "One of the reasons fall is the best season is because of the holidays."

Next, choose a sentence on a different topic and underline it in blue. Find other similar sentences and say, for example, "These sentences all have to do with sports that occur only in the fall." Perhaps a set of sentences speaks to the beauty of the season. Underline them in green. An argument sentence to connect these might be "Yes, fall is Mother Nature's best-dressed gal!" As you look back, you have organized your thinking around three main arguments—but you discovered them by grouping sentences that seemed to belong together.

Shared/Guided Writing: Invite students to try creating a list just like you did. You may want to start with a shared experience, or you could place students in groups of three or four and ask them to choose another season. Have books on hand such as *Changing Seasons* by Henry Pluckrose, *When Summer Comes* by Robert Mass, *Spring* by Ron Hirschi, *Summer* by Ron Hirschi, and *When Winter Comes* by Nancy Van Laan.

Students can collaborate to make a list. Any ideas should be welcome. Students can work together to find similar thinking and come up with a way to name their main ideas or arguments. In whole group or small group, they can also share ideas that they were going to delete or ideas that could not be categorized. They can also share sentences that support a big idea but could not be developed enough or that did not seem as powerful or appropriate.

Independent Practice: Invite students to try out this strategy with another piece of persuasive writing. It can be a piece about another season—for example, "Why Winter is the Best Season in My State"—or it can center around another topic, such as "Why My Community Needs a Rollerblading Park." When students come to writing conferences, have them bring their list and explain how they used it to help them come up with their main arguments and organize their information.

Reflection: After students share their lists and how they found their arguments and supporting details, ask them to reflect on what they did.

How did using the listing strategy help you begin?

How do you think your piece will improve by beginning with a listing such as this?

How did categorizing with color help you discover the main ideas/arguments?

How did this strategy help you be more selective?

Was it easier or more difficult to begin your plan this way? Explain.

When could you use this again? Would you change anything?

Nonfiction Writing in the Real World
(and Other Interesting Formats to Engage Student Writers)

What we as teachers must do is help children discover what the types

of nonfiction writing look like and the structures and features that

competent writers use when writing for specific purposes.

—Tony Stead, *Is That a Fact? Teaching Nonfiction Writing K–3*

135

In elementary school, the focus in reading, and therefore writing, often has been the narrative, including both personal narratives and fictionalized/fantasy stories. With the greater demands of an information age that require students to become not only critical readers but also accomplished writers of information, it is important for us to introduce our students to the varied purposes and formats for information writing. According to Duke and Bennett-Armistead (2003), "If we are going to prepare children for this world, we need to be serious about teaching them to read and write informational text" (21). Duke also points out that including more informational text in classrooms may help educators address the interests and questions of more of their students. We have seen firsthand the level of enthusiasm and energy that students put forth when real-world writing opportunities are offered to them. They clearly see that this kind of writing is for a larger audience, not just their teacher. If it is important to them (the students), they will be more willing to take risks, try out new formats, research more extensively, and be willing to take the extra time to revise their thinking. In addition, the continued practice of nonfiction writing helps students own vocabulary in content areas, therefore building their word power and style.

Postcards, Letters, and Email— Familiar Formats

There is comfort in beginning a nonfiction writing project using a familiar format. Even in this age of technology, students still receive postcards from relatives and friends who travel, and the occasional friendly letter. Although letter writing is becoming a lost art, letters are welcomed treasures—gifts to grandparents who live far away or parents who want to hear from their child who is away at summer camp. Email still is not an option for every child when he or she is not in school. Furthermore, a letter allows a child to write in a friendly voice but still attend to the conventions of written language. For older students, opportunities to write business letters can provide a powerful avenue for introductions, opinions, and requests. Both fiction and nonfiction texts can provide the mentors your students need to understand the letter and postcard format. We include email in this chapter as a form of letter writing because it is quick and easy, and it often provides a vehicle for an almost immediate response from the target audience.

Short and Sweet—Writing a Postcard

Denise Allard's *Postcards from the United States* provides a simple format (the text is presented as postcards) that uses students' interest in photos to help them create their own postcards. Writing a postcard is not an easy task; after all, there isn't much room. Allard shows us how to personalize the postcard writing by offering factual information and sometimes including what we are doing, thinking, or feeling. By doing this, the writer makes it "real" for the reader. The postscripts included at the bottom of each page often extend the content with an explanation or an interesting example. The following postcard entry from this book focuses on a photograph of the Chicago River, which connects to Lake Michigan:

> *Dear Alan,*
> *We flew north to Chicago. It is beside Lake Michigan.*
> *The weather is cooler here. Our hotel is near the lake and the stores. Today we are going on a boat ride down the river.*
>
> > *Your friend,*
> > *James*
>
> *P.S. Mom says that Lake Michigan is one of the five lakes called the Great Lakes. The Lakes are very big. They look like the ocean. Lake Superior is the biggest lake.*

In Ray Nelson Jr. and Douglas Kelly's *Greetings from America: Postcards from Donovan and Daisy*, readers can travel vicariously through the United States, living the experiences of Donovan and Daisy, the writers of the postcards. Postcard examples from this book also show students how to write an address. The postcards can help students imagine interesting leads and see how to add in local flavor, or voice. In addition, they also show us that element of personal touch—an important component of postcard writing.

> *Howdy pardner!*
> *Texas is huge. It's actually the second largest state in America. There is a bunch of great stuff to see here. We've been to the Alamo, which was a famous fortress during the Mexican-American War of 1836. We also visited the Johnson Space Center in Houston. Texas got its name for an Indian word meaning "friends." I got a new cowboy hat. It's really big and covers my eyes. We'll bring one back for you.*
>
> > *Love,*
> > *Donovan*

As you can see from this example, postcard entries can serve to drive home the importance of proper nouns for specificity. A practical tip for writing postcards is to use names of places, events, and people that are specific to your topic.

Lynne worked with two fourth-grade teachers, Barbara Hollish and Gretchen Elfreth, to plan and create an Alex's Lemonade Stand, a real-world outreach project to raise money for cancer research. To set the stage, Lynne read Patricia Polacco's *The Lemonade Club* to the fourth graders. She wanted to get them excited and involved immediately, so she chose the postcard format as a way for the students to send their thinking about the book and their plans for the lemonade stand to author Patricia Polacco. A postcard is short and sweet and would allow the students to experience immediate success. Students were instructed to inform Mrs. Polacco about their project and offer a response to or opinion about her book. They drafted in their notebooks, conferred with several partners, and eventually wrote and sent their final drafts (see Figures 6.1 and 6.2).

In Mickey Moore's third-grade classroom, students were studying the solar system. *Postcards from Pluto* by Loreen Leedy provided yet another opportunity to make use of the postcard format. After sharing Leedy's book as a read-aloud, Lynne and Mickey began by modeling what it might sound like to write a postcard to a family member while working as part of a NASA team aboard a spaceship. They tried to include factual information gained from reading widely about one planet across many texts and added a sentence or two

FIGURE 6.1
Donna's postcard to
Patricia Polacco

> 3/19/08
>
> Dear Mrs. Polacco,
>
> Your book, The Lemonade Club inspired me to have courage. When you said, "When you dream it, you can be it" really inspired me to follow my dream and to help kids with cancer so they can follow their dream. Our school is making an Alex's Lemonade Stand to raise money to help save a childs life. This makes me proud.
>
> Your reader,
> Donna

FIGURE 6.2
Chianna's postcard to
Patricia Polacco

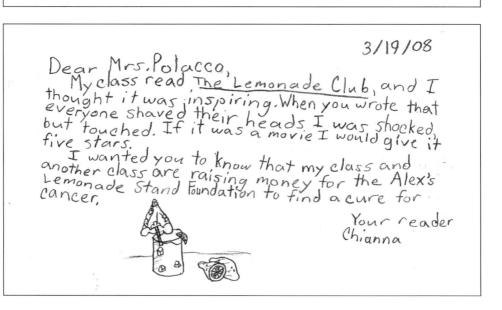

> 3/19/08
>
> Dear Mrs. Polacco,
> My class read The Lemonade Club, and I thought it was inspiring. When you wrote that everyone shaved their heads I was shocked, but touched. If it was a movie I would give it five stars.
> I wanted you to know that my class and another class are raising money for the Alex's Lemonade Stand Foundation to find a cure for cancer.
>
> Your reader
> Chianna

within the text or as a postscript to add voice and a personal touch. To help the students sharpen their focus and build content, Lynne and Mickey asked them to develop a different idea for each of three postcards for their particular planet. As a class, they looked through the planet books to pick out the big ideas that were discussed. These included weather, moons, surface features (canyons, deserts, mountains), solid or gas, and water forms (if any existed). Lynne modeled from notes she wrote in a bulleted format on the board about her planet, Jupiter.

Dear Sandy,

    I hope you are missing your big sister as much as I am missing you. We have finally reached Jupiter and have been orbiting the planet for the last two weeks. The weather is rather violent on Jupiter. The Great Red Spot is actually a storm that has been raging for over three hundred years. The hurricane force winds are much stronger than anything on our planet! I hope you will get this postcard before I return home, but you never know about interplanetary mail.

Love,

Lynne

P.S. Please take care of my Welsh Corgis. I hope you are not feeding them too many goodies.

Keegan studied the planet Venus. After reading widely, he decided to develop his postcards around surface features, atmosphere, and temperature. He took notes using important phrases and words and used them to develop the content of his postcards. Each postcard ends with a personalized message to his target audience:

April 15, 2099

Dear Mom and Dad,

    I visited Venus today. It is so hot that it could melt zinc. The temperature is close to 900 degrees F. That is almost three times as hot as a kitchen oven. How's Otis doing? I miss him!

Love,

Keegan

April 16, 2099

Dear Dad,

    I'm here orbiting Venus. The planet has about 430 volcanoes. Each of them is 12 miles wide, more than 80% by lava flows. It's truly a volcanic world! The planet has small valleys and high mountains, but this place is nothing like Earth. I miss you very much.

Love,

Keegan

April 18, 2099

Dear Mom,

I'm still here orbiting Venus. In the night Venus looks like a star. Unfortunately, Venus is not a beautiful place to live! The atmosphere is what we breathe out—carbon dioxide. Clouds are made of sulphuric acid. I miss your cooking. Can't wait to get home.

Love,
Keegan

From their postcards and notes, the students were asked to write a report in the voice of a NASA astronaut to answer the essential question: Could humans live on this planet? Lynne asked the students to use the scaffold from *Somewhere in the World Right Now* by Stacey Schuett to create their lead sentence. This book uses the scaffold "Somewhere in the world right now . . ." and variations of it to describe what could be taking place across the twenty-four time zones on our planet:

Somewhere in the world right now, it's deepest night. Fog hugs the shoulders of buildings and bridges. A baker slides long loaves of bread into an oven. Somewhere, somebody watches a movie, a mouse hunts for crumbs.

Lynne asked the students to write their descriptions based on the three big ideas from their postcards and wait until the end of their piece to state their topic and point and name the planet. Notice how Keegan successfully combined all of his ideas into his report:

Somewhere in the solar system a planet shines like a bright star. Poisonous yellow clouds made of sulphuric acid surround this planet. The pressure of the air is so strong it can crush a space ship.

There is no water on this planet. It never rains because it is too hot. Rain would turn to steam before hitting the ground. The temperature is three times as hot as a kitchen oven.

It is a solid planet with a rocky core. Small valleys and high mountains cover its surface. Asteroids and comets blast out powerful shock waves.

Life could not exist on Venus. Spaceships couldn't even land on its surface. This planet is not for human beings.

Even though the students read widely to become mini-experts on their planets, the postcards helped them to focus in on three big ideas, which in turn helped them answer one essential, real-world question—the heart of good research writing.

Letter Writing: An Old Familiar Friend

Many books, both fiction and nonfiction, offer examples of letter writing. From books such as *Dear Peter Rabbit* by Alma Flor Ada, *The Gardener* by Sarah Stewart, and *First Year Letters* by Julie Danneberg, students can easily imitate the format for a friendly letter. They can also learn how letters of correspondence answer questions that have been posed and ask new ones.

Some authors, such as Jennifer Armstrong and Elvira Woodruff, have used the familiarity of the letter format to interest students in different historical times, places, or people. In *Thomas Jefferson: Letters from a Philadelphia Bookworm*, part of the Dear Mr. President series, Armstrong presents an imagined letter exchange between Present Jefferson and a twelve-year-old girl. Although the letters are fictional, the information is factual, based on extensive research and primary source documents.

Woodruff's *Dear Austin: Letters from the Underground Railroad* is an adventure story set in the years just before the Civil War. The letters help the reader experience the emotionally charged times and events of that period, while adding to their background knowledge. In the following excerpt, you can see how Woodruff weaves some bits of information into the story:

> *Dear Austin,*
>
> *. . . I can't think why Darcy should not be allowed to learn to read and why she's got to plead to do it. There's plenty in my class who would plead not to do their school work. I don't know how there can be a law that keeps folks from learning. I wonder at the men who thought up such a law and why they were so determined to keep a young girl from reading the Bible—just because of the color of her skin. It makes no sense, Austin . . .*

Letters can provide a real-world experience for students to explain what they have learned. At Rose's school, third-grade teachers Sally Owens and Stephanie Pisano were looking for a unique way for their students to show what they had learned from a unit on air pollution. Since they knew that one of their local state representatives, Mrs. McIlvaine-Smith, would be coming to visit the school, Sally and Stephanie decided to have the students write persuasive letters about the dangers of air pollution. The third graders used the information they learned in class and included thoughts about how air pollution affects their lives.

> Dear Rep. McIlvane-Smith,
>
> My name is Connor. I go to Fern Hill Elementary. A favorite subject of mine is P.E. because it is fun. By the way I am a nine year old boy. Also my teacher is Mrs. Owens.
>
> In science we are studying air pollution and its effects on forests, buildings, stone, and our world. Air pollution is affecting our world and

you will know in the following ways. Air pollution makes acid rain and the rain kills forests. If our forests are gone where will our animals live and where will we get our oxygen? It is also hurting our buildings. If the buildings fall someone may get hurt. Acid rain also falls in lakes and may kill fish. It's affecting our drinking water.

Hopefully there are ways to reduce this happening to our world and to us. Air pollution is hurting us and I want you to do something about it. You could make laws of electricity use which would help get rid of air pollution. You could make laws about car pooling so we won't have so much exhaust. There could be a limit of factories in West Chester. Now you know how you can help our world, us, and me.

Sincerely,
Connor

The letters were presented during a school assembly, and Rep. McIlvane-Smith visited the third-grade classrooms to answer questions and to further discuss air pollution with the students.

In Lynne's school, fourth graders from Barb Hollish's and Gretchen Elfreth's classes continued their work on the lemonade stand project by writing letters to mail home to their parents. The students' job was to announce the project and explain its purpose. Their goal was to get their parents excited enough to come to the fairs and make donations. Ultimately, they needed permission to work at the lemonade stands as part of the outreach project. Lynne began by asking students to brainstorm possible leads in their writer's notebooks, turn and talk, revise, and eventually share in whole group. She charted their ideas for leads on the board as a way to help students get started with their letters. Here are a few of their ideas:

- Would you like to save a child's life?
- Have you ever wanted to make a real difference in the world?
- People say that when life hands you lemons, you make lemonade.
- Would you like to help support kids with cancer?
- Our class is participating in an exciting and challenging project.
- Would you like to save a life today?
- Did you know that buying a cup of lemonade will bring us one step closer to finding a cure for pediatric cancer?
- Sit down and relax while I tell you the story of a little girl named Alex Scott.
- Imagine a day when you are hot, tired, and thirsty from all the chores you've completed. Why not buy some lemonade and help save a life at the same time?

Once the students got started with effective leads, they were able to continue with an explanation of the events and end with an effective close that would grab at their readers' (in this case their parents') hearts.

March 14, 2008

Dear Mom and Dad,

Would you like to save a child's life? Did you know that buying one cup of lemonade is one step closer to finding a cure for cancer?

Our class is trying to raise over $300. We want to help save kids with cancer at the Curriculum Fair and Family Fair Night.

Help cheer us on! Buy a cup of sweet lemonade to save a life and refresh yourself at the same time. We can all raise money TOGETHER!

Your daughter,

Samantha

March 14, 2008

Dear Mom and Dad,

Our class is participating in a fascinating and challenging project. Would you like to save a life today? Have you ever had a dream that you've made a reality?

Our fourth-grade class is trying to raise money to fight children's cancer. We want to help save kids by having a Curriculum Fair on April 21st and the Spring Fling on May 16th. You can buy a cup of delicious lemonade at both of these events.

Now won't you help save a life? Together we can find a cure to beat cancer.

Your son,

Aidan

Notice how both students used a rhetorical question as a powerful persuasive tool. These fourth-grade students understood that asking a question that is loaded—in other words, the writer already can predict how the audience will answer the question—is a good way to begin to win your point. What parent would not answer the question "Would you like to save a child's life?" with a resounding, "Yes!"?

A Variation on Letters: The Email

In the real world, emails often replace the traditional letter because they are faster and less trouble. One reason for teachers to use email as a vehicle for delivering powerful commentary by students is that there is a better chance for an almost immediate response. This was the case when Joanne Costello's third graders wrote to Governor Crist of Florida about their concern for the manatees. She and the class had read *Saving Manatees* by Stephen Swinburne, as well as a host of other books on manatees and ocean creatures. Joanne's unit on the ocean was based on a literature anthology selection that highlighted the nonfiction genre.

Joanne invited Lynne into her classroom to work with her students on creating emails to the governor so that the children could feel empowered by writing. This email was a multigenre piece because it included a lot of information the children had gathered, but the global structure for the writing was the persuasive mode.

Lynne began by allowing the students to talk about what they already knew about manatees. She listed their key points on the board. If students debated a piece of information, then the student researchers were assigned the task of exploring the classroom library of related books to check on those facts. Lynne explained that many of the facts they had collected would be part of the body of their email.

Next, Lynne turned her attention to the introduction. Lynne shared some well-written introductions from mentor texts (see Chapter 4). She told the students that because the governor did not know them personally, it would be helpful to let him know that a third grader was writing the piece so he could have a picture of the writer in his mind as he read the email.

Then she asked the students for some topic and point statements. "What is our purpose for writing the governor?" Lynne asked them. "What do we want him to be thinking about throughout our writing? How are we feeling? Why are we feeling this way?" Again, Lynne wrote some of their thoughts on the board under the heading "Introduction." The students began by drafting their introductions and sharing them with a partner and with the whole group. As they finished their introductions, they turned to their list of facts and began writing the body of their email.

By the next day, the third graders were ready to think about pulling the email to a powerful close. Lynne reminded them that Ralph Fletcher (1993) says that endings are very important because these are the last words that you will leave in the reader's mind. Lynne added that they wanted to stamp these words on their readers' hearts as well. It was here that she introduced the idea of the rhetorical question. She asked the students to write down some of their thoughts in their notebooks, and as they shared, she placed some of their powerful words, phrases, and sentences on the board. After the students finished drafting, they shared in small and whole groups.

As students revised their emails, Joanne and Lynne reviewed the letter format but talked about the more formal conventions needed for a letter to a government official. They taught students about the use of a colon in the salutation and about appropriate closings, such as *respectfully, sincerely,* and *truly yours.* They also added that signatures must be first and last names, although in the samples we've included here last names have been omitted.

Dear Governor Crist:

My class and I are studying manatees, and I got concerned when I noticed that manatees are endangered. I hope you can take care of manatees the way you take care of Florida. Would you like to see manatees vanish from the earth forever? My classmates and I would not. You can save them, so why not do it? As governor, people will listen to you.

I know you would not let boats run over people, so why let boats run over manatees? I do not know everything about the laws. I do know I want them to stay strong to protect these unique creatures. I want my grandchildren and great grandchildren to see manatees. You can make the laws more strict so that people will take care not to hurt these gentle giants.

Manatees need our help. They cannot talk, so we're talking for them. As governor of Florida we need you to help the manatees. We are counting on your support.

Respectfully,
Alec

Another student, Andrew, included information about what the class was doing before asking what the governor would do:

I am a third grader, and my class and I think that manatees should be protected. I don't want them to be taken off the endangered list. We are very worried that manatees might become extinct. My class held a bake sale to raise money for manatees. We raised $120 and adopted a manatee named Dana.

Elizabeth knew the power of a rhetorical question when she ended with this thought:

Don't you want your grandchildren and your great grandchildren to see the real natives of Florida?

Sydney's close tugged at the heartstrings of her reader:

I would really love to have my grandchildren and their children see these gentle giants for themselves. The world would not be the same without them, I think. Manatees love Florida. After all, they are the true natives of the sunshine state. Thank you for your time. Don't forget the manatees.

Of course the students were very excited when they received reply emails from the governor's office. The emails thanked the children for presenting their views and informed them that the manatees have actually increased their numbers due to the protection of the Florida Fish and Wildlife Commission. This organization voted unanimously to postpone a reclassification of the manatee status. The students were very glad to hear that the manatees would remain on the endangered species list.

Here is a great example of how real-world writing can demonstrate to the students in our classroom that the pen (or keyboard!) can be a powerful tool—that through writing, they can make a difference in their world. Lynne and Joanne were amazed at how easy it was to get every child to produce an effective email in a timely fashion. They attributed the success of this writing project to the wonderful texts that were shared as read-alouds and guided and independent reading experiences. The students' extensive background about manatees and their work to raise money to adopt a manatee gave them the knowledge, the wisdom, and the heart to write these pieces.

Nature All Around Us

Young children are intrigued with the world around them. They are curious about how things work, what things mean, and what their place is in the whole scheme of things. As JoAnn Portalupi and Ralph Fletcher (2001) remind us: "Researching involves more than simply copying facts out of a book. It is being alive to the world, and valuing one's perceptions of the world" (21). At Rose's school, kindergarten teacher Connie Harker was looking for a way to engage her students in exploring their world and at the same time nudge them beyond simple personal narratives into new writing territories. She had recently used *Where I Live* by Eileen Spinelli as a read-aloud. Her students had connected to the main character Diana's love of nature and poetry. In the book, Diana is invited to attend a poetry workshop conducted by a famous city poet, Mary Elmore DeMort, who offers her audience of young poets this advice:

> *write what we feel,*
> *tell the truth,*
> *love who we are,*
> *share,*
> *keep a notebook,*
> *take it everywhere,*
> *open our eyes*
> *and our hearts.*

When Diana returns home from the poetry workshop, she takes her notebook outside to look for poems in her neighborhood:

> *to Mr. Burt's dog, Tucker,*
> *who likes to lick my knees . . .*
> *to Mrs. Martin's gazebo,*
> *painted pink as*
> *strawberry ice cream . . .*
> *. . . I take out my pencil.*
> *I open my notebook*
> *and my heart.*

Connie decided that having her students keep a notebook similar to Diana's would encourage them to notice things in the real world, wonder about them, and investigate and learn through writing. After all, it was spring, and what better time of year to notice changes in nature? The class had always done a great deal of writing, and by this time in the year they had enough command over conventions to make their thoughts and ideas understood. So each student transformed a small copybook into their personal nature journal.

Mentor texts like *Three Days on a River in a Red Canoe* by Vera Williams, *Crinkleroot's Nature Almanac* by Jim Arnosky, and *Take a Backyard Bird Walk* by Jane Kirkland are good models for young students, showing them that nature journals can include drawings, photographs, or even artifacts. The One Small Square series by Donald M. Silver are also excellent resources for young nature explorers. Each book in this series focuses on a different part of nature, such as a backyard, the woods, or the seashore. The author offers step-by-step directions on how to map out a small area and revisit it from time to time for exploration and discovery. The books are filled with information on plants and animals as well as suggestions for notebook entries and other activities.

Connie began by modeling with her nature journal and showing her students how she was exploring nature with her daughters at home. She composed the first few entries together with the class, then the students were encouraged to take their journals home and record observations from their neighborhoods. Connie's weekly newsletter home to the parents offered suggestions that might serve as a follow-up to something done in class or offer a new way of recording information. For instance, one day the whole class went out to observe clouds and recorded their thoughts and observations in their journals; then, Connie suggested they repeat this activity at home. On another occasion, she suggested that the children try adding labels to their drawings.

Every Wednesday during writing workshop, the students shared their entries. Their writing offered opportunities for revision as Connie taught different mini-lessons on topics such as unpacking sentences or adding details to descriptions. The results of this activity were amazing! Notice how Nancy used headings, facts, diagrams, and labels in her entries (see Figures 6.3 and 6.4).

FIGURE 6.3
Nancy uses headings and facts in her nature journal.

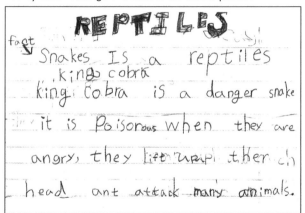

FIGURE 6.4
Nancy uses labels for her diagram.

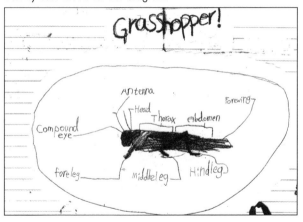

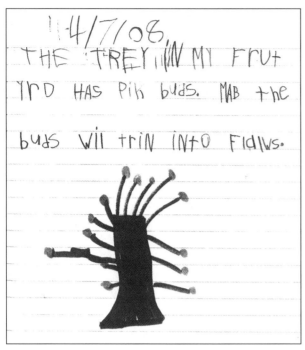

FIGURE 6.5
Entry from Kyle's nature journal (The tree in my front yard has pink buds. Maybe the buds will turn into flowers.)

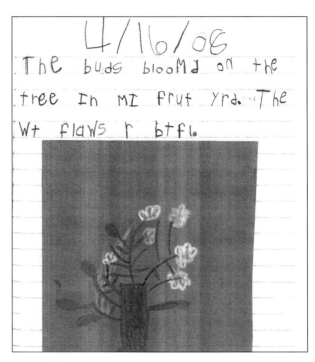

FIGURE 6.6
A later entry in Kyle's nature journal (The buds bloomed on the tree in my front yard. The white flowers are beautiful.)

FIGURE 6.7
Entry from Graham's nature journal (I went out my backyard and I found creepy crawlers like worms and isopods.)

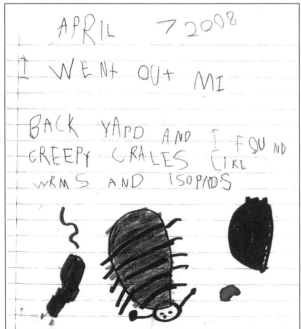

Kyle wondered about the trees in his front yard and returned to this thinking later as the trees bloomed (see Figures 6.5 and 6.6).

Graham used specific words and drawings to show what he learned about bugs (see Figure 6.7).

One morning the class gathered to reflect on what they had learned from keeping the nature journals. Children commented on the opportunities they had to "look at some things very closely and find out the differences" and "go outside and pick stuff up and bring it in." Alex turned to a page in her journal pasted with some feathers she had found. "I think they're from a hawk," she commented, "or maybe a blue jay." The children understood the value of what they had done as they continued to wonder about their discoveries. Many planned to continue the journals through the summer vacation.

Even children who live in urban areas can keep nature journals. Jane Kirkland's *Take a City Nature Walk* is a good mentor text for them. Kirkland provides field guides and talks about city places where nature can be observed—zoos, parks, and even city buildings where birds can nest.

Up Close and Personal

Sometimes we forget that human beings and what they create are part of nature. The world is so enormous that it is often difficult for students to contemplate or write about their world without first focusing on something that is very tangible or concrete to them. Writing about themselves—starting with something as basic as their hands—can provide a powerful writing opportunity for students of all ages. In a selection from *The Alphabet of the Trees: A Guide to Nature Writing*, Christian McEwen and Mark Statman offer this advice:

> *In the same way that nature writing depends on close looking and attentive listening, so too it benefits from a considered sense of touch. Like so many of us, children take this sense for granted. They don't realize what touch has already taught them, or how that expertise translates into their connections with the larger world.* (2000, 106)

We liked their suggestion for using a scaffold in order to have students think about and write about their hands. We also were intrigued with the student writing found in *The Best Part of Me: Children Talk About Their Bodies in Pictures and Words* by Wendy Ewald. This book combines photography with writing to have students create self-portraits of their favorite body parts. We adjusted McEwen and Statman's scaffold slightly and used the following sentence stems to get our children started:

> The best part of me is my _____.
> My _____ love . . .
> My _____ remember . . .
> My _____ hope/wish . . .
> The best part of me is my _____. (or any sentence that brings
>   closure to the piece of writing)

The scaffold helped our students see a part of their history since they were talking about present, past, and future. It helped them realize that they didn't have to go far to describe something—they could start with themselves. In addition, it helped them make self-discoveries. Melissa, a third grader who wrote about her hair, talked about donating it to people with cancer. So as much as Melissa loved her hair, she wanted to do something with it that would help others. Taylor, another third grader, noted how her hands are important because they help her do her favorite thing, writing. Lauren wrote that her ". . . brain helps me remember all my friends, new and old." Especially for the second graders, writing about their favorite body part showed what is most important to them at this particular time in their lives. Graham, who suffers from severe asthma, wrote about his lungs; Shannon wrote about her teeth that she hopes "won't be crooked for long." The writing activity fostered a sense of community and helped students rediscover who they are and who their classmates are.

After modeling with our own examples, we suggested that the students begin with a description. If your students describe their hands, they can trace them. A facial part can be examined in a mirror. Or, you can begin as Wendy Ewald did, with a photograph. Linking the visual component with the writing piques their interest and can lead to more specific observations. Students from Clare Silva's class in Upper Moreland and Barb Norton's class in Fern Hill chose their favorite body part and had fun writing.

The best part of me is my hands. My hands are small, but they do a vast amount of things. My pink-as-a-peach hands grip the smooth pages of a book. They write for me because I love to write. My hands, cold and tired, pull the covers up to my chin every chilly night. My hands, soft and warm, give massages to my family. My mom likes them the best! My hands love to curl up in a ball. My warmed, washed hands remember me sucking on them when I was a baby. Today they dream of marking papers as a teacher, my wish come true! My wonderful hands are a special gift.

Rebeka, Grade 3

The best part of me is my eyes. My eyes help me see shooting stars, constellations, and planets with a telescope. My eyes dream of seeing my cat feel better again. They love to look at my mom and dad. My eyes remember Gracie that moved away to Washington. They help me see my new friend Brianna. My eyes wish to be an artist when I grow up. My eyes, blue and beautiful, look around the world. I love my eyes.

Lyric, Grade 3

The best part of me is my fingers. They are made of German skin. My fingers have a little hair on them. They get a lot of cuts.

My fingers love to hold my pencil and write all day. They love writing the answers to math questions with my pencil.

My fingers remember gripping the ball I threw for the first time. After that I felt so good.

My fingers wish to be playing Tchaikovsky's Nutcracker Suite in front of a huge audience. When I was done they would clap so loud it would hurt my ears.

The best part of me is my fingers.

Matthew, Grade 2

Using Interviews to Create Family Histories

We live in a fast world. Sometimes we don't even have time to get to know our family history—the stories of the people who came before us. One way to help students learn about family members is through the interview. Students learn how to ask good questions and follow up with other questions that might pull out interesting details. They learn how to abandon interview lines that lead to nowhere. Finally, they learn how to take their information and organize it into a piece of writing to be shared and celebrated with family members—creating a real-world opportunity to give the gift of writing (and teachers get to find a new audience for their students' writing!).

In Maribeth Batcho's classroom, fourth graders had spent several weeks studying women in history. They were ready to begin learning about the skill of interviewing for a new writing project centered on women in their families. Lynne read Betsy Hearne's *Seven Brave Women* aloud to the students. She asked them to listen for the kinds of things the author included as she described the women in her family. The students noticed that all the stories demonstrated how the women in Hearne's family showed courage. As the students turned and talked with a partner, Lynne and Maribeth listened in. The students could vividly remember certain details the author had included. One anecdote about Hearne's great-great-grandmother was talked about by many groups:

> *Once, a sharp knife slipped and cut her finger open. She used the other hand to sew it up with a needle and thread.*

Lynne asked the students to make a list of women in their families who they might want to interview in order to make a short book of family history. She asked them to come up with four to five names and then limit their list to their top two choices. Lynne advised them to choose people who would be available for interview in person or by phone or email. All of the students would ask the same questions of themselves as they asked their interview subjects—in other words, their family book would end with a little history of themselves. That is just the way Hearne had ended her book.

Lynne modeled with some interview questions on the board—good and bad—and asked the students to evaluate the questions. She reminded them of the work they had done in literature circles with thick questions (questions that go beyond a simple "yes" or "no" answer). After the students wrote some questions in their writer's notebook, Lynne recorded these on chart paper for further reference. The students came up with some excellent questions, including the following:

1. What was the biggest accomplishment of your life? Explain.
2. What brave thing did you do that you didn't want to do, but you did it anyway?

3. What was your dream in life?

4. What is the best advice you ever received and gave?

5. What do you treasure? Why?

6. What was the gutsiest thing you ever tried in your life? Explain.

7. What did you want to be when you grew up?

8. What is/was your favorite quote?

9. What is the hardest thing you've ever done? Explain.

10. Did you ever want to do something brave? Explain.

11. What advice did your mom and/or grandmom offer you?

12. Has anyone purposefully hurt you? What happened?

13. What was the best thing that ever happened to you?

14. What is the most important thing you've ever done? Explain.

15. What was/is your life goal? Have you reached it?

16. What was life like for you growing up?

17. If you could change something about your life, what would it be? Why?

18. What moment in your life was so incredible that you'll never forget it? Describe.

19. What was your most embarrassing moment? Explain.

20. What story about your mother/grandmother will you always remember?

Generating lots of questions provided choice and gave options if some questions just didn't work for a specific interview. All the students chose three questions that they liked, but chose three more for backups. Some questions were revised in order to draw out more information from the person being interviewed. For instance, to the third question, the students added a follow-up: Did you accomplish it? To the seventh question, students added: Did that change?

The next day, Lynne shared three interview questions and answers about herself. She reviewed question words with the students and wrote them on a chart as a visual cue. Then the students practiced asking her more questions to flesh out deeper responses. This practice was important so that the students would be able to obtain the best possible information from the people they interviewed.

Now the writers had the job of gathering the wonderful information and bringing their notes back to class. This took about a week or more to accomplish. Your Turn Lesson 2 at the end of this chapter shows how the information from the interviews was used to create the family history piece. Yachana interviewed her grandmother and her mother and applied the same questions to herself to create a family history as a Mother's Day gift (see Figures 6.8–6.10).

Ralph Fletcher discusses autobiographical writing in *How to Write Your Life Story* (2007). This book is an excellent reference for either teachers or students. As with many of Fletcher's other books, it can be used as a read-aloud or studied in small groups within the writing workshop. Fletcher offers advice on how young writers can begin to write their life story. He suggests pulling out

My Grandmother

My grandmother's name is Urmila, a strong name for a strong woman. My grandma grew up in India. When she was four her father died. Her grandma never remarried.

When she was in fifth grade she got an illness. She stayed in bed for two months. My grandmother was very bored because she was an active person (and that hasn't changed). She wanted to go to school. My grandmother missed her friends. My grandmother's family couldn't get any medicine because there wasn't any medicine for that disease. She got that sickness in the middle of fifth grade. That was bad because she was sick till the end of the year.

When my grandmother had to repeat fifth grade, she had to do some things over again. She got to learn new things as well. My grandmother was sad because she missed her friends that she made in the beginning of the year but she made new friends.

When she had children she took care of them like they were precious jewels. When one of her sons (my dad) left to go to America from India she let him go, but she couldn't stop thinking about him. She wondered how he was feeling. Did he know anyone there? She found these answers when she visited America. She felt relief.

We have no heirloom from her but we have my father who was most precious to her.

FIGURE 6.8
Yachana's interview with her grandmother produced this family history piece.

My Mother

My mom's name is Meena. It calms me to say her name. To me it sounds like the water flowing when everyone is quiet.

My mom has a special relationship with her mother, my grandmother. My mom remembered the time when she used to come home from school. She wouldn't eat without her mother.

My mom learned how to knit from her mother. It was very hard, but she had fun doing it. The first thing she made was a design of a flower on a handkerchief. Today, she still knits hats and scarves – sometimes even blankets. One day she will teach me how to knit. My mom loves spending time with her mother, and misses her.

Now she can't spend time with her mother because her mother lives in India, and she lives in America. My mom came to India with two children alone for the first time because she wanted to visit her mother, my grandmother. That was the most horrible twenty hours. She remembered the time when our plane landed late so we had to run to catch the other plane. Then when everything was going all right, three out of five bags didn't come! They were sent to our home in India (Thank goodness!). Before that, my sister got annoying because she was tired and my mom got angry. When we finally left the airport, it was four o' clock in the morning. We didn't see anyone so we had to call my aunt (she came to pick us up) until we saw her. My mom was happy that the horrible twenty hours were over.

My mom is going to give me the handkerchief with a flower design which she knitted for the first with her mother. My mother gives me her memories of growing up in India and her love.

FIGURE 6.9
Yachana's interview with her mother helped her create this piece.

Yachana

My name is Yachana, a sweet name for a brave girl. My name means to pray in Hindi. There are many ways to be brave.

One time I fell down on the tiles in the bathroom. It was slippery and I also ran. I screamed very loud, but I didn't cry. I screamed so loud that even the neighbors could hear me. When my mom, dad, and aunt came, my aunt carried me to the hospital by walking because the hospital was near our house. I got six stitches on the back of my head.

Something else I did that was brave was when I stayed with my mom's and dad's friends for a week without my mom and dad (I didn't know them very well). I was worried because my sister was only two years old. I was so worried that I couldn't sleep for the whole night.

Another time was when I was at school in India. It was pouring hard outside. By recess time the streets looked like rivers. We had a half day because of the flood. When my mom came and we tried to walk home on the road, the water came up to my chest! I was scared, but I didn't cry. It's okay to be scared. That doesn't mean you're not brave. I got home without an injury. I am lucky because many people got injured and died.

I am not a woman yet, but I can do great things. I can play the violin and tell stories and play video games and write stories. I will make history like my grandmother and mother did. When I have my own family, I am going to teach my children a quote: "A person's a person no matter how small." This is to teach them to respect everyone. There are billions of ways to live a good life.

FIGURE 6.10
Yachana interviewed herself to create this family history piece.

the writer's notebook and listing key events that might be included as a "menu of ideas" to choose from. Fletcher also talks about collecting family stories and asking questions of family members to pull out important details. In addition, he advises writers to gather artifacts to reach into their memory banks and pull the memories associated with the artifact to surface level. Neighborhood maps and heart maps are also suggested as ways to help students dig up the stories of their lives.

ABC Study: A Useful Organizational Format

The ABC format is a great way to take any topic and offer information about it in an interesting way. Using this format also allows teachers to divide the class into small groups for cooperative work to create a class book.

In Hillary McCartney's and Lisa Labow's third-grade classrooms, students collaborated in small groups to write entries for an ABC book about their own school. The third graders were very excited. Not only were they creating a book for the school library, as well as an office copy for parents and other visitors to read, they were also creating a work presented in PowerPoint format that would be shared in assembly programs, open house introductions, or Grandparents' Day celebrations. As fourth graders, they would have another opportunity to see their work displayed and used for real-world purposes.

Together with Lynne, the teachers shared examples of ABC books. Lynne's favorites, *Appaloosa Zebra: A Horse Lover's Alphabet* by Jessie Haas, and *G Is for Galaxy* by Janis Campbell and Cathy Collison were shared as read-alouds. The students studied the ABC picture book genre with the school library collection and the teachers' additions. They made a list of the kinds of things they noticed about the craft. One thing that stood out to them was the use of alliteration by some of the authors (they had all studied alliteration and loved including it in their poems and narratives!). Margriet

Ruurs uses alliteration in *A Mountain Alphabet*, a book about the mountains of western North America: "A gigantic grizzly digs for grubs in the grassy meadow." In another mentor text, *Away from Home*, Anita Lobel uses alliteration to take her readers on a journey to cities around the world. In another book, *Alison's Zinnia*, the author uses alliteration for each letter but with a different twist. She ends each line with a word that begins with the next letter of the alphabet: "Maryssa misted a Magnolia for Nancy."

The students volunteered ideas for the ABC projects. Lynne wrote their ideas on the chalkboard. Combining the two classes for these initial conversations was powerful. Ideas flowed freely. As a group, they decided to use a photograph wherever possible, an alliterative line to introduce the letter, and a paragraph of explanation. As the work was divided by letter among the writers, other discussions included how to gather information to include in the paragraph of explanation. Some students decided they would need to take a survey, and others, who chose *nurse* to represent the letter *n*, decided they would have to conduct an interview.

Small, flexible group instruction on interview questions and survey techniques followed. Here, Lynne offered this advice: "When you interview people, try to write down one important thing they tell you so you can quote them. You will also have them sign a permission slip so their words can be used in our book and PowerPoint presentations. It is important for people to know that their thoughts will be made public." Erin and Christian followed that advice while interviewing the school nurse: "The most important thing a nurse decides is whether a child is healthy enough to stay in school," says Mrs. Donahue.

Students enjoyed creating surveys and collecting the data as well as finding an appropriate question to end their paragraph—one that would invite reflection from their readers or assembly audiences. Their excitement and enthusiasm for the project reinforced the value of writing for specific purposes and specific audiences. The ABC format is easily converted into a real-world writing opportunity for students of any age (see examples in Figures 6.11 and 6.12).

FIGURES 6.11 AND 6.12
Using the ABC format for real-world writing

Ff

F is for Friends
Friends are fun, faithful, and forever lasting at UMIS.

Making friends at UMIS is an easy thing to do. The children are friendly. Playing with friends at recess is easy. We can play jump rope and basketball. Whether we're eating together at lunch or working together in the classroom, friends at UMIS are loyal and faithful and never will let you down!

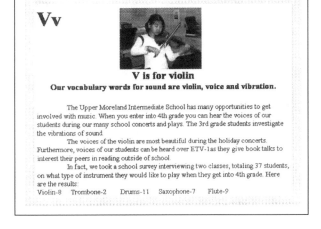

Vv

V is for violin
Our vocabulary words for sound are violin, voice and vibration.

The Upper Moreland Intermediate School has many opportunities to get involved with music. When you enter into 4th grade you can hear the voices of our students during our many school concerts and plays. The 3rd grade students investigate the vibrations of sound.

The voices of the violin are most beautiful during the holiday concerts. Furthermore, voices of our students can be heard over ETV-1 as they give book talks to interest their peers in reading outside of school.

In fact, we took a school survey interviewing two classes, totaling 37 students, on what type of instrument they would like to play when they get into 4th grade. Here are the results:

Violin-8   Trombone-2   Drums-11   Saxophone-7   Flute-9

Using Primary Source Documents

One way to help students become better researchers and make connections to social studies is to introduce them to the concept of primary source documents. In Kate Tiedeken's and Kathy Randolph's fourth-grade classes, the students were learning about primary sources. They would eventually be responsible for finding three primary sources around their home. They could also enlist the help of parents or grandparents, if necessary. After talking about these documents with family members, the students would bring them to class and talk about them with their peers. Finally, they would create a poster including a sketch of each object and a paragraph explaining what the document or object revealed to them.

Lynne used several mentor texts to show students what a primary source document could look like and what we could learn from studying it. She used *Airborne: A Photobiography of Wilbur and Orville Wright* by Mary Collins, which contains a copy of a Western Union telegram from Orville Wright announcing his successful flight. This book also houses many black and white photographs of the Wrights' plane and family members as well as a photograph of the actual notebook where the Wrights recorded important information. Also included in this book are quotes from publications of the time, such as Scientific American, headlines from newspapers about the Wright brothers' famous feats, and a cartoon advertisement from a foreign newspaper. Lynne also returned to *Yours for Justice, Ida B. Wells: The Daring Life of a Crusading Journalist* by Philip Dray to linger on the afterword that contains photos of Ida B. Wells and her family, a political cartoon, and a photograph of a protest march. Frank Murphy includes a photograph of a letter written from George Washington to General Howe in his book *George Washington and the General's Dog*. Lynne used Murphy's book to explain to the students that sometimes an entire piece of writing can evolve from one primary source document. She also pointed out that primary source documents lend the voice of authority to a work of nonfiction and demonstrate that the author was willing to go the extra mile and do some good research.

After examining these mentor texts and others, Lynne asked the students what we could learn from these primary source documents. Even though these were not the actual artifacts, the students understood that they were authentic facsimiles of the actual documents, which the authors viewed and studied for their books. Together with the students, Lynne and the teachers came up with a list of general categories that tell us the kinds of things we learn by examining primary source documents, including technology, culture, economy, and traditions.

Next, they imagined where they could go to look for primary source documents in the larger community and in their homes, and what they might be. This list included such things as newspaper articles, photographs, cartoons, currency, birth certificates, letters, recipes, receipts, coins, diaries, magazine articles, advertisements, identification cards, as well as many others. Since the fourth graders were going on a trip to Pennsbury Manor, William Penn's house on the Delaware, Lynne and the fourth-grade teachers asked them to imagine what primary sources they might find there.

Finally, Lynne asked them to think of other possible places to discover a primary source document. They came up with the following:

- Textbooks
- Trade books
- Government agencies
- Schools and libraries
- Community agencies (hospitals, police stations, courts)
- Newspaper archives
- Radio and television stations
- Art galleries
- Museums
- Local businesses
- Homes (attics, basements, family records, albums)
- Flea markets
- Garage sales
- Antique shops
- The Internet
- CD-ROMS
- Diaries and journals
- Writer's notebooks

The students were given a few days to find primary source documents. Many chose to start at their own homes with interviews of their parents and other relatives. What a great way to begin to discover some family history! Enthusiasm ran high as students began to share their discoveries each day for the rest of the week. Elizabeth found a picture of an old gristmill that was one of the first buildings in Hatboro. The picture was taken in 1950, but Lynne suggested that she try to find out more about the mill. As it turns out, it was built around 1720 and used as a lookout by the Revolutionary troops during the Battle of Crooked Billet. Amanda brought in a hand fan that belonged to her grandmother, Kathleen brought her great-grandmother's neck watch, and Aiden brought in a postcard from 1889 that shows a picture of the Columbian Exposition at the World's Fair held in Chicago. Julia found the hospital bill from when her great-great-grandmother was born and her certificate of naturalization.

Lynne wanted the students to go beyond just discovering the artifacts. She wanted them to reflect on the significance of their finds before they created their posters. So she asked them to do the following in their written descriptions:

- Tell what it is (photograph, newspaper, yearbook, birth certificate)
- Tell from where and when it came (approximate decade or historical era if possible)

- Tell who it is or to whom it belonged
- Tell what it means or reveals to us—what we can learn from it (about the culture, traditions, economy, technology)

Lynne modeled with a photograph of her grandfather's store taken in the late 1920s. First she showed the photograph and talked about what she could learn from its contents. Then she revealed her written description and asked the students to evaluate how well she included all of the necessary information (listed above). The students examined her piece and identified the key components of the scaffold for this writing project (underlined below):

> This photograph shows my <u>grandfather's</u> store on <u>Wyoming Avenue in West Philadelphia</u>. The picture was taken <u>in the late 1920s</u>. My grandfather sold fresh fruits and vegetables. As you can see, the shelves are stacked high with <u>canned goods</u>. At that time, there were <u>no frozen food packages</u> because that technology was not available yet. There is a sign that advertises cans of Norwegian <u>sardines</u> in olive oil for <u>15 cents a can</u>.
>
> Today, a can of sardines costs about three dollars! A <u>pound of cheese</u> in 1924 was <u>38 cents</u>, and a <u>pound of coffee</u> was <u>47 cents</u>. Today, we would pay about four to five dollars, depending on the brand. The floors were wooden, so they were easy to sweep and clean.
>
> There is also a sign for <u>Bond Bread</u>. In 1929, the cost of Bond Bread dropped to <u>one cent a loaf</u>. The <u>Great Depression</u> lasted from <u>1929 to 1939</u>. My grandparents lived through hard times during this era.

Lynne told the students that some of the things in her passage were discovered by researching on the Internet, but the clues were all in the photograph. Both classroom teachers, Kathy and Kate, also provided models with their primary source documents. Before letting the students write their own descriptions (see Figure 6.13), they practiced with newspapers—looking at headlines, advertisements, and photographs to discover what they could learn about today's world. They used the categories established for this project: technology, culture, and traditions.

At the conclusion of the project, Lynne asked the students to reflect on what they had learned. She asked them to think about the purpose of the primary sources they used in their projects. For instance, were they meant to inform or persuade, or did they have another purpose? She also asked them to list any "still wondering" questions they had and to think about how they might find the answers. Many students questioned why the people in all of the old photographs were not smiling. They wondered if this was meant to imitate portrait painting or the fact that it might be easier to stay still for the length of time needed to take a photograph with old-fashioned equipment. One student hypothesized that it could have been because the teeth didn't look good because of poor dental care. As a whole, this was a highly successful project.

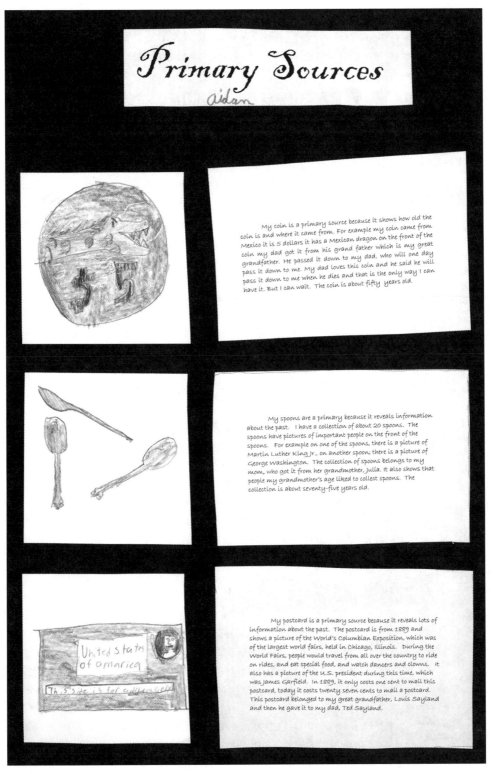

FIGURE 6.13
Aidan's examples of primary source documents

The students experienced firsthand another strategy they could pursue to find a nonfiction writing topic and possibly engage in an interview or additional research to learn more about their family histories and their world.

Newspapers as Mentor Texts: Writing an Obituary

Newspapers can often serve as primary source documents. Here students have rich models for many forms of real-world writing, including weather reports, feature articles, movie reviews, letters to the editor, and want ads to name a few. The obituary is a unique form of writing and can be useful to students in upper elementary grades through high school and beyond. It demonstrates how to capture essential information and present it in a "nutshell" format (brief and to the point).

One way to include the obituary as a form of writing in your classroom is through a multigenre approach to the study of a famous person or a particular event. Teresa Lombardi's fifth graders easily learned this format while studying people who lived during the Civil War period. They were working on biography scrapbooks (a collection of multigenre writing). They had already tried out preparing a birth certificate, a journal or diary entry, and a letter to a colleague or relative. Lynne and Teresa felt that an obituary would make an appropriate final entry. A useful professional reference for multigenre writing in social studies is *Eyewitness to the Past: Strategies for Teaching American History in Grades 5–12* by Joan Schur (2007).

Lynne cut out approximately fifty obituaries from local newspapers. She tried to choose obituaries that varied slightly in format, including some larger articles with headlines. As the students explored the different examples, they were asked to keep track of the things they noticed about the writing. David noticed that the people were often referred to by their last name. Carly commented that people were often quoted saying something complimentary about the person. The students all noted that many times the obituaries gave a brief description of where the person lived and highlights from the person's life. The students also found sentences that talked about family members, funeral services, and donations. Jimmy commented that there were a lot of dates and numbers. Alexa was surprised that their seemed to be an absence of craft, or what she expected to see in a piece of writing. Things like similes, metaphors, and rich descriptions just weren't there. But Erin felt that the craft was found in

FIGURE 6.14
Obituary written by a fifth-grade student

**Bethany Veney,
Plantation Slave, 78**

Bethany Veney, of Luray, Virginia, born on a plantation, worked as a slave her entire life. She died in 1893 at the age of 78 of natural causes.

Veney's life as a child was tragic. She never met her mother who died when she was only nine years of age. Later, she married a fellow slave, but after a year he escaped. Again, she was alone. In 1858, Ms. Veney was sold for the price of $775 together with her son at a plantation on Rhode Island.

She served many different masters and was separated from her family for a time. After the Civil War had ended in 1865, she and her son were freed by her owner, G.J. Adams, a Northern businessman. Veney finally settled in Worchester, Massachusetts with her daughter and three grandchildren.

In 1889 she told her story in her autobiographical work, *The Narrative of Bethany Veney: A Slave Woman.* Her book included details from her childhood, how she received her freedom, and what her new life in the North was like. Throughout this work, Veney stressed the importance of faith.

She will be missed by friends, but her words will be read and talked about for generations to come.

the quotes and the precise language. (See Your Turn Lesson 3 at the end of this chapter for a more detailed explanation.)

While some of the information that the students wanted to include in the obituaries they were writing needed additional research, they were easily able to imitate the language and format of an obituary (see Figure 6.14). What made this successful for the fifth graders was the fact that they knew their subject so well by this point in the project that they could easily transition to this new form of writing.

How-To: Writing Recipes, Poems, and Procedures

Think of all the times you are asked to write procedures for something. We write procedures or directions to others on topics that range from how to care for our pets to how to bake our famous blueberry muffins to how to get to next Friday's after-school get-together. We even write directions to our students for how to complete classroom activities. Procedural writing is real-world writing, and we can engage our students in understanding this mode from the start. In fact, you may be surprised at what they already know about how-to writing.

Consider this recipe dictated by Christopher, a kindergarten student:

Chocolate Cake

flour to the top of the measuring cup
spoonful of sugar
2 bags of melted chocolate
2 chocolate frostings
3 eggs

Crack the eggs. Pour the flour in. Put the chocolate stuff in. Stir it. Wait until all the little dots are done. Pour it into a glass pan and put in the oven. Cook it for 1 hour at 2 degrees.

Although following this recipe as written probably would not yield the kind of cake Christopher had in mind, he understands that recipes list ingredients and sometimes equipment, are specific with listing how much or how many of something you need, and use special vocabulary. He is using his background knowledge from watching and helping his mother bake to begin to understand how to explain a procedure to someone else.

Writing Recipes for Food We'd Really Eat

Knowing that all students had, like Christopher, dictated recipes in kindergarten, Rose wanted to extend this knowledge in Cindy Algier's first-grade class. She began by returning to parts of a book the class had been introduced to earlier in the year, *Discover the Seasons* by Diane Iverson. In this book, each season includes kid-friendly recipes such as sunshine tea, fruit kabobs, and spiced nuts. Rose and the students revisited some of the recipes they (the first graders) had written in kindergarten as well as the recipes in *Discover the Seasons* to begin to chart the students' understanding of what needs to be included in a recipe. Then, working in pairs, the class examined cookbooks for more ideas. There are many wonderful cookbooks written for children that include simple language, photographs, and diagrams. Some that the first graders explored include *Pink Princess Cookbook* by Barbara Beery, *American Grub: Eats for Kids from All Fifty States* by Lynn Kuntz and Jan Fleming, and many others. As a shared writing experience, Rose and the students charted what they considered to be must-haves for a recipe—a list of ingredients, numbers that tell the amount of each ingredient needed, and step-by-step directions in the proper order. The first graders also explored what they termed "cooking words"—words like *cut, pour, mix, stir, blend, spread*—and added them to the chart.

The fun started when Rose asked the first graders to brainstorm some of the things they thought they could write a recipe for. Suggestions included ants on a log, lemonade, toast, salad, waffles, ice cream sundaes, and sandwiches. The students were quite thoughtful about the kinds of foods they could make without much supervision. Rose modeled writing a recipe for making popcorn, then together the class created a shared recipe for ice cream sundaes. Rose asked the students to do a little thinking and research at home that night in preparation for writing their own recipes. The next day they had a chance to discuss their ideas in partnerships. The most difficult part of the assignment was thinking about the order of the steps. As they drafted their recipes, some students acted out the steps, and others drew a few simple diagrams. They all decided that it was most important to list the steps in order, because otherwise it "just won't turn out right." The finished products demonstrated this new knowledge of procedural writing and served as an extension of the thinking begun the year before in kindergarten.

Ants on a Log
by Emily

1 piece of celery
1 package of cream cheese
1 box of raisins

1. Take out the piece of celery and wash it.
2. Spread the cream cheese on the celery.
3. Put the raisins on top of the cream cheese.
4. Start eating.

Nachos
by Donovan

1 bag of tortilla chips
1 big cup of cheese
2 bags of beef

1. Cook the beef.
2. Put a handful of chips on a plate.
3. Pour the cheese on the chips.
4. When the beef is done cooking, put the beef on the chips with the cheese then you have yourself a yummy snack.

Turn Up the Heat on Social Studies! Recipe Writing Adds a New Flavor

It's not a stretch for students to grow in their understanding of how to write the traditional recipe. There are numerous cookbooks written for children at all different levels that can serve as mentor texts (see the Treasure Chest for this chapter for some of our favorites). Once students understand the basic format and vocabulary of recipe writing, you may want to have them extend their thinking to include writing "recipes" on topics across the curriculum.

At Upper Moreland Intermediate School, fifth graders were finished with state testing and ready to think about topics for their wax museum presentations. In a wax museum, students "become" a person from a period of history and dress in costume to speak about an event or a "day in the life" of their famous person. This project spans two days every spring. The hallways, library, and large-group instruction pods are decorated with artwork and lined with "wax museum" figures (the students themselves). Parents, board members, administrators, and senior citizens tour the school to hear the presentations.

The nine fifth-grade classes were excited about the plan to present their work around different themes for the wax museum project—most of which related to American history or social studies in some way—to the community at large. Their excitement spurred Lynne to think about the possible use of recipe writing as a creative and useful format to organize their new learning. Barry Lane (1999, 2003) discusses how research can be used to create a recipe poem, and Lynne used some of his ideas in her planning.

As always, the first step in imitation of a mentor text or author is deep study. Lynne and fifth-grade teacher Valorie Hawkins immersed the students in the sounds, smells, and tastes of recipe writing. According to Routman (2005) teachers should "provide more time for browsing nonfiction (after you've modeled how to browse) and immersing children in the genre before expecting them to write" (196). The school library collection was extensive—enough to put a book in every student's hand.

Lynne modeled some of the things she noticed while browsing, including the nomenclature of the kitchen—both equipment words and cooking verbs. A wonderful mentor text is Abigail Johnson Dodge's *Around the World Cookbook*. It provides a road map for how to use the book, kitchen safety tips for elementary school children, and so-very-useful pages with definitions of the lingo, pictures and descriptions of essential tools, and last, but not least, cleanup advice! Lynne asked the students to pass the books around and use their writer's notebooks to make a list of strong verbs, cooking equipment, headings for sections, and ways the publisher made the layout attractive and easy to follow.

Lynne also shared Shar Levine and Leslie Johnstone's *Kitchen Science*, a book that demonstrates another way to learn about recipe formats and, at the same time, discover the scientific principles behind the chemistry of cooking! Sections also include "What Happened?" and "Did You Know?"—and sometimes, a bit of fun history:

> *Do you like eating toast in the morning? If you wanted toast 1500 years ago, you couldn't just drop a slice into the toaster and wait until it popped up. Instead, you would have to stick your bread on a long fork and turn it over a large pit fire in the middle of the room.*

Furthermore, Levine and Johnstone include a well-written introduction for the book as a whole and intriguing introductions for each kitchen experiment with food. Consider the following lead for "Salted Popcorn":

> *If you wanted to mix something up, you might put all the ingredients in a jar and give the jar a good shake. The up-and-down movement should combine all the foods and evenly mix everything together. That's what you'd think, but is that what really happens?*

After students had a day or two to study cookbooks, Valorie and Lynne charted their work, including a list of strong verbs and a list of cooking equipment. In order to work their recipes into the wax museum presentations, they agreed upon a format that included a catchy title describing an event or person from the Revolutionary War period (their theme for the museum), a list of ingredients combining facts and/or food items, directions written as a paragraph or bulleted list, and the number of servings. Lynne wrote an example from a different time period on the board using what she knew so well about Abe Lincoln.

Honest Abe Apple Stew

Ingredients:
- 10 pounds of honesty potatoes
- 9 ounces of bravery butter
- 14 cups of desire-to-learn carrots
- 13 cups of onion tears
- 10 gallons of sweet apple cider sensibility
- 12 pints of humble behavior cream
- a dash of sideburns pepper
- a sprinkle of tall stature salt
- 20 pounds of lean sirloin
- 1 tablespoon of shocking reality cornstarch

Directions:

Wash and dry a large bowl. Marinate the lean sirloin with apple cider sensibility overnight. Add sideburns pepper and stature salt. Season to your liking. Chop the honesty potatoes in large pieces, add strips of desire-to-learn carrots, and place in the bottom of a deep cooking pot with diced onion tears. Cook for five minutes before adding the sirloin. Cover and allow to simmer. Bring to a full boil, then slowly stir in the humble behavior cream. Cook for one hour over a low flame. Thicken mixture with a tablespoon of shocking reality cornstarch. Add a score of poetic words as a garnish. Serve steaming hot in wooden Gettysburg bowls.

Serves: a grieving nation

Lynne directed the students to turn and talk about what they noticed and liked about her recipe. After cautioning them not to try out her creation (Lynne is a disastrous cook and could not create her own recipe in a million years!), she decided to turn their attention to an event they had just read about in social studies. Using information concerning the Boston Tea Party from their textbook and Pamela Duncan Edward's *The Boston Tea Party,* Lynne and the students created a recipe as a shared writing experience. After that, most of the students were ready to take an event they had been studying and turn it into a recipe. Some students returned to more cookbooks before drafting their ideas. Peer and teacher conferences followed the writing of their first drafts. Students revised for recipe words and details to describe their person or event before publishing. Figures 6.15 and 6.16 provide samples of the finished products.

How-to-Be Poems

In Tina Madison's and Kathy Randolph's fourth-grade classrooms, Lynne introduced how-to-be poetry to inspire the young writers first to write about themselves and then transfer that experience to writing about other people in the real world. Lynne read Lisa Brown's *How to Be,* in which the author gives directions for how to be various animals. Lynne asked the students to tell her what they noticed about Brown's writing. Immediately, the students talked about how the author began her sentences with verbs and sometimes limited her sentences to one word. For instance, Brown offers some advice about how to be a snake:

> *Shed your skin.*
> *Slither.*
> *Dance in a basket.*
> *Be charming.*

The students were asked to turn and talk about where they might have seen this type of writing before. They offered these insights: directions for how

Bunker Hill Home Fries
By: Jake

Ingredients:

3 ounces of diced brave patriot peppers
2 ounces of General Washington Hot Sauce
3 fresh independence scrambled eggs
4 cups of pure, raw courage
5 scared redcoat potatoes
1 bushel of newly gained confidence
2 quarts of fresh Nathan Hale herbs
1000 British soldiers killed or wounded

Directions:

1. Shred 5 scared Redcoat potatoes.
2. Mix with independence scrambled eggs.
3. Sprinkle Nathan Hale herbs and diced patriot peppers on.
4. Pour pure raw courage on mixture,
5. Blend best as possible.
6. Add in newly gained confidence.
7. Mix with 1000 British soldiers killed or wounded.
8. Stir well one last time.
9. Cook at 342 degrees for 30 minutes.
10. Pour General Washington Hot Sauce on top of everything.

Serves: one Continental Army

FIGURE 6.15
Jake had fun with his "Bunker Hill Home Fries."

King George III's Jambalaya
By: Samantha

Ingredients:
- 1 cup of Proclamation Broth
- 1 cup of war salt
- 1 cup of French Chicken
- 1 cup of Indian Rice
- 2 cups of American Parsley
- 1 quart of British Beans
- 2 cups of George Washington's Victory

What to do:
1. Pour the Proclamation Broth into a pot.
2. Let the broth heat up until it reaches about 100%.
3. Then pour and mix 1 cup of war salt.
4. Add the cup of French Chicken.
5. Sprinkle the cup of Indian Rice.
6. Chop 2 cups of American Parsley, then add to pot.
7. Immediately add 1 quart of British Beans.
8. After that, place two cups of George Washington's Bravery.
9. Take the gallon of British victory, and pour into pot.
   Serves 3 British Soldiers.

FIGURE 6.16
Samantha's "King George Jambalaya" is almost good enough to eat!

to play a card or board game, cookbook recipes, and directions in kits for assembling things such as model cars and airplanes. Tyler shared that his mother had tried to follow directions for assembling a bookshelf, and that she had complained that the written directions were not very friendly. Shannon added that her father had easily assembled a fan just by using the pictures. Lynne told them that they were going to write a how-to-be poem about themselves. She reminded them that this piece of writing would be easy to do—after all, they were the experts here.

Lynne had the students list the characteristics that Brown shared for each animal in her book. She told them that Brown tried to give them a picture of what it would be like to actually be that animal. "What would we have to know about you, what would we need to be able to do, what would we need to like and dislike, in order to be you?" Lynne asked. She made a list of things that came to mind about herself and asked the students to do the same in their writer's notebook. Then she had them turn and talk. Later, as they shared in whole group, Lynne charted the interesting verbs they used on chart paper. These included *adore, practice, remember, follow, design, choose, enjoy, despise,* and many others. Lynne used the chart to model a poem about herself:

How to Be Dr. Dorfman

Dream of becoming an elementary school teacher.
Go to school for years and years and years.
Gobble your lunch in less than ten minutes flat.
Be crazy about dogs, horses, whales, and children.
Dream of going to New England to see the humpback whales.
Write in a writer's notebook every day.
Own Welsh Corgi dogs like the Queen of England.
Teach horseback riding to children and adults.
Love your twin goddaughters with all your heart.
Shop for shoes with your sister, Sandy.
Love to receive flowers, especially daisies and roses.
Despise house cleaning and avoid doing it at all costs.
Wear turtlenecks as often as possible.
Dream of writing a children's book.
Write a book about mentor texts.
Keep believing you CAN make a difference!
Never stop dreaming.

The students used the list of things about themselves they had brainstormed and expanded it to include any important instructions that would be essential to explaining who they are to someone else. Brooke found a way to scaffold her piece by beginning with waking up and ending with going to sleep:

How to Be Brooke

Be sure to wake up early for school!
Don't be shy or quiet.
Write a speech for K-Kids as the fourth grade representative.
Sing a few songs to mom every day.
Be sure to eat healthy foods and try to eat NO SWEETS!
Adore Yorkies and Cocker Spaniels!
Keep the house and your room extra clean and tidy.
Use good manners at the dinner table.
Practice your clarinet every day or a few
times a week.
Be prepared for your little brother, Mark, to come
into your room and wake you up on weekends.
Remember to smile and be kind and considerate to others.
Shop at Justice for clothes.
Sleep with three blankets and a stuffed penguin!
That's how to be Brooke.

These two fourth-grade classes were also studying biographies in reading workshop, so extending this scaffold to writing about famous people was a logical next step. Lynne found support for this type of writing for primary through intermediate grades in Barry Lane's *Reviser's Toolbox* (1999) and *51 Wacky We-Search Reports* (2003). Lynne asked the students to return to the picture book biographies they were using and bullet the facts that stood out to them. She cautioned them to limit the dates and number facts used since this would take away from the voice of the poem. However, she also asked them to revise for chronological order. Before writing, they enlarged the list of verbs that were originally charted to describe themselves. Brooke easily transferred what she had learned about the how-to-be scaffold to her piece about Theodore Roosevelt:

> *Be born with no strength and kept indoors.*
> *Cherish your favorite subjects, nature and science.*
> *Author 35 books in your lifetime.*
> *Journey to Britain, Europe, North Africa, and the Middle East by*
> *the time you are 15.*
> *Enjoy riding horses and hunting.*
> *Become a father of six children.*
> *Be elected the 26th president at age 42.*
> *Have your image carved on Mt. Rushmore.*
> *Don't forget your spectacles.*
> *After your first wife dies, don't be afraid to marry again.*
> *Lead your nation with pride.*
> *Enjoy your lifetime, for it will shortly fade away.*
> *Follow your dreams for they will come true.*
> *That's how to be Theodore Roosevelt!*

Shannon had read about Rosa Parks and captured her essence in this poem:

> *Marry a barber that works at Maxwell Air Force Base.*
> *Work as a seamstress, and be the best one.*
> *If someone threatens you to call the police, answer quietly,*
> *"Do what you must."*
> *Be arrested for never giving up your seat on a bus.*
> *Never back down,*
> *even when people are telling you to give up.*
> *Debate the unfair laws.*
> *Dream of fair laws.*
> *Love your people who are African American.*
> *Fear nothing, especially threats from police and people*
> *who are ignorant of the truth.*
> *Be brave even if you have to go to jail.*

Writing Paragraphs of Explanation

Almost every writing curriculum at every grade level explores writing paragraphs that offer explanations or directions for how to do something. Although students may have experience reading and following directions in school and at home, you can use mentor texts to introduce them to some of the aspects that make this type of writing interesting and more effective. *How a House Is Built* by Gail Gibbons offers a study in the use of transition words, especially for a younger audience. The simple text is enhanced with labeled illustrations and offers step-by-step procedures in paragraph form to explain how a house is constructed. In *How People Learned to Fly* by Fran Hodgkins, simple transitions are also used to indicate time-order relationships and help readers think about a step-by-step sequence without numbering the steps.

When students begin writing procedures, they naturally use the transition words that are most familiar to them. Notice how Ryan, a first grader, uses simple transition words such as *when, next,* and *then* to explain how he and his father built a pinewood derby car:

> I learned how to build a pinewood derby car from my dad. When we opened the box it was just a block of wood, but my dad and me carved it. Next me and my dad scrayped the nals and wheels with sandpaper. Then me and my dad painted the car until it was smooth and didn't feel like wood anymore. Next we grout the nals. I was glad that it was dun!

As students grow in sophistication, new transition words and phrases can be introduced. Students will try them out for size and, as usual, will litter their writing with more transitions than are necessary. Like everything else about good writing, a sprinkle of transition words will make the writing clear and easy to follow, but a word of caution here—the use of too many transition words and phrases creates writing that sounds stiff and unnatural. The piece of writing tends to lose voice if overwhelmed with a stampede of transitions. *Lacrosse in Action* by John Crossingham provides examples of how to effectively use transition words while offering directions and explanations.

In another text, *How to Talk to Your Cat,* Jean Craighead George uses transition words and phrases effectively and sparingly. Consider this example, in which we've underlined the transition words:

> *You and your cat are speaking in scent when you exchange touches. A cat touch is silent talk. Scent glands lie along the flank and the lip, under the chin, on the top of the head, and along the tail of the cat. <u>When</u> you are rubbed by flank, lip, chin, head, or tail, you are being told, "You are my property." <u>Although</u> you can't smell the message, you will probably answer by picking up or petting your cat. <u>Now</u> you have scent marked the fur. <u>However,</u> you have not said, "You*

are my property." You have said, "Yes, I am your property." That's cat talk. They own you. You cannot own a cat.

You can also show your students how Jean Craighead George uses a conversational tone that is friendly and talks directly to the reader using the second-person voice (*you*).

The following list of possible transition words and phrases may be useful as a handy reminder to use with students throughout the year.

after	all at once	along with	also
as a result	before	besides	consequently
during	earlier	eventually	for example
for instance	for this reason	however	immediately
in addition	in conclusion	in the same way	instead
last	later	meanwhile	not long ago
quickly	slowly	soon	suddenly
therefore	to begin with	to sum up	whenever

When writing paragraphs of explanation, students need to use concise language and the special vocabulary of their subject area. Revising for precise language will keep the explanations or directions from becoming too wordy. A helpful mentor text for teaching this concept is *How To Catch a Fish* by John Frank. Consider the following example, which explains how to use dip-netting as a fishing method:

We strip the bark from limbs of fir
and make them into poles as tall
as three men head to toe combined,
and lash to them a white-oak hoop—
a supple branch shaped over fire—
and netting from wild iris twined.
Our dip nets now complete, we climb
the rocks between the steep cliff walls,
and swing the long poles through the roar
of rapids carving canyon floor—
to catch the fish that scale the falls.

Notice the exact nouns, such as *wild iris*, to describe the twine and the special vocabulary of fishermen—*dip nets*. The strong verbs—*lash, carving, scale*, and *strip*—also help to limit the number of words needed to create an image.

When writers become more accomplished in explanatory writing, you could introduce other possible strategies, such as offering cautions, options, or tips to your readers. A mentor text to illustrate how to embed cautions within the text is *Walk On! A Guide for Babies of All Ages* by Marla Frazee. Her tips also add a touch of humor (or at least will bring a smile to your face). Here are a few cautions about learning to walk:

Be careful of things that are wobbly.
You don't want anything to fall on top of you.
Stay away from fragile stuff, too.
You don't need something new to cry about.

Josh, a fourth grader in Steve Grant's class, wrote about planning a surprise party. Here are his cautions:

Often fill the snack bowls so your guests don't get hungry while waiting for the person to surprise. Only put out chips and a fruit and vegetable tray. You can put out peanuts, but make sure no one is allergic.

Another fourth grader, Alyssa, wrote about how to wash a dog. She also offers cautions, using capital letters to make sure the reader will not miss her suggestions:

Next, squirt the dog's back, neck, and legs with the dog shampoo. WARNING: Do not put any on the head. The shampoo can irritate your dog's eyes and ears. Then, gently scrub the shampoo into the dog's fur (Don't forget the legs and under the belly!). WARNING: Dog might shake!

Kendra wrote about hamster care. When giving directions on how to fill a water bottle, she provides the following caution:

Slide the bottle back into the cage and if it is dripping, tap the top of the bottle until no water escapes (You don't want to drown the hamster!).

As you can see, Kendra provides a helpful hint to her reader, using humor in parentheses as a gentle reminder of the importance of her advice. Writing helpful hints can be used in creating procedural guides (for example, "How to Care for a Pet Hamster") that are friendly and fun for readers in elementary and middle grades. These guides are a form of how-to writing that are practical venues for writing about the real world.

Paragraphs of explanation add content to any piece of writing—narrative, informational, and persuasive. Because procedural writing is a natural part of writing workshop at many grade levels, it is a good idea to help students write with precision while simultaneously creating interest in the topic they are writing about.

Survival Guides: Practical Advice in Practical Formats

Dan Monaghan's fifth graders at Upper Moreland were ready to try something new. They had bonded as a collaborative community of readers and writers and trusted one another. Dan's students believed in themselves as writers. When Lynne suggested to Dan the idea of a fifth-grade survival guide to extend opportunities for real-world writing, he was eager to help her plan the project. Lynne and Dan knew it was important to take the advice Regie Routman (2005) offers to teachers:

> *When the purpose of writing is to teach how to write a letter, essay, persuasive piece, or fiction, we make writing harder for kids. Focus first on meaningful purposes to real readers.* (193)

Lynne and Dan felt that a fifth-grade survival guide had definite purposes and a specific target audience. The fifth graders would leave their guide behind for next year's fifth graders. Their reasons for writing would be clear, and many of the sections included in this guide would be written as the fifth graders navigated their way through their fifth-grade year. The guidebook would be completed in June around fifth-grade graduation time, even though the conversations about the process—how the work would be divided and shared and what everyone would include (such as "Helpful Hints" and "Did You Know . . .?" entries)—began in January.

Lynne and Dan began reading parts of survival guides to the fifth graders. They wanted the students to understand the purposes for writing guides and clearly see the long-lived usefulness for this kind of writing. Students were already familiar with Jane Kirkland's Take a Walk Books. Using a visualizer or document imager, Lynne displayed some pages from *Take a Beach Walk* to share Kirkland's inviting introduction, her nature identification pages, and her helpful tips in sidebars. Kirkland includes her personal connection to seashore adventures before moving into the purposes and goals for her guidebook. She explains the various sections and concludes with this heartfelt advice:

> *Once you know where to look and what to look for you'll see just how exciting a beach walk can be! There's so much nature at the beach that soon you'll wonder how you didn't notice it before! You can read this book in any order you wish. Just remember that this book isn't finished until you go outside to explore! Are you ready to discover nature at the beach?*

Lynne also shared Meghan McCarthy's *Astronaut Handbook*, written in a conversational tone in the second-person voice. The author presents important information and embeds advice into the running text:

It's also important to be a team player. While in space, you'll be eating, sleeping, and working in very tight quarters with many other people, so be nice to your neighbor and no fighting!

The handbook includes diagrams of a space suit and even what a space toilet looks like (the kids will love it!), as well as a list of fascinating facts and places to visit for additional information.

Dan shared bits and pieces from Diane C. Clark's *A Kid's Guide to Washington, D.C.*, a guide that includes maps, games, puzzles, travel diary pages with sentence stems to get your thinking started, and "Did you know . . .?" pieces placed throughout the book on the wide margins to enhance the information on the two-page spreads. For example, in the section about the Library of Congress, you would find these "Did you know . . .?" entries and more:

The Library of Congress collection grows by 10 items a minute.
If you spent 1 minute looking for each item in the Library of Congress for 8 hours a day, 5 days a week, it would take you 648 years to see everything.
Four hundred seventy languages appear in the library's collection.

Another useful mentor text for guidebooks is Ellen Sabin's *The Greening Book: Being a Friend to Planet Earth*. The first page offers a definition of what it means to be "green" and establishes a rationale and purposes, followed by an explanation of how the book works. Like Kirkland's books, this guide provides space for written response—thus, it becomes interactive and particularly meaningful and useful. The author is always drawing her readers in, asking them to participate. In the section "Be Green by Giving to Others," Sabin describes three ways to reduce trash and be green by giving. She ends with a question: "Can you think of other things that you or your family throws out that might be nice to give to other people instead?"

After studying and collecting many guidebooks, the students felt they understood the form and genre and were ready to write. Lynne and Dan had asked the students to help them divide up the school year into key events and brainstorm other important areas to include in their fifth-grade survival guide. These topics included students, teachers, specials, subjects, the fifth-grade penny drive, the diversity feast, field trips, and promotion. Next, the students submitted a paper listing the three topics they thought they would like to gather information and write about. Dan took a long time to make sure that all students received a topic that would interest them and made sure that partners and small-group members were compatible. Each partnership or small group was assigned a topic. A few groups handled several topics, depending on the size of the topic to be covered. Because Dan had firsthand experience as a fifth-grade teacher, he could make these decisions.

Students studied *You Wouldn't Want to Sail on the Titanic! One Voyage You'd Rather Not Make* by David Stewart for the helpful hints the author included to spark humor and thought. Then they created their own list of helpful hints to be spread throughout the fifth-grade survival guide. The fifth graders wrote these hints so they would also be helpful to students who were entering the district's school system for the first time as fifth graders:

- It pays to work hard from the beginning. Then the whole year will be easier for you!
- You will find the third-grade classrooms in our school closest to the office and front of the building. The fourth grades are in the middle, and the fifth-grade classrooms are closest to the back of the school by the playground. The second floor is organized the same way!
- During a field trip, always stay with your group.
- Remember to do your assigned job if you have one.
- For the egg drop competition, the more padding you have—the better!
- During fifth-grade concerts, sing your best. It's about teamwork!
- Don't be afraid to try out for the talent show. It's so much fun—even more so when you participate!
- Try new things and take responsible risks to grow as a learner.
- Continue to work hard for the penny drive—anyone can win! But never take change from home unless you ask first.
- Be prepared to set aside 30 minutes for independent reading every night.
- Find creative ways to handle stress during tests—especially state tests (exercise, read, play games, listen to music).
- Use appropriate audience behavior as it is expected and appreciated. (Don't forget, you are the role models for the entire school!)
- During the wax museum, know your speech and deliver it in a clear, crisp, voice.
- Always provide a worthy and interesting topic for presentations and demonstrate your commitment through your specific and accurate research.
- Treat substitute teachers like your everyday teacher—with RESPECT!
- Be the best you can be every moment of every day. (Remember what Rudyard Kipling said about the "unforgiving minute"!)

Throughout this project, the students had periods of time when they worked independently or with their group. Sometimes they had to conduct interviews. Other times they carried their writer's notebook with them to record observations, such as on the field trips to Camden Aquarium, Fort Mifflin, and the Keswick Theater. A few groups, especially the group reporting on the history of the township and special landmarks, needed to do online research and seek out our most veteran teachers and community members for help. Students

brought their drafts to teacher and peer conferences. Finally, as a class the writers decided on
the font, type size, page layout, and order. The
introduction for the guidebook (Figure 6.17)
shows an understanding of purpose, a sense of
audience, and what these writers know about
giving voice to a piece of nonfiction writing.

Opportunities Abound

We know that our students will write more passionately and sustain writing for longer periods
of time when they are given the chance to write
for different purposes and different audiences.
Sometimes it is hard to find an outside audience
other than the teacher and the parents, but if we
look into the real world, we will find that opportunities abound.

   One place students can look is in their
expert, or authority, lists. Right away you can be
sure that students will find a topic of keen inter-
est that will give them ownership of their writing piece and help them sustain
writing through multiple drafts and revisions. Another place to find real-world
writing opportunities is in classroom, school, or community events. Often, it is
easy to make ties with subject matter across the curriculum. For example, we
described about how Joanne Costello's class studied the ocean and its creatures.
Their study of the manatees led to a real-world writing project—writing to the
governor of Florida via email to voice their concerns.

   We also know that when students know their target audience—the specific
audience they are writing to and for—their writing has voice. The real world
can give us many opportunities to share our passions and make our voices
heard.

> ### Introduction
>
> Are you ready for fifth grade? If not, this survival guide put together by former fifth graders will give you ALL the information you need!
>
> This guide will tell you about the fifth grade staff, amazing activities, landmarks of the Upper Moreland community, the finish line (graduation and class picnic) and MUCH, MUCH more. This guide includes tips in all subjects and activities.
>
> Everything you need to know about mastering the PSSA writing is here (Yes, there is a writing PSSA!). Help on winning and beating Mr. Monaghan in the Penny Drive conducted by the fifth grade class appears in this book, so read carefully from start to finish!
>
> ### Helpful Hint:
> It pays to work hard from the beginning, and then the whole year will be easier for you!

FIGURE 6.17
Introduction to the fifth-grade survival guide

An Author's Voice: *Some Tips for Writers*

Jen Bryant
Author of *Georgia's Bones* and *A River of Words: The Story of William Carlos Williams*

1.   Be patient (it's hard, I know!). Good writing is a skill and a craft that
     takes as much time and practice as learning how to play soccer, master
     the flute, or become a dancer. Brainstorming lists, rough drafts, and sec-
     ond, third, and fourth drafts are a necessary parts of the process and are
     just as important as that final polished copy.

2.   Allow yourself to be messy and nonlinear in the beginning. Don't judge your earliest rough drafts, just write when you begin a work (or a new section of a work). Remember that you don't always have to start a novel, poem, short story, or essay at the beginning. Start where you feel the most passionate about your topic and write "around" that. Later on, you can put on your editor's hat and begin to think about the order of your ideas and about more specific things, such as word choice, rhythm and length of sentences, and transitions.

3.   Practice your observation skills: Slow down and listen, watch, smell, touch, hear . . . For this, you need to get away from the TV and the PC! Go outside or to a public space with living things and real human beings. Especially in our technology-driven world, this is very, very important! All good writers have keen sensory perception—they use their five senses to take in information about the world around them, then they translate that into sentences, lines, or paragraphs.

4.   Read literature, not just "books." Learn the difference between the two. (Hint: The magazines in the checkout line at the grocery store are not literature—you might learn who's making what movie in Hollywood, but you won't learn how to write well by reading them!) Ask your teacher, librarian, or local bookstore owner for their recommendations. Most library websites have links to lists of recommended books for each age group and genre. Use them often!

5.   Learn to take constructive criticism. This is also very difficult for most of us—but aside from patience, it's the most important aspect of being a good writer. You must learn to think of your rough draft as something that is separate from you as a person, even if the topic is something very personal and you've spent a lot of time thinking and writing about it. If you can do this, it greatly increases your ability to correct your weaknesses and to improve your structure, style, and voice.

6.   Honor your own personality in the writing process: Do you need quiet and solitude? A little background noise? What time of day do you write best? While it's not always possible to create the ideal circumstances in which to write, you should pay attention to your own preferences for when and where you tend to do your best work. (I do almost all of my brainstorming and rough drafts in my car, which I park at a nearby lake. I also have a favorite desk in the back stacks of my public library.)

7.   Imitate the style of writers you admire the most. You can do this by trying one or more of the following: Complete or continue a scene in one of their novel chapters; write a poem using their pattern of rhythm and rhyme (but choose your own topic); take one descriptive paragraph and notice how they vary their sentence length, if they use repetition, and if they include any poetic devices such as simile, metaphor, or personification. Then (again choosing your own topic/person/place), imitate these aspects in a descriptive paragraph of your own.

Your Turn Lesson 1

How-To (Procedural Writing)

In the book *My Friends=Mis Amigos* by Taro Gomi, the main character tells the reader all the things she learned from her animal friends (*I learned to walk from my friend the cat*). The author uses the repeated refrain "I learned to . . . from my friend . . ." throughout the book. This refrain can be used to spark how-to writing with young writers. It can be used to help students reflect on how they learned to do something, then how they might offer advice or tips to others learning how to do the same thing. Older students may not need this help to get started, but can benefit from thinking about the things that are included in procedural writing.

Hook: Gather as many how-to books as you can and let your students explore. These could be books the students are already familiar with, or they could be new books on familiar topics. Books such as *How a House is Built* by Gail Gibbons, *From Wax to Crayon* by Michael H. Forman, *Games (and How to Play Them)* by Anne Rockwell, *The Most Excellent Book of How to Be a Magician* by Peter Eldin, *How Baseball Works* by Keltie Thomas, and *Walk On! A Guide for Babies of All Ages* by Marla Frazee are good choices. Give students time to discuss with each other the kinds of things they notice about how these books are written. For example, they should note the special words some authors use such as *first, next, then,* and *finally.* They might also note the use of numbers to sequence steps and sentences that begin with a verb. As students share, be sure to record their observations on the board or on chart paper.

Purpose: *Writers, as we read* My Friends *I was thinking there are probably lots of things we have all learned how to do from friends just like the little girl in the book. But as I read the book, I wanted to know more. How did that little girl learn to walk from the cat, or kick from the horse? So, I thought we could start our pieces the way Taro Gomi did, then take what we've learned about explaining how to do something and use it to add further explanations to our own writing.*

Brainstorm: Ask the students to think about some things they learned how to do from a friend, a brother or sister, their moms or dads, or any other person. For example, someone may have taught them how to ride a bike, jump rope, cast a fishing line, swing a golf club, or play checkers. Record the students' suggestions on chart paper so there will be lots of ideas to choose from.

Model: Choose something from the list and write an example for the class. As you write, talk about the kinds of things you are including, such as special transition words, strong verbs, and practical tips. Here is an example from Rose's notebook:

> I learned to ride a bike from my friend Ruthie. First, she showed me how to get on and balance. All the while, she held on to the back. Tip: Make sure you have someone hold on for you, too. Then, I put my feet on the pedals and the bike began to move. Tip: Move your feet slowly at first so you don't go too fast. Next, we rode up and down the block with Ruthie still holding on. Tip: Practice until you think you have the hang of it. Finally, Ruthie let go and I was riding on my own. It made me feel like I was flying!

Shared/Guided Writing: Have students return to the list and decide on what they want to explain how to do. Invite several students to come to the front of the room for a guided conversation. As they explain how they learned how to do something, ask clarifying questions and engage the students in some oral writing. Ask them what tips they would offer at different places in the process. Students can then turn to a partner and talk through their piece.

Independent Writing: Students can return to their notebooks to draft their pieces. They might want to vary the structure by including other things they noticed in the books they examined, such as illustrations or numbered steps in a sequence.

Reflection: After sharing in small or whole group, students can reflect on the process. The following questions can help guide their thinking:

How did thinking about how you learned to do something help you explain it to someone else?

What did you learn about how-to or procedural writing? Was it easy or hard to write?

What other strategies could help you write directions for something?

When could you use this kind of writing again?

Your Turn Lesson 2

Writing a Family History from an Interview

Through scaffolded conversations created by interview questions, writers dig up memories connected with people, places, objects, or events. For this lesson, Lynne and fourth-grade teacher Maribeth Batcho asked the students to interview two or three women in their family and use the same questions to interview themselves. (See the section on using interviews to create family histories in this chapter). Variations of this lesson are endless, as the final product could be written up in interview format; as a series of casual conversations, diary entries, or letters; or in the form of this lesson—an informational narrative created as a book of collected family histories. Try this out on your own so that you have a model to share with your students.

Hook: Familiarize your students with *Seven Brave Women* by Betsy Hearne (you will need to return to this book many times for this lesson). Read two or three excerpts. Through whole-group conversation, invite students to make connections to events that were shared by the people they interviewed (students should already have interviewed someone before you use this lesson plan). Be sure to participate in the discussion and share your own connections (you need to interview someone or write down the imagined interview).

Purpose: *Writers, just like Betsy Hearne told many stories about things that happened to the women in her family, today we will learn how to use our interview questions and responses to help us record memories as a family history. Our collection will be published as books. You can choose to keep it or give it away as a gift, but whatever you do, I hope you will share it with all the wonderful women you chose to interview.*

Brainstorm: Ask students to reread their interviews, then have them turn and talk with a partner to share some of the things they have discovered and would like to include as they write their informational narrative pieces. Ask students to circle or star two places in their interview notes they would like to sketch and write about.

Model: Here you need to display your interview notes on an overhead, a television linked with your computer, or a visualizer or document imager. Use the board or chart paper to draft a narrative about one of the people you interviewed (or the imagined interview) or your self-interview. As you draft, you can point to or refer to your interview notes. Return to the mentor text by Betsy Hearne. Look at your piece and see if there is something you can add. For instance, you might be able to include an anecdote or a rich description of a place, a person, or an event. Hearne also includes a description of an object—an heirloom that was passed down by each female family member she interviewed. The author notes that her grandmother, Margaret, didn't have much herself, but she left them her most precious treasure—the author's father. (The students in Maribeth's class were all asked to try to include information about family heirlooms as part of their interview.) Continue to model by choosing one object that evoked a special memory or story.

Shared/Guided Writing: Return to your model and talk to the students about places in your piece where you may have to go back to the person and pull out a little more information. Use this scaffold for leads: My _____'s name is _____—a _____ name for a _____ lady. ("My mom's name was Betty—a beautiful name for a beautiful lady." Or, "My grandmom's name was Dorothy—a strong, old-fashioned name for a woman with strong, simple beliefs and dreams.") Ask the students to try writing a lead sentence for each person they are going to write about. Write some concluding sentences from Hearne's book on the board where she talks about an heirloom that is being passed on. Have your students try this out. Share leads and concluding sentences aloud.

Ask students to turn and talk again with their neighbor about their interviews and what they will include in their written narratives; this serves as an oral rehearsal. As they talk, circulate and listen in—ask clarifying questions often to guide their thinking.

Independent Writing: Ask students to begin to draft their pieces. Every student should have a self-interview and at least one other completed interview about his or her mother, grandmother, aunt, great-grandmother, or another important female mentor. Some writers will choose to have three finished pieces. Some students may find it easier to begin with the piece from their self-interview. You may want to refer to the last chapter in Hearne's book. She describes all the things she is able to do and connects them with "and" as a way of emphasizing the length of the list. The sentence leaves the reader breathless with the accomplishments of the writer. This technique can be easily imitated by young writers. On the day following, or as revision work, have students share their work with leads and concluding sentences.

Make sure notes about leads, concluding sentences, and ways to include an heirloom (if you choose to include this piece) are somewhere visible—on chart paper or on the board.

Reflection: Invite students to reflect on the strategy.

Did the interviews help you to focus your thoughts? How so?

How did the mentor text guide your thinking?

When could you use this strategy again to gather information for writing?

Students can first share in pairs, then share ideas with the whole group. After reflecting on the strategy, ask students to reread their writing and think about the things that they do well as a writer. What revisions could they make? Some students might choose to continue to work on their pieces during subsequent workshops or create a series of narratives about the men in their families.

Your Turn Lesson 3

The Newspaper as Mentor Text: Writing an Obituary

There are many ways a newspaper can be used as a mentor text. Students can write food reviews, travel articles, sports articles, comic strips, and letters to the editor. As we discussed earlier in this chapter, the most satisfying writing often comes from its relationship to real-world purposes and audiences. For young writers, discuss the format of obituaries so they understand that obituaries often include the highlights of a person's life written in nutshell format; that is, no frills—just the facts. This type of writing may be used as part of a biography scrapbook or a variation to a biography book report. In this lesson, we demonstrate how to teach students to write an obituary for a famous person in history.

Hook: Choose some obituaries from local newspapers and examine the headlines. Write them on the board. Ask the students to turn and talk about the purpose of this kind of writing. Ask them to talk about the target audience. Look for the larger articles in the obituary section and some of the smaller pieces. Think about the kind you think your students can best imitate in their attempt to write an obituary about a famous person.

Purpose: *As we have been discussing, real-world writing takes many different formats. Obituaries are a very important part of newspaper writing. This writing may be the last thing that is written about a person and publicly acknowledged. What you say must be memorable and satisfying, but it must also be concise. It is a terse version of an entire life. Since each life is significant, it is the writer's job to capture the highlights and interests and provide important information the readers will need.*

Brainstorm: In the case of this lesson, brainstorming is closely tied to the examination of obituaries from the local newspapers. As students examine articles, ask them to jot down their thinking about what kinds of things are included in an obituary. For example, they will probably notice that in the larger articles, friends and family members are often quoted. These discoveries can be charted and referred to when students are drafting independently.

Model: Read an obituary and share it on the visualizer or document imager, or as an overhead. Think aloud, first noting how the headline includes the person's full name, age at death, and occupation or the way he or she was known. Look at the opening paragraph and talk about the format—the repeated information from the headline, the cause of death, time, and location. Continue to go through the article, one paragraph at a time. Note that the last two paragraphs are reserved for information about funeral services, burial, and memorial donations.

At this point, you can either muster up enough gumption to write your own obituary, or write one for a deceased family member or friend. Sometimes, this is too hard to do. In that case, take a famous person, such as Abraham Lincoln, or write an obituary for a book character, such as Wilbur or Charlotte from E.B. White's *Charlotte's Web.* You will get older students' attention if you use a character from a J.K. Rowling book, such as Professor Dumbledore or Snape.

Shared/Guided Writing: Ask students to return to the newspaper clippings of obituaries. You should have a collection of these on hand. The cut-out articles are easier to handle and pass around than entire newspaper sections (and a lot less noisy as well!). The students can use your example and these clippings as models to draft their piece about a famous person in history. (Lynne worked with Teresa Lombardi's fifth-grade students, who were creating a biography scrapbook for a person who lived around the time of the Civil War.) Invite some students to offer their obituary pieces for group revision or hold two or three scaffolded conversations in front of the group. Talk about the straightforward writing style of obituaries and the absence of figurative language. Point out things such as the use of proper nouns for specificity, quotes for feeling tone, and transition words for clarity, organization, and flow.

Independent Writing: Ask students to write an obituary for a famous person they have studied in social studies or have read about in current events (maybe in *Weekly Reader* or *Scholastic News*). Students may also wish to include an obituary as part of a biography scrapbook project or as a unique way to offer up a biography report.

Reflection: After students have the opportunity to revise or write, ask them to share in whole or small group. The following questions can help guide their thinking:

How did you grow as a writer from writing an obituary?

How is your obituary satisfying for all the readers who may have known the person?

Does the obituary you wrote fit the format and sound like an obituary? How so?

What kinds of things do you think you should include but didn't?

Your Turn Lesson 4

Writing a Recipe—Listen, List, Think!

This lesson format was developed by Jacqueline Sham, supervisor of curriculum and instruction for Upper Moreland Township School District. Jackie is a fellow of the Lehigh Valley Writing Project. She had fun collaborating with Lynne and fifth-grade teacher, Teresa Lombardi.

Hook: *Amish Horses* by Richard Ammon provides an excellent model for this format for recipe writing. For this lesson to be effective, this book should be a very familiar read-aloud. Return to it often so that students find examples of actions and text-based vocabulary.

By this time, students should have already browsed myriad cookbooks and obtained a working knowledge of recipe nomenclature (the strong verbs and exact nouns) and equipment, measurements, and utensils.

Purpose: *Writing without specificity leaves too many unanswered questions and makes writing fuzzy. Today I will show you how to organize your thinking about your reading by listening for actions you hear, listing the special vocabulary that goes along with your topic, and thinking about how you can use this information to create a recipe. Writing this information in lists will help you think of the details to add to your writing so that it is clear to the reader. You can decide to actually use food words and recipe measurements or leave them out!*

Brainstorm: Ask students to think about some things they recently did or perhaps places they recently went. For example: played soccer, went to the aquarium, or went to a concert practice. Ask students to jot down these ideas in their notebooks, or have them share orally and record some ideas on the board. Share some of your ideas about things you recently did or places you recently went. Then, choose one and record details about it in three lists on a chart or overhead: actions, special vocabulary, and how I can use this information to create a recipe.

Model: Choose a book that interests you or links to an area of expertise. As you share it with your students, ask them to listen for actions and text-specific vocabulary. Students can jot the words and phrases in their writer's notebooks. When you finish, create two lists (one of actions and one of text-specific vocabulary) of your own words and phrases on the board. For *Amish Horses* by Richard Ammon, your actions list might include the following: help with chores, care for horses, draft horses that work in the field, stable them together, break open a hay bale, clean stalls, currycomb each horse, introduce new horses to fence boundaries. The text-specific vocabulary might include: *Amish, Memm's garden, Datt, Percherons, fertilizer, manes, geldings, mares, trough, draft horses, saddlebreds,* and *Belgians.* Ask the students to check their list and volunteer any actions or vocabulary words that are directly related to your lists that you might have missed. You can add these in a different color.

Then, think aloud about the ways you could use this text to find topics that can be written as recipes. For this book, you might write a recipe for life as an Amish boy or as a working horse on an Amish farm. Then, use the actions and vocabulary words to write a draft of your recipe. You can write your piece as an explanation or as an actual recipe. Here is the example that Jackie used:

Recipe to Live as an Amish Boy

If you wish to live as an Amish boy, it is important to understand our way of life. We are farming people with strong religious beliefs that define our lifestyle. Our values based on the simple life are mixed with hard work and a blend of daily chores. We do not rely on engine-propelled machines to help us with farm work but use horses for our transportation, plowing, and planting.

One of my daily chores is to tend to the draft horses. A draft horse pulls buggies or farm equipment. On our farm we have saddlebreds, Percherons, and Belgians. Some people prefer mules. When preparing to plow the fields, we attach a bridle and harness to one of the Percherons or Belgians. I alternate them, depending on how much work they have done on a day-to-day schedule. It is important to keep horses fresh and strong. One day a horse may pull a planter and on another day, a hay baler. Keeping horses healthy is important since they are our main tools.

Every eight weeks we hitch one of our saddlebreds to a buggy and visit the blacksmith. He trims their hooves and fits them with new shoes. A blacksmith must stay bent over for a long time! The shoe is nailed on very carefully, the end is nipped off, and the sharp edge is filed. Horses sometimes throw a shoe or need corrective shoes. They all outgrow their shoes—just like I do!

Sometimes, we need to purchase a new horse. We will go to the auction and carefully look over the stock before making a bid. Luckily for me, Datt knows horses very well. I become the lucky Amish boy with a new black gelding. Since I am in charge of the horses, I get to ride him around the boundaries of the farm surrounded by fences. Life as an Amish boy is full of work and play!

Shared/Guided Writing: After you reread the book aloud, students can create lists of actions, text-specific vocabulary, and recipe topics. Some possible topics may include making hay, the life of a blacksmith, driving a buggy, training a new horse, and a horse auction. Students can use the standard recipe headings of "ingredients" and "directions" to make use of actions and nomenclature lists. Teresa's fifth graders chose to create a recipe for a horse auction. As a whole group they listed these ingredients: standardbreds, stalls, cribbing straps, soaring bids, sinking heart, vet checks, narrow aisles, chestnut mare with foal, handsome black gelding, bidding wars. They also listed actions starting with the verb for directions (for example, "Tie the horse to the back of the buggy."). After they created the list of actions, they revised it to put the directions into a meaningful order:

Tie horses with other buggies, head to the stall barn, cross out horses with glassy or headstrong eyes, walk up and down aisles, lead horses down run, watch to see if horses jog "sound," bid on horses, sing-songy auctioneer calls out bids, lift little finger, heart soars when gavel announces a sale, tie horse to back of buggy.

Students can all do the same recipe topic or work on different topics (training a new horse, planting a vegetable garden, making hay, etc.) while the teacher circulates to confer with any group that needs help.

Independent Writing: Students can return to their brainstormed lists of actions and vocabulary around a topic of interest and/or browse nonfiction books on a wide variety of topics. Once they find

FIGURE 6.18
Sharon's close
imitation of Jackie's
format

Recipe for a Life as a Talented Artist
By Sharon

Ingredients:
- Goals/dreams
- Observations
- Amazement
- Curiosity
- Planning
- Sketching
- Carefulness
- Exactness
- Perseverance
- Patience
- Feeling for project

Follow this Life for a Talented Artist

If you would like to be a talented artist, you have to have goals and dreams. You should have something to accomplish. You should also observe. To create a work of art, you should observe things that will help you. Observe and be amazed! When you are amazed, you become more involved with the subject. You cannot work without full concentration.

Curiosity is something you'll always need. Find. Discover. To be talented, you should always look for new ways to improve your art.

If you have a project to work on, you should always plan. You should be able to think if you are organized.

When you are ready to begin your project, you should start sketching. This is just your rough draft, so mess around! Try new strategies.

Once you're done your sketching, you can start on your final copy. Here, you should be very careful. This is it, so tray not to mess up! Being exact is also very important in this step. You want it to be perfect, and the best it can be.

Say your finaldraft is done, and you're not satisfied with it. DON'T give up. Try again. You shouldn't throw away a good idea. ALL ideas are good. If you are one of the people in this situation, then patience is very important. It could take awhile for it to come along.

The last thing is most important! All talented artists should follow this rule. You MUST put your feelings into the project. This is YOUR project. It has to have a part of you in it.

If you follow this recipe, and try and try again, you should be able to live the life of a talented artist!

a topic to their liking, they can use this strategy—listen for actions, list text-specific vocabulary, and think of ways the text can be used to create a recipe—to plan their writing. Jackie's student Sharon (Figure 6.18) closely imitated Jackie's scaffold for recipe writing, and Carly added her own twist to recipe writing (Figure 6.19).

Reflection: Ask writers to reflect on how this strategy worked for them. As a group, discuss how the writing became clearer as students used the actions and nomenclature from their lists. Ask them to think about how they could use this strategy during independent writing time. Think about anything in the piece they would add or omit.

FIGURE 6.19
Carly writes her recipe
with her own creative
twist.

Recipe for a New World Salad

By Carly

Ingredients

1 tablespoon daring butter, melted
1 ½ cups curious carrots, sliced
2 teaspoons spilt, planning walnuts
1 ¾ gallons shredded, never giving up lettuce
3 pints chilled finding sponsors tomato
1 pinch learning maps and stars peppers, diced
2 ½ bushels grilled, courage to explore chicken, cold
2 chopped praying-because-of-superstition pink peaches
½ bottle of wild waves dressing

Equipment

1 large bowl
2 tablespoons
1 teaspoon
3 measuring cup
1 charcoal grill

Courage Chicken

Make sure your chicken comes from Spain! Place wings on grill and grill on high heat. Flip them over every calm day. Take off when streaked with black lines. Cut from the bone and chop into gold sized wedges. Refrigerate until you leave port.

Salad

Scoop never- giving- up lettuce into a large bowl. Sprinkle on planning walnuts and daring butter. Throw in sponsor tomatoes, maps and stars peppers, and curious carrots. Toss. Spread courage chicken throughout never giving up lettuce. Carefully arrange praying peaches on top. They split if you handle them roughly. Pour on wild wave dressing with wind in your hair.

Serves one brave crew in the middle of nowhere.

Voice, Syntax, and Conventions in Nonfiction

It is a writer's voice that gives me the best sense of his or her potential.

—Donald Graves, *A Fresh Look at Writing*

Donald Graves (1994) charges teachers with the task of recognizing each student's potential in writing. But how do we get our young writers to reach their full potential? When writing nonfiction, an important element to consider is voice. JoAnn Portalupi and Ralph Fletcher (2001) tell us that primary students often lose their voices when writing in the informational mode, often resorting to a list of facts devoid of personal feeling and thinking.

It is the voices of the nonfiction writers that draw us into their world. Their interests and the things they know best can also become things we know and love if we hear their voices in our head and in our heart. That is why nonfiction mentor texts introduced in classrooms as read-alouds are so important.

In *Bat Loves the Night*, Nicola Davies draws us in to learning about a sometimes not-so-pleasant subject by the way she describes the pipistrelle bat.

> *Bat is waking, upside down as usual, hanging by her toenails. Her beady eyes open. Her pixie ears twitch. She shakes her thistledown fur. She unfurls her wings, made of skin so fine the finger bones inside show through. Now she unhooks her toes and drops into black space.*

Notice how Davies refers to Bat as if it is her name. The use of the pronouns *she* and *her*—instead of the pronouns *it* or *its*—is more familiar and personal. Her choice of words helps us visualize the bat waking in much the same way we wake—providing a personal connection that allows us to begin to love bats almost as much as she does. Helen Frost does much the same thing in her book *Monarch and Milkweed*, referring both to the butterfly and the plant in this manner:

> *A breeze bends Milkweed side to side. Monarch chooses its best leaf. Swaying in the breeze with Milkweed, she curls her underneath the leaf and glues one pale yellow egg to its soft underside.*

The voice of Martin Jenkins in *Chameleons Are Cool* is humorous and lighthearted, providing a way to pique and maintain the interest of the reader.

> *And I suppose you wouldn't exactly call many of them beautiful. Their skin is wrinkly and bumpy, and they've got big bulgy eyes, while lots of them have the most ridiculous . . . noses! (I think it's their noses I like the best.)*

The use of parentheses provides the author's personal commentary in a friendly, whisper-in-the-reader's-ear style. His enthusiasm for these creatures is obvious and delightful. We laughed when we read the "About the Author" for this book. Apparently Jenkins had his first encounter with wild chameleons in

Madagascar, where, despite his gentle touch, he was bitten on the finger. Jenkins goes on to say that he still finds chameleons wonderful but has learned to look but not touch.

Jim Gigliotti displays his enormous respect and admiration for firefighters in his book *Smoke Jumpers*. He begins with a page heading that says it all: "One-of-a-Kind Job!" Then he goes on to create a scene, letting the reader know how impressed he is with the heroes who do this kind of work:

> *Rick Rataj stands in the open doorway of an airplane. He is flying high above a forest where a fire is raging. Most people would be worried, but Rick is ready to go to work.*
>
> *Rick is a smoke jumper—a special kind of fire fighter who uses a parachute to jump into the forest to fight fires. Without smoke jumpers, it might take many hours—even days—to reach a remote fire.*

Even first graders can make their voices heard and lead us into sharing their interests. In the following example, Tessa explains the process of learning how to do a karate kick. She uses interjections and personal feelings to pull the reader in:

> I learned karate from my brother Ian. At first I was tarubool [terrible] at it. Then my brother said lets try something different. I was grate at kicking. Yay! It goes like shrate [straight], bend, kick, then shrate. It was the best day in the whole entire world!

It's almost like Tessa is talking directly to her reader. Don't you want to find out more about karate kicks?

The Importance of Oral Writing to Establish Voice

In discussing how students write research reports, Lucy Calkins (1991) poses the question: "How can we help kids write in their own voices?" We as teachers are always concerned about plagiarism issues. Calkins suggests that if our objective is to teach children how to write about informational topics in their own voices, then the issue should not be copying but learning how to step outside of their own lives to experience new ideas and new worlds—in fact, to let other people's thinking in and make it their own. We can help students find their voices in nonfiction writing by providing opportunities for them to read widely, take specific notes, reread their notes, and add their thinking and feeling about those notes. Then they can talk about it with peers and/or their teacher, revise their thinking, and use it to write their pieces.

Talking is a powerful way for writers to plan and rehearse what they are going to say. Graves (1994) discusses the importance of writing for a specific audience and developing voice through oral writing. This technique is especially useful with nonfiction writing because it helps the young writer paraphrase important ideas from other texts and write about those ideas in his or her own voice. Often students will first become mini-experts on a topic by reading widely in an area of interest. After much reading, they will take some notes. We need to remind them that their notes should be rich in detail and wonderful language. As Lucy Calkins (1991) tells us:

> *I want my notes to be tools to think with, and so they must be very particular. Then too, often what I value most are the words someone has used; the words aren't disposable peanut shells that carry extractable kernels of meaning. I don't want my notes to be filled with summaries any more than I want my library filled with plot outlines.* (201)

In order to develop their own voice, students need to reread their revised notes in chunks and then put them aside to record their thinking from those notes with vigor and feeling. A final check will involve rereading both notes and revised drafts to make sure that facts have not been altered or omitted.

In Lynne's school, the librarian, Sue Powidzki, often uses oral writing with note taking to help students write research reports and projects. In one fourth-grade classroom, Tina Madison's children read about places in Pennsylvania in preparation for creating an interesting lead paragraph that might introduce a pamphlet or brochure about one particular place. After reading sample brochures and taking notes, the students orally shared in small and whole group some of the magic and mystery of their Pennsylvania places. They wrote using their own language combined with their note taking and imitated the scaffold used by Stacey Schuett in *Somewhere in the World Right Now* to open their pieces. Lynne suggested that they extend the use of the scaffold by using it as a closing as well, and to wait until the very end to reveal the specific place. The sights and sounds of each place came alive with this kind of writing.

Somewhere in Pennsylvania tourists observe black iron cannons. Knowledgeable guides show tourists the living quarters of soldiers. The Delaware River thunderously roars downstream. Visitors catch a glimpse of the original blacksmith shop. Tourists notice the weapons used back then, somewhere in Fort Mifflin.

Josiah, Grade 4

Somewhere in Pennsylvania, wonderful wizards make magic seem real. Pretty princesses wait for a prince to marry them in the medieval castle. Royal fools entertain everyone every minute, every hour, every day. The mud show makes people laugh out loud, somewhere at the Pennsylvania Renaissance Fair.

Shannon, Grade 4

During the last few weeks of school, Lynne teamed up with two fourth-grade teachers, Bruce Bloome and Kate Tiedeken, to do some collaborative nonfiction writing that included oral rehearsal. Bruce shared *If You're Not from the Prairie* by David Bouchard. In poetic verse, Bouchard tells us about all the things he loves and knows best about the prairie.

> *If you're not from the prairie,*
> *You've not heard the grass,*
> *You've never* heard *grass.*
> *In strong summer winds, the grains and grass bend*
> *And sway to a dance that seems never to end.*
> *It whispers its secrets—they tell of this land*
> *And the rhythm of life played by nature's own hand.*
> *If you're not from the prairie,*
> *You've never* heard *grass.*

Although this powerful example is written in verse, the students were not required to limit themselves to this form. Bruce and Lynne wanted to hear their voices and felt that it would be more natural for the students to write in paragraphs, so that is the way they modeled the writing. After sharing what he loved best about Hatboro, the town where he grew up, Bruce asked the students to brainstorm places they loved. Lynne recorded these places on the board so that the students could form collaborative groups around these topics in order to write a book. Since the students came from two different classes, they had the opportunity to hear new voices as ideas were shared prior to writing. Each student wrote his or her own paragraph but collaborated on the title page and the closing paragraph.

The students shared again during writing and then again after their drafts were completed. They revised for strong nouns and verbs. They added interesting tidbits—inside information that would lend specificity to their writing. Hailey wrote "If You're Not from the Pocono Mountains." Her selections were specifically about a resort. Her writing was effortless since she knew the place so well and was eager to share her knowledge with others. In this selection, Hailey describes the activity and setting with specificity:

If you're not from Pocmont Resorts, you don't know paddle boating—you can't know paddle boating!

You are in a two-seat paddle boat, with a turning stick and foot pedals for your driver and passenger. You take one turn at the pedals at a time, turning left and right in the pond, seeking a glance of a great blue herring, taking a mid-day snack on the edge of the pond, or searching for frogs in the thicket of cattails or other pond weeds. If you're not from Pocmont Resorts, you don't know paddle boating. There is just no way!

Rianne, Lexe, Maggie, Amanda, Leanna, and Michelle wrote a book entitled "If You're Not From Willow Grove" (a community in the township). Notice the specificity created by proper nouns and the rhythm of the pairing, as well as the appeal to the senses that helps the reader hear their voice:

> If you're not from Willow Grove
> you don't know Lawnton Road,
> you can't know Lawnton Road.
> You can't know Gimlet or Xingu, Junior or Sally, or even Duke or Dominic. You can't know time with friends or slip 'n slides, laughing and swimming in your neighbor's pool. You can't know picking blackberries off the vine and plopping them in your mouth when they're just right from Mr. and Mrs. Lighter's garden.
> If you're not from Willow Grove,
> you don't know Lawnton Road.

The Conversational Tone

Portalupi and Fletcher (2001) say that voice is "an intimacy or closeness between writer and subject, writer and reader" (45). In nonfiction writing, this intimacy can be established through a conversational tone—writing that includes not only the surprising details that bring a topic to life, but all the emotions we feel when we read and write about topics we care about. In an article titled "Expanding the Web of Meaning: Thought and Emotion in an Intergenerational Reading and Writing Program," Anne DiPardo and Pat Schnack (2004) explore the notion that comprehension—meaning making—involves both head and heart. Readers want to feel something when they read a piece, regardless of mode or genre. In our conversations, we can use this head and heart combination to engage a response from others. Through our writing we can do the same.

One technique for writing in a conversational tone is to ask the reader questions. Debbie S. Miller uses this technique in *River of Life*, a book about a river in Alaska.

> *Beneath the surface, a rainbow trout chases salmon fry. The trout catches a glimpse of something shiny. Will it take a bite?*

In his book about the Costa Rican rain forest, *The Forest in the Clouds*, Sneed B. Collard III invites his readers to examine the pictures by asking a question.

> *Camouflage shapes, patterns, and colors help animals blend into their surroundings. Look carefully. Can you tell which camouflaged animals are predators and which are prey?*

In *How Big Is It? A Big Book All About Bigness*, Ben Hillman discusses the "bigness" of mountains. Notice how he uses a question to establish a conversational tone with his readers.

> *And speaking of the tallest mountain on earth, did you know that it's not Mount Everest at all? It's Mauna Kea in Hawaii.*

Other examples can be found in *The Girls' Life Guide to Being the Best You!*, edited by Kelly White. Questions such as "Ever been put on the spot in class?" and "Does Megan's story sound familiar?" and "So how come the second the test hits your desk, you feel doomed?" are posed throughout the book to establish a sense of intimacy with the readers. And don't miss *G Is for Googol: A Math Alphabet Book* by David M. Schwartz. Its use of questions to create a humorous tone will draw readers in, even though the content may appear to be difficult (after all, it is a book about mathematical concepts!). Schwartz's voice is delightfully pleasant and engaging. In explaining the rhombicosidodecahedron, he writes:

> *"Excuse me?"*
>
> Rhombicosidodecahedron. *(ROM-bi-cosi-DOE-DECK-a-HEE-dron.) Say it a few times, and it'll roll right off your tongue. You can impress your parents and your friends. You can say things like, "Do you happen to have a rhombicosidodecahedron I can borrow?"*
>
> *Now that you can pronounce it, perhaps you'd like to know what it is. A rhombicosidodecahedron is a special kind of polyhedron.*
>
> *"What kind of polyhedron?" you say. "And what's a polyhedron, anyway?"*

Other authors, such as Barbara Brenner in *Thinking About Ants*, Sandra Markle in *Creepy, Crawly Baby Bugs*, and Maya Ajmera and Michael Regan in *Let the Games Begin!* establish a conversational voice by offering advice. We expect to get advice from people who know us well—our parents, our teachers, and our friends. So when we read this type of writing we feel right at home. Barbara Brenner begins by telling us how we should think if we are to understand ants:

> *Think about living in dark places. But imagine lots of company—sisters, brothers, a family. Living and working together because an ant can't live alone.*

Sandra Markle calls the reader's attention to a photograph that looks as if the ants are attacking a caterpillar when, in fact, they are protecting it. She advises the reader: "Don't worry."

Laurie Halse Anderson offers a more sophisticated technique for establishing a conversational tone. In both *Thank you, Sarah: The Woman Who Saved Thanksgiving* and *Independent Dames: What You Never Knew About the Women and Girls of the American Revolution*, she uses sarcasm to deliver her point. In *Independent Dames* she asks the reader to consider the women, not just the men, who were involved in the American Revolution:

> *Look, another school play about the heroes of the American Revolution. How sweet.*
>
> *We've got George Washington, Thomas Jefferson, John Adams, Ben Franklin, and Thomas Paine. Famous guys who did important things.*
>
> *Wonderful. Just wonderful.*
>
> *Of course, you're missing part of the story. In fact, you're missing about half of it.*
>
> *Hello? How about the women? What about the girls?*

Did you laugh out loud while reading her text? Did she get your attention? Notice the artful use of short sentences and the absence of exclamation points. It's a purposeful monotone until she asks her questions. As soon as she poses "Hello?" she shifts into a conversational stance you would take with someone you knew fairly well. Then you can hear a forceful, purposeful tone take over. Before she begins telling the stories of these women, she advises the reader to "listen up."

Katie Wood Ray (1999) discusses a technique she terms "whispering parentheses."

> *Writers use this technique to communicate directly with readers, stepping "outside" the regular text for a moment to whisper something in the reader's ear. These are usually asides of explanation that are more characteristic of spoken language than written language, but the form they take in texts is often parenthetical. Whispering parentheses give texts a conversational tone, making readers feel like insiders with an author.* (78)

We have found that it is not only authors of fiction but also authors of nonfiction who use parentheses to enter into a conversation with the reader. Laurie Halse Anderson in *Independent Dames: What You Never Knew About the Women and Girls of the American Revolution* writes, "Some soldiers brought their wives (and children!) with them when they enlisted." Notice how the use of the short phrase followed by an exclamation point offers a dramatic pause in the rhythm of the sentence—an aside that would be offered in a juicy story.

In *Lightning*, Stephen Kramer uses parentheses to share important wisdom with his readers:

If you are in an area with lots of trees, look for shelter underneath a group of trees that are all about the same height. . . . (When you are camping, be sure to chose a safe place to pitch your tent.)

Consider the well-placed parentheses in *Johann Gutenberg and the Amazing Printing Press* by Bruce Koscielniak:

As each book required numerous artisans and many months to make, it's no surprise that books were not cheap! They were so valuable that only monasteries that had scribes in residence, libraries (which were open only to clergy and scholars), and some wealthy patrons could own books.

The use of parentheses lets the reader in on the fact that libraries in the middle ages were not open to the public as they are today.

Catherine Thimmesh's book *Team Moon: How 400,000 People Landed Apollo 11 on the Moon* deals with a complex topic. Imagine writing (or reading) an account of a project that involved that many people! Thimmesh uses parentheses to make the text more considerate for the reader:

The stories herein are but snapshots. Just a handful of players pulled from the bench of the greatest team ever. Just a few of the 400,000 people (imagine about ten large stadiums full of fans) who set out to do an impossible task: to land man on the moon and return him safely home.

Frank Murphy makes good use of this technique in *Thomas Jefferson's Feast*, truly a delightful read! Murphy clearly understands his target audience of young readers and uses parentheses to offer explanations and comments to elicit a smile. Writing for an intended audience is crucial to writing with voice. In the following example, Murphy uses parentheses to help his young readers understand the text:

Thomas liked food so much, he sometimes spent as much as 50 dollars on groceries in just one day! (That would be like spending 750 dollars today!)

Sometimes the parentheses are used to define a foreign word. Other times Murphy makes a friendly comment that would appeal to his readers: "And to this day, Americans enjoy eating love apples. (Especially on pizza!)" The use of parentheses is something young writers can study and imitate effectively.

In writing about spring as her favorite season, first grader Tessa lets us in on a secret about herself:

I love it when time gets pushed forward because we have more time to play. Sometimes we ride our bikes (I always fall).

Another first grader, Sara, uses parentheses to offer her readers an explanation:

I know it is spring when me and Marlee (my best friend) have play dates at her house.

Patrick, a fourth grader, wrote a biographical piece about Norman Rockwell. His humor comes through in his use of parentheses:

His [Rockwell's] first wife, Irene, he divorced because things weren't working out (She loved to play and he loved to work!). His second wife, Mary, died in his midlife. (That wasn't his fault!)

In Tyler's piece about Dr. Seuss, the fourth grader offered an astute comment in parentheses:

His mother went to the library with him and helped him choose books. At night she would read lots of stories and nonsense verse to him. (Something he became quite good at writing himself!)

When writers establish a conversational tone, you hear them talking directly to you—you hear their voice. Sometimes the most simple, direct writing has great emotional appeal. Listen to Sneed B. Collard III's voice in *Leaving Home*:

Sooner or later, we all leave home. Some of us walk. Some of us crawl. Some of us fly. And some of us swim . . . But no matter who we are . . . Or what we look like . . . We all leave home. A few of us even . . . find our way back.

The Poetic Voice

One genre that is sometimes overlooked for nonfiction, but should definitely not be forgotten, is poetry—a wonderful vehicle to deliver information with a powerful voice. Students can use poetry to introduce or conclude their informational pieces or to break up a collaborative work into sections. Research reports that are multigenre in nature are often much more interesting to read because they can sound like a blend of voices. Poetry can add the harmony to the melody of a larger work, or it can stand on its own.

Discover the Seasons by Diane Iverson is a multigenre work about each season that includes informational paragraphs, articles on things to do in that particular season, and recipes for kids to try. All of this is held together by the accompanying poems, which offer vivid description through powerful verbs and well-placed adjectives. From "Summer" we read:

> *Red Fox ventures out*
> *   to explore and grow*
> *In golden-green*
> *   meadow grass.*

"Winter" includes these lines:

> *The Cedar Waxwing*
> *   bounds along*
> *His frosty winter perches.*

Another book that focuses on seasons with rhyming poetry is *Prairie Born* by Dave Bouchard. His voice, heard through the rhyming verse, gives us the experience of living on the prairie.

Diane Siebert chooses to write in other voices, taking on the persona of her subject matter. In *Sierra* she uses first person to talk about the history of the mountain range, how it has changed, and its value as a home for many creatures:

> *I am the mountain.*
> *   From the sea*
> *Come constant winds to conquer me—*
> *Pacific winds that touch my face*
> *And bring the storms whose clouds embrace*
> *My rugged shoulders, strong and wide;*
> *And in their path I cannot hide.*

J. Patrick Lewis writes in the persona of the Empire State Building in *Monumental Verses*, a book of poems about timeless monuments. From "Empire State Building":

> *I am ten million bricks of unshakable faith.*
> *I capture imagination at its peak.*
> *I hugged King Kong, he hugged me back.*

This book contains many examples of free verse. This is needed if you want to encourage students to let their voices be heard through poetry. Rhyming can be difficult for many students, and forced rhyme is voiceless. Another example of largely unrhymed poetry written about a nonfiction topic, in this case strange and unusual animals, is *The Originals: Animals That Time Forgot* by Jane Yolen.

When students begin to use poetry to tell about nonfiction topics, they must first think about the specific words that reveal their topic to them and to their reader. Poetry is a great vehicle for teaching students how to become wordsmiths. Young writers should be picky about the words they choose to carry their ideas. This is what style is all about—making conscious decisions to use one word over another.

At Rose's school, first-grade teacher Cindy Algier helped her students develop voice through poetry by helping them to first attend to their words. After studying parts of the solar system, she decided to offer the cinquain as a way for her students to express their wonder about the moon while weaving in some of the factual information they had learned. She began by reading poems from *Long Night Moon* by Cynthia Rylant and *When the Moon Is Full* by Penny Pollock. Both of these books follow the moon through the months and offer the names the Native Americans gave to each of the full moons. Factual information about the moon came from the final pages of *When the Moon Is Full* as well as from *The Moon Book* by Gail Gibbons, which Cindy read aloud to her class.

Together they brainstormed and charted adjectives and verbs that could be used to describe the moon. The students returned often to the books to pull out words such as *bright, reflecting, shimmering, lunar, changing, glows,* and *shines.* They also charted facts that they had learned about the moon. After teaching the cinquain format, Cindy modeled with her own poem, and the class did some shared oral writing. The first graders also created chalk drawings of the moon on black construction paper, keeping the interest in the project high. Notice the students' word choice in Figures 7.1 and 7.2.

Another excellent text written as a series of poems is *Comets, Stars, the Moon, and Mars* by Douglas Florian. Use of colorful and specific words abound in this informational work about space for students of all ages.

In Teresa Lombardi's fifth-grade class, students had read *Freedom Crossing* by Margaret Goff Clark to build a foundation for a larger biography scrapbook project. Lynne and Teresa decided that found poetry would be a wonderful way for the students to represent their thinking about the book they had just read. Found poetry is exactly what it sounds like—words, phrases, and sentences can be borrowed from a piece of writing to become part of a poem. Students can be encouraged to use other techniques they know about poetry writing, such as

FIGURES 7.1 AND 7.2

Annabelle and Evan use cinquain to write about the moon.

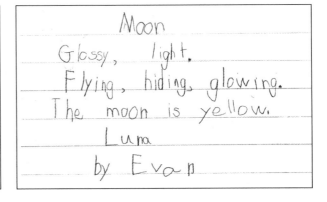

Moon
Shimmers, bright.
Peeking, floating, dazzling.
Friend glowing up above
Orb
by Annabelle

Moon
Glossy, light.
Flying, hiding, glowing.
The moon is yellow.
Luna
by Evan

effective repetition and figurative language, to make their own voice heard. (For a more detailed explanation of found poetry, see our previous work, *Mentor Texts: Teaching Writing Through Children's Literature, K–6* [2007].)

Teresa had provided many reading materials from various websites that complemented the text so that the students could pair nonfiction material with the historical fiction they had read. This served to broaden their knowledge base and bring the events in the book to life for them. Lynne modeled by writing a found poem using the same materials the students had. She talked to them about effective repetition, which she included in her model, and encouraged the students to try it out in theirs. After completing a shared found poem, Teresa and Lynne gave the students ample time to write, share, and revise their poems. It is particularly important with poetry to have students read their work aloud. Only then can they truly hear the rhythm of the word choice that becomes the voice they want their readers to hear. Notice the effective repetition in Jenna's found poem about Lewiston:

> *Lewiston had a secret.*
> *Lewiston kept a code of silence.*
> *Lewiston, New York—the last stop for*
> *escaping slaves.*
> *People smuggle thousands of slaves*
> *across the border.*
> *Lewiston had a secret.*
> *People hid slaves and kept them safe*
> *in their homes.*
> *Lewiston, across the river from*
> *Canada, safe for escaping slaves.*
> *When the boat comes for them*
> *they will be free . . .*
> *Lewiston had a secret.*

Establishing an Audience Connection: Writing in the Second Person

Most students are already familiar with writing in the first and third person through their work on personal narratives and research reports. In order to establish a one-on-one relationship with their audience, students might like to try out writing in the second person. The Backyard Books by Judy Allen employ this technique effectively to teach young students about ants, bees, dragonflies, ladybugs, spiders, and more. Even though they are written for primary students, they can be used as writing models for students of any age. The author offers rich description, practical advice, cautions, and words of encouragement as she guides you through your "new life." For example, in *Are You a Spider?* the author offers you some hunting and dining advice:

When a fly flies into your web, it will stick there. Run and bite it. Your bite will make it go to sleep. You can eat it now. Or you can wrap it in silk thread and save it for later.

When examining this second-person writing, ask students what they notice about the author's craft. Hopefully they will notice the pronouns *you* and *your* repeated in the writing and the absence of other pronouns, such as *I* or *me*. This kind of writing lends itself to beginning a sentence with a verb, just like the how-to-be poems we mentioned in Chapter 6. When you are writing in the second person, you are going to be offering advice or explaining how to do things. Consider the following from *Are You an Ant?* that not only explains how to hunt for food but also gives you an evaluation of your skills:

Bite your prey and spray it with acid from your tail. Actually, you're not a very good hunter. Look for bugs that have been stepped on. They're easy.

Joanne Ryder would be a perfect mentor author to study this second-person writing. It's one of her fingerprints—it can be found in almost all of her books. In *The Snail's Spell*, Ryder has us imagine that we are becoming a snail:

Your small black eyes rest at the tips of these feelers . . . Now you can see the darkness there.

Ryder's book *The Goodbye Walk* helps students write about special places using the second-person voice. It is a powerful mentor text that contains many examples of figurative language and varying sentence structures. The use of the second person in this text makes the readers feel like they are taking this walk with the author. The scaffold is easy for students to imitate and is often very meaningful to them. Many have had to take a goodbye walk when they have moved to a new home, graduated from elementary school to middle school, or left a vacation spot. However, students need to be very familiar with the book by hearing it or reading it several times in order to understand the structure and imitate it. You may have to help them make these discoveries. In her book, Ryder begins by defining a goodbye walk, points out landmarks, talks about things you might do on that walk, and describes the places where you may linger and the things you may never have seen before. She speaks about your secret place, and then brings it together with a memories-that-linger ending.

On a goodbye walk you can stop as you please—on the bridge where young fish hide below, waiting for you and your bread . . . on the hill where eagles soar above you like dark kites without strings.

After reading the book aloud to two fourth-grade classes, Lynne helped the students chart their discoveries about Ryder's craft and her organizational structures. She returned to the book and reread pieces when it was necessary. Lynne and the classroom teachers, Steve Grant and Kate Tiedeken, all modeled possible topics for their goodbye walk pieces and had the students do the same. A list was made of all their choices so that students could have options. Students began their work by sketching four to six drawings to be included in their piece. These drawings served as anchors for their writing. After drafting, several lessons were conducted for revision purposes focusing on Ryder's craft—appeal to the senses, use of similes, and adjective pairs placed after the noun they describe.

Amanda wrote her goodbye walk about the Cape May campground (see Figure 7.3).

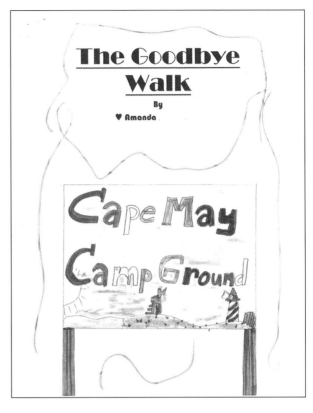

FIGURE 7.3

Amanda's good-bye walk about Cape May, New Jersey

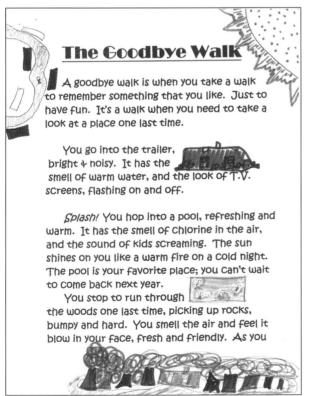

The Goodbye Walk

A goodbye walk is when you take a walk to remember something that you like. Just to have fun. It's a walk when you need to take a look at a place one last time.

You go into the trailer, bright & noisy. It has the smell of warm water, and the look of T.V. screens, flashing on and off.

Splash! You hop into a pool, refreshing and warm. It has the smell of chlorine in the air, and the sound of kids screaming. The sun shines on you like a warm fire on a cold night. The pool is your favorite place; you can't wait to come back next year.

You stop to run through the woods one last time, picking up rocks, bumpy and hard. You smell the air and feel it blow in your face, fresh and friendly. As you

joyfully jog through the woods you say "Goodbye" until next summer.

You go back home empty handed, but you still have memories that can't fade away... memories that you'll have forever.

Daniel wrote about hiking through the woods at a special vacation spot:

You are taking a good-bye walk. Emotions of every kind are welling up in you. Now it is the time to leave your sanctuary and head home. You have gained everlasting memories that no one can take away from you. Time is running short to say good-bye to something special that you've loved so dearly for so long.

On a good-bye walk, you pass the beauty of wonderful landforms of hills and plains. This nature overwhelms you, but at the same time puts joy into your soul. When the sun sets and the moon rises, sounds of crickets echo through your head again and again.

On a good-bye walk, you can stop to see the glimmering water of the pond one last time. The wonderful woods with all its magnificent creatures fill your mind. The deer stand has a great view of what seems like the whole world, and you stand there for an eternity. And the old dirt hill, rocky and dry, calls to you.

Today, you notice that in silence everything seems so much smaller and peaceful—like a newborn baby at its first wink of sleep. The tremendous trees tower over you like a green skyscraper. Peck! Peck! A woodpecker's peck is louder and more powerful than any sound you've heard, and you can pinpoint exactly where it is coming from.

At the end of a good-bye walk, you feel sad to leave, but happy to go home again. You're thinking that it's not the end of this joy, but just the beginning. You dream of seeing this "part of heaven" next summer. You remember just arriving and never wanting to leave. Now it is time to go. A good-bye walk is saying good-bye to a friend.

Some authors, such as Laurence Pringle, don't use the second-person writing throughout the book. They might use it just in the beginning to get your attention and draw you in. In *Bats! Strange and Wonderful*, Pringle writes:

If you were a bat, you could stay up all night. You could hang by your thumbs, or hang upside down by your toenails. You could fly through dark woods and even darker caves and not bump into anything.

If you were a bat, you would be afraid of people. A person, even a child, would look like a huge monster to you. When a bat is afraid it opens its mouth wide and shows its teeth.

Notice how Pringle transitions from second person into third person in this last paragraph. The rest of his book is written in the third person, but he cleverly chose to begin his book by establishing an intimacy with the reader through second-person writing.

Our students come to us each with a different voice, but like a singer whose voice can be trained to reach a larger range of notes, their writing voices can also be trained. It is through this training and practice that a voice is enriched. We can help our students reach a larger range of possibilities by trying the craft they have gathered from mentor texts. It is with their new voices that they will sing new songs.

Purposeful Use of Fragments

As teachers, we might shy away from teaching students how to use sentence fragments. After all, we might think, they do it unconsciously all the time already and think they are writing a sentence! But the key to using fragments effectively is in understanding how to use them purposefully. According to Arthur Plotnik (2007), fragments commonly occur in spoken language as well as in written dialogue. They may be used by authors to capture the thoughts of a character, or to create a special mood. Plotnik goes on to say that fragments "provide refreshing variations of rhythm and tone within paragraphs" (156). In *Sky Boys: How They Built the Empire State Building*, Deborah Hopkinson effectively uses fragments in describing the building:

> *They're getting ready to make something new, bold, SOARING. A symbol of hope in the darkest of times. A building, clean and simple and straight as a pencil. And tall, so tall it will scrape the sky.*

Hopkinson creates a rhythm to her words that emphasizes their meaning and makes us relish their sound.

In *Thinking About Ants*, Barbara Brenner uses fragments to appeal to her young audience. She wants them to imagine what it would be like to be an ant, so she does it in short bursts, providing just the right amount of information at a time for her young readers. This listing also helps contribute to the rhythm of the words:

> *How would it be to have an ant face? Two huge eyes, a mouth, a pair of scissor jaws to bite and tear with. No ears. No nose. Instead, two hairy feelers on your head to wave around like magic wands.*

Some authors use fragments simply as a way to create a list that would emphasize each item. In nonfiction writing, a list of this sort could also be represented with a drawing or photograph to further the reader's understanding. Frank Murphy does this in *Always Inventing: The True Story of Thomas Alva Edison*:

> *Thomas invented other important things, too.*
> *A movie camera. A movie projector. A copy machine.*
> *A phonograph. A talking doll . . . and more!*

Murphy could have written this list as a complete sentence with commas, but perhaps he felt that these inventions were so enormous a contribution that each one deserved to be mentioned on its own.

Sometimes fragments are used to create that conversational voice that pulls the reader in. It can be especially effective to use when the audience is unfamiliar with the vocabulary or topic. Then the familiar conversational tone tempts the reader to keep reading. In *Creepy, Crawly Baby Bugs*, Sandra Markle uses fragments in the form of questions:

> *Spittlebug nymphs make bubble nests that they hide inside. Wondering how? The young bug feeds by sucking juice from plants . . . Wondering why this bug is called a spittlebug?*

Nicola Davies, in *Bat Loves the Night*, uses fragments to emphasize the importance of Bat going out into the night. Notice the effective repetition of the word *out*, which adds a poetic quality to the writing:

> *Bat is flying. Out! Out under the broken tile into the nighttime garden.*

Cynthia Rylant uses a fragment as her very last sentence in *The Journey: Stories of Migration*:

> *Tiny birds, great whales, fragile butterflies, persistent eels, humming locusts, and brave caribou: These are all miracles in motion. Travelers on a remarkable road.*

Her powerful writing leads you to that last remark—written as a fragment—because she doesn't need to say anything else. Rylant's readers have already learned the where, the why, and the how of the remarkable migration stories she has shared. The beauty of the fragment is in its simplicity to sum up one of earth's most magnificent mysteries.

Fragments are used quite effectively by masterful writers who break the rules when it is appropriate and effective to do so. The simple truth is that our written language is much more interesting and full of voice because of rules that are broken. However, for our young writers in elementary and middle school, an awareness and understanding of grammar and mechanics is also important. A sense of sentence does not come easily to some of our young writers. We must realize that over time and with practice, they will imitate many sentence structures successfully. But to close our eyes and pretend that our young writers are not reading fragments in published work, or are not using them effectively—and sometimes naturally—would be a shame. In conferences, guided writing experiences, and whole-group shares we can lead students to a deeper understanding of the use of fragments in their writing. It is through these spontaneous and purposeful conversations that we can help students recognize what they do well, why it is working, and when they might be able to use it again. Jeff Anderson (2005) provides additional help with sense of sentence in "Two-Word Sentence Smack Down" and "Two-Word Sentence Search" for writer's notebook work.

Finding a Toe-Tapping Tempo to Share Information

Lynne has been a fan of lyric summaries ever since she found the idea in Barry Lane's *51 Wacky We-search Reports*. Lyric summaries are words put to a familiar tune to summarize information. It is a way to accomplish many things at the same time: Get students to reread information, create a powerful scaffold to remember information, and present a unique way to summarize and share information. In addition, it's a wonderful way to walk around in the syntax of the author (lyricist), using the rhythm of the music to create the flow of words. Lynne has had a chance to see Barry Lane present his workshops, often with the additional help of some songs he plays on his guitar to tell a story or make a point. Lynne had been itching to try out song writing with students when an opportunity presented itself.

Teresa Lombardi's fifth graders used the biography scrapbook as a vehicle to share information in several distinct writing formats. They had read widely about a person who lived just prior to and/or during the Civil War period for a fifth-grade "Wax Museum," an annual event that gives students an opportunity to dress in period costumes and present history through the "people" coming to life and talking about their experiences. The Wax Museum is always open to the public as well as the third- and fourth-grade classes. All fifth grades participate and share information in a variety of ways. Lynne suggested that one of the scrapbook entries could be a lyric summary about the person's life.

Teresa agreed right away and decided that the students could help one another perform their songs—even dress in costume—and share them through a video as an activity choice for her class's presentation during the Wax Museum. The students understood that their audience would be the community at large, raising the bar and challenging them to do their best.

The students had not used this format before, but Lynne and Teresa used their enthusiasm for this project and the promise of group collaboration for performances to create excitement. They shared a few books that featured songs, such as *The Teddy Bears' Picnic* by Jimmy Kennedy, *Yankee Doodle* by Mary Ann Hoberman, and *Summertime* by Gershwin and Heyward, as well as other songbook collections and DVD recordings, including ballads sung by Pete Seeger, Woody Guthrie, and Peter, Paul, and Mary. Lynne then modeled with a song she wrote about Harriet Tubman.

She had read several books about Tubman including *Minty: A Story of Young Harriet Tubman* by Alan Schroeder, *Barefoot: Escape on the*

Underground Railroad by Pamela Duncan Edwards, *Go Free or Die: A Story About Harriet Tubman* by Jeri Ferris, and *Moses: When Harriet Tubman Led Her People to Freedom* by Carole Boston Weatherford. Lynne used the information and a simple tune, "Oh, Mary, Don't You Weep," to create her lyric summary of Tubman's life. Notice the effective repetition imitated from the original song and the change in the scaffold for the last two lines. (Teresa was brave enough to sing Lynne's song to her class!)

"Minty and the Freedom Train"
Harriet Tubman is a famous name,
Leading her people on the freedom train.
North Star pointing to freedom,
Oh, Minty, don't you weep!

Please, slave catcher, don't follow me,
You just can't breathe if you can't breathe free!
North Star pointing to freedom,
Oh, Minty, don't you weep!

Nightfall hides you but your heart beats fast,
Find Pennsylvania 'fore your legs don't last.
North Star pointing to freedom,
Oh, Minty, don't you weep!

Gather berries; find cures from roots,
Don't get captured by the "Heavy Boots."
North Star pointing to freedom,
Oh, Minty, don't you weep!

Your feet may bleed and your guts may churn,
But you won't turn back—no you'll never turn!
North Star pointing to freedom,
Oh, Minty, don't you weep!

Fool the dogs with a water wade,
You'd rather die than remain a slave!
North Star pointing to freedom,
Oh, Minty, don't you weep!

Hiding in a potato hole,
Reaching freedom is your steadfast goal.
North Star pointing to freedom,
Oh, Minty, don't you weep!

A couple in a wagon stops to take you in,
Believing that slavery is a sin.
North Star pointing to freedom,
Oh, Minty, don't you weep!

Reaching Philadelphia you begin to sing,
Feels to you like you've sprouted wings!
North Star pointing to freedom,
Oh, Minty, don't you weep!

But now you realize you must go back,
Following the Underground Railroad track.
North Star pointing to freedom,
Oh, Minty, don't you weep!

You become a Conductor; you become a guide,
And you lead your people on their freedom ride.
North Star pointing to freedom,
Oh, Minty, don't you weep!

Nineteen trips with a price on your head,
Lots of people want to see you dead.
North Star pointing to freedom,
Oh, Minty, don't you weep!

Never lost a passenger—that's her claim,
Harriet Tubman is a famous name
That brought her people to freedom,
Harriet Tubman is her name!

The students selected a familiar song with a simple tune to write their lyric summary for the biography scrapbook and presentation. Peter was successful in finding the right tune for his information and an effective line to repeat at the close of each verse. The lyric's simplicity is perfect for this simple, lively tune.

My Life Story: Booker T. Washington

(To the tune of: "Do Your Ears Hang Low?")
I was born a slave,
My mother was a cook.
My mother got married
So we had to move.
Then I worked in a salt mine
At the age of nine.
I am Booker T!

I wrote a book,
It was mostly about me.
It was called Up From Slavery,
A life history.
I wrote it with a friend,
Frederick Douglass was his name.
I am Booker T!

They considered me
The nation's most
Dominate black leader
So they cast a vote.
In the Hall of Fame,
Remembered for all times,
I am Booker T!

Peter manages to tell us lots of important information about his famous person's life, including some major accomplishments.

Writers Love Words!

If you are a writer, then you have to love words. You as the teacher are very instrumental in developing a love of language in your students. There are many books whose main characters can inspire students to become lovers of words. These include *Donovan's Word Jar* by Monalisa DeGross, *Winston the Book Wolf* by Marni McGee, and *Miss Alaineus: A Vocabulary Disaster* by Debra Frasier. We hope that our writers become wordsmiths; that is, we hope they pay close attention to the words they choose to use and the words they choose to eliminate from a text they are crafting.

Students need to have opportunities to have fun with words—not limited to crossword puzzles, word searches, and tongue twisters. They can incorporate word play into all genre work. In one fourth-grade classroom, Lynne and Maribeth Batcho shared *Why?* by Lila Prap, a nonfiction text that uses a riddle format to create interest. Each page asks a specific question about an animal, then answers it in different ways—sometimes very humorously, sometimes more practically. She always includes a factual paragraph that answers the question as a good researcher would. For example, Prap's question about the camel is "Why do camels have humps?" Her answers include:

To confuse their riders.
They didn't sit up straight when they were little.
Because it's better than not having any.
Out of habit.
They aren't humps; they're sand dunes that camels carry across the desert.

Prap also includes a sidebar that explains the factual reason for the humps. The beauty of this book is that students can use it as a model to ask one essential question about any topic they are studying and imagine the possibilities for answers after they research. The research and reading will allow them to come up with amusing responses that can play on words or use information in a clever way.

As Maribeth shared Prap's book, she asked the students to add humorous answers of their own. After hearing about the camel, Kyle added, "Camels have humps so that when someone offers them a cup of tea they can ask for two humps or one, please." This oral rehearsal shared as a class was important in developing the students' understanding of the activity and in helping them develop an ear for word play.

The fourth graders had spent a great deal of time reading biographies of famous women. Their task was to come up with one essential question they felt was important to answer and that would highlight that person's contribution to the world. After the students found the right question, they did the research to answer it. The students were familiar enough with the life of their person to begin to play with language as they went about answering the question in humorous ways. Christian was able to incorporate words that could be associated with the environment, then use them in a different way, in the answers he gave to his question about Sacagawea (Figure 7.4). Emily and Julia used homophones and synonyms to play with words (see Figures 7.5 and 7.6).

FIGURE 7.4
Christian asks an essential question to research and answers it in humorous ways.

FIGURE 7.5
Emily has three fun answers for her research question, "Why did Rachel Carson like writing about the sea?"

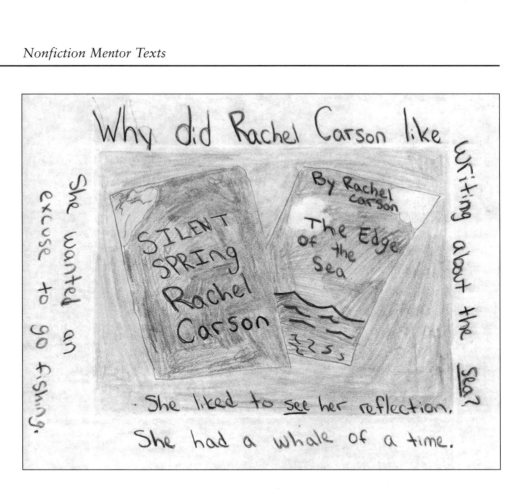

FIGURE 7.6
Julia's plan for her display, which will eventually include her research about Amelia Earhart

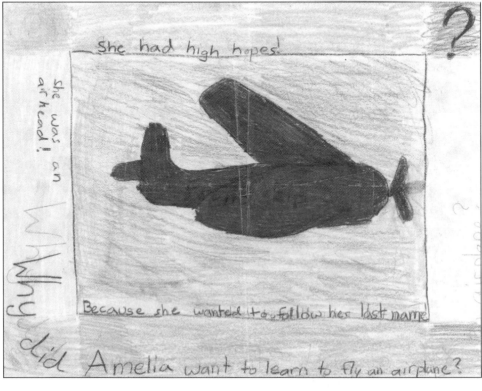

Author Study: An Investigation into Craft and Conventions

One of the easiest ways to embark on a study of conventions is to link it to the craft of a mentor author. It is important to choose an author that your students can study and then imitate in their own writing. Authors such as Jim Arnosky, Gail Gibbons, Sneed B. Collard III, Joanne Ryder, Frank Murphy, and other picture book authors are good sources for texts students can easily investigate. As students make discoveries, they can record them in their writer's notebooks, then share their findings in whole-group discussions. All of this new understanding can also be charted to become a product of collaborative thinking and a reference for everyone in the class.

Charting has been advocated by many as a way to make thinking visible. Janet Angelillo (2002) provides numerous examples of the use of charts in the study of punctuation. Charts displayed in the classroom serve as a reminder to students of the work they have done as a community. They offer a valuable reference to students as they write. They remind all of us of the collaboration present in an inquiry-based classroom. But we must remember that charts should never become something to fill a space on a wall or bulletin board. They are most useful when they are interactive, created collaboratively, and frequently revised to add new discoveries and thinking.

Figure 7.7 is an example of the kind of chart that could be used by students to study the craft and conventions of an author, in this case Frank Murphy.

Murphy's books lend themselves to all sorts of study in craft and conventions—the use of question marks, exclamation marks (even a combination of the question mark and exclamation mark), italics, quotation marks, commas, commentary dashes, ellipses, interjections, fragments, rhetorical devices, apostrophes, the rule of three, noun-verb sentences, proper nouns, and hyphenated adjectives (to name a few!). While we would not advocate studying all of these devices at once, you could certainly choose according to the needs of your students and embark on a month-long, or even a year-long study.

Begin by choosing a craft technique or convention that you feel your students need to understand more deeply and that will help them grow as writers, and point out how the author uses it. An example from Figure 7.7 is how Murphy uses the comma after an introductory phrase. This study will serve not only to help students more deeply understand the use of the comma but also will perhaps lead them to trying out a different way to begin a sentence. Point out an example or two from one of Murphy's books, then talk to your students about what the comma does and why the author needed to put it there. You can then have pairs or teams of students find other examples of the same use of the comma in other books by Murphy.

These discoveries can be written on the chart, added to the chart on sticky notes, or recorded by students in individual charts in their writer's notebooks. You can also have students find examples of the use of the comma after an

Craft/Convention	Why It Was Used	Example	Our Example
Noun-verb sentence	To emphasize the previous sentence or vary the sentence length To create rhythm	He did! *(BR)* They worked! *(BF)* Guns fired! . . . Cannons roared. *(GW)*	Soon the caterpillar cannot fit inside its skin. It eats. It grows.
Commas	To set off an introductory phrase To separate items in a series	In the fall of 1777, George's troops went to Pennsylvania. *(GW)* In that year, something bad happened to baseball. *(BR)* He checked on the oxen, mules, and sheep. *(GW)*	In the winter months, the monarch spends its time in Mexico.
Dashes	To add drama to a sentence closing	In 1919, Babe hit the most home runs ever—29. *(BR)* George's dog Vulcan jumped up and stole the ham—right off the table! *(GW)*	Inside the chrysalis, the monarch waits for its wings—twelve days and twelve nights.
Proper nouns	To give the writer the voice of authority and provide the reader with a clearer picture	Teddy wandered through the wooded valleys of Pennsylvania and climbed the towering peaks of the Colorado Rockies. *(Legend of TB)*	Monarch butterflies migrate from the eastern part of North America to Mexico.
Combination of exclamation and question mark	To show a combination of both surprise and disbelief	That name was William Howe. *William Howe!?* *(GW)*	Each monarch lays hundreds of eggs. *Hundreds of eggs!?*

FIGURE 7.7

Charting the craft and conventions of Frank Murphy

Murphy's books are coded as follows: BR=*Babe Ruth Saves Baseball;* BF=*Ben Franklin and the Magic Squares;* GW=*George Washington and the General's Dog;* Legend of TB=*The Legend of the Teddy Bear*

introductory phrase in the works of other authors and add an additional column to the chart to record what they find. It is important to remind students what it is they are searching for and to encourage the types of conversations that will help them reflect on the use of the comma.

Perhaps the most important part of the chart is composing the original examples. Try it out in the context of a topic you are investigating as a class. You may notice that all of the examples in our chart are about butterflies. This is another way to review what your students are learning across the curriculum. Examples should probably first come from shared writing experiences, then opened up to include examples from individual students. During your conferences, be on the lookout for opportunities to celebrate the use of a convention or craft you are studying in the individual work of your students. Acknowledge their efforts by having them record their work on a sticky note and add it to the chart.

Tying It All Together

We believe that creating voice in writing, no matter what the mode—narrative, persuasive, or informational—is closely tied to the understanding of syntax and conventions. That is why we chose to discuss them together in this chapter. Writers need to understand the power of words as well as have options for incorporating interesting conventions into their work, experimenting with the flow of language by varying the rhythm, structure, and length of their sentences. As Barry Lane (1999) says:

> *As teachers of writing, a big part of our job is to help our students to sway their hips, to find their own voice and experiment with forms. Many teachers seem to encourage this in what is called "creative writing" (fiction and poetry), but stop when it comes to "expository writing" (report writing). This is very ironic because in the real world boring informational writing demands a lively and creative presentation.* (120)

An Author's Voice:
Bring Your Writing to Life —Painting a Clear Picture

Steve Swinburne
Author of *Turtle Tide* and *Wings of Light*

Hi!

Do you really want your writing to sparkle? Do you want to be totally happy with the story you wrote about your walk in the woods? You can make your story come alive by writing with specific information that shows the reader what is happening rather than telling the reader what is happening. Maybe you've heard your teacher or an author say "show, don't tell." What they mean is, try to paint a very clear picture in the reader's mind.

Here's how it works. Look at these two examples. One is a "telling" sentence and one is a "showing" sentence. Which one is stronger, more alive? "The squirrel was active." OR "The squirrel dashed up the tree, scampered along the branch, flicking its tail, chattering like your teeth on a cold winter day."

The first sentence tells you the squirrel was active but the second sentence shows you how active the squirrel was. It helps the reader picture the image of a dashing squirrel and hear the sound it makes. By replacing general words with concrete, specific details you can "see" what the writer is saying. Your writing comes alive. A sentence that shows may take a few more words, but it's worth it.

See if you can turn these sentences that tell into sentences that show:

The mountain is high.
The forest was dark.
My backyard is nice.

If you practice, you get better at turning boring telling sentences into sentences that are alive with strong verbs, interesting details, and vivid images. Have fun!

Happy writing,
Steve Swinburne

Your Turn Lesson 1

Creating Voice with Second-Person Writing

The use of the second-person voice creates an immediate rapport with an audience. The friendly tone invites the reader in to learn more. Second-person stance is an easy structure to use when offering advice, practical tips, and cautions to a reader about how to do something.

Hook: Many of the books by Joanne Ryder are written in the second person. Read aloud or return to *White Bear, Ice Bear* or *The Snail's Spell* and ask the students to listen for the second-person voice (you, your) and to think about how it affects them as listeners.

Options: The Backyard Books by Judy Allen, *Sky Boys: How They Built the Empire State Building* by Deborah Hopkinson, the One Small Square Books by Donald M. Silver, and the Take a Walk Books by Jane Kirkland.

Purpose: *Writers, today we are going to examine how writing in the second person can be useful to a writer—the purposes it might serve and the effects on the writer's relationship with the reader. We've been talking about ways to create voice, and writing in the second person may be one way to make your voice heard.*

Brainstorm: Ask your students to return to their expert or authority lists to find a suitable topic for writing in the second person. If they don't have an expert list, here is the perfect opportunity to write one. An expert list is simply all the topics you feel you could write about with limited or no research. If students share aloud, it will give classmates more ideas to add to their lists. Record ideas on the board or chart paper so that the thinking of the class is visible. Make sure to include your own topics.

Model: Choose from the list a topic that you are comfortable writing about and draft in front of the students. Try to include some humor, practical advice, and a caution or two if you can. Whatever you do, make sure you let your students know who your target audience is since voice is closely connected to a sense of audience. An example might go something like this:

Today I think I'll write about how to bathe a dog. I have lots of experience with that so I think I can do a good job. I'm going to write it as advice to people who may just have gotten a dog and want to know more about how to give their dog a bath.

For this example, the writing would then look like this:

If you are about to tackle the enormous task of bathing your dog, be prepared for battle. Bathing a dog, big or small, can be difficult. But don't worry. Follow these simple steps and you'll be OK.

First of all, gather all your necessary supplies—shampoo, a tub of warm water, towels, sponge, and a garden hose. Make sure you have a collar and leash on your dog or your slippery, soapy canine might escape before his bath is over! Please take this advice—it is always best to dress in a bathing suit or a T-shirt and shorts. Wear flip-flops or go barefoot. Chances are you will get wet!

Coax your canine friend into a tub of warm water. You may need a doggie treat to get the job done. Firmly holding your dog's collar, begin to wet his fur. Now place some shampoo on your sponge and begin to rub in small circular motions. Be careful not to get any soap in your dog's ears or eyes.

Finally, rinse your dog with the garden hose (if it is a hot day) or empty the tub and refill it with clean water. Make sure you get all the soap out! Dry vigorously with a towel.

Now you have a spanking-clean canine. Most likely, you'll be spanking-clean, too!

Talk with your students about what you just did—how you spoke directly to your reader, offered tips and cautions, and (in this case) developed a humorous tone. Another option is to take the same piece and rewrite it in the third person and have your students compare the two, deciding which one has more audience appeal.

Shared/Guided Writing: Collaborate with your class to choose a writing topic that everyone is able to contribute to. For example, you might use "How to Grow a Friendship," or return to the framework presented by Joanne Ryder in her books and write a piece imagining you are becoming the class pet (or some other familiar animal you have studied in science class). Draft together on the board or chart paper so the class has a visual model.

Independent Writing: Students can return to the brainstormed authority list to choose their own topic and write about it using the second-person voice. They could also return to a previously written report and rewrite it in the second person.

Reflection: After sharing, ask your students to think about how this type of writing worked for them.

What did you notice about writing in the second person?

Did writing in the second person help you connect to your audience in a variety of ways?

When would it be best to use this type of stance?

Was it easier or more difficult to write using second-person voice? How so?

Your Turn Lesson 2

The Dash—Purposeful Panache

Many young writers are still developing their understanding of how to read and use punctuation marks. Authors can use dashes for many purposes—a listing or summarizing technique, a way to interrupt the sentence, a way to replace commas of apposition, or a simple alternative to comma or parentheses use. Students can play around with different ways to use the dash in their writing. One word of caution: Like anything else, dashes should not be overused!

Hook: Cathy Camper's *Bugs Before Time: Prehistoric Insects and Their Relatives* demonstrates many wonderful reasons why an author might choose to use the dash. Other options for mentor texts include *Turtle Tide* and *Saving Manatees* by Stephen Swinburne, *The Journey: Stories of Migration* by Cynthia Rylant, and *The Real McCoy: The Life of an African-American Inventor* by Wendy Towle.

Purpose: *Writers, today I'm going to show you how you can use a dash to add variety to the punctuation you might use in your writing. We've already talked about a few different ways that authors use punctuation to get a reader to pause for dramatic flair or to note that a list or something very important is going to follow. Commas help readers to slow down and take breaths. Colons often signal a list or important information. Today we're going to practice writing with dashes to help us imagine the possibilities for the use of the dash in our own writing.*

Brainstorm: Reread various parts from *Bugs Before Time: Prehistoric Insects and Their Relatives* or another book that makes use of dashes. As you read the places where dashes are used (make sure you read a paragraph or sentences around the sentence containing the dash as well), ask students to make a list of the things that the dash does for the piece of writing. What are the various purposes for using the dash? Continue to add to the list as you read passages throughout the book.

It is helpful if the book can be displayed on a document imager (visualizer), or you may have to make overhead transparencies of these passages or scan them into your computer to project on a whiteboard or TV screen. You can always copy them onto chart paper to display for the class if you don't have the technology (we like to use chart paper as well!).

Model: Use the ideas from the brainstormed list and add some of your own to create a list of reasons why a writer might use the dash. Return to a previous piece of writing you may have completed. As you go through your piece, star places where you might have use for the dash. Add or change some sentences to include the dash in the sentence structure. Think aloud while you work so you can let your students in on your thinking. Here is an example from Lynne's notebook:

Built in 1950, the Empire State Building rises into the New York skyway—a total of 1,454 feet of majestic beauty! A colony of workers—masons, carpenters, brick layers, plummers, and electricians—performed their jobs like tireless bees to complete the project in record time. The building's design—the clean, simple lines of a pencil—was the invention of architect William F.

Lamb. The Empire State Building—New York's finest gem—gives New Yorkers and visitors from all over the world—which are considerable in number—an incredible view of all of Manhattan.

Although Lynne purposefully overused the dash, her example includes a variety of reasons why a writer might choose to use the dash. The first set of dashes is used to close the sentence with dramatic flair. The second set is used to present a list. The third set offers an explanation. The fourth set replaces commas used with appositives. The last set interrupts the flow of the sentence with an aside.

Shared/Guided Writing: Invite students to study the craft of writing with dashes. Provide books for each group of three or four students to examine and then have groups collaborate to make a list of examples and purposes for using dashes. Students can work together to find similar thinking and come up with a way to name the purpose and describe its function. In whole or small group, they can share ideas for purposes, and example sentences can be charted.

Here are some books you could use: *I Wonder Why the Sea Is Salty and Other Questions About Oceans* by Anita Ganeri, *Smoke Jumpers* by Jim Gigliotti, *Otter* by Sandy Ransford, *A Drop of Water* by Walter Wick, *Animals in Flight* by Steve Jenkins and Robin Page, *The Wonder in Water* by Diane Swanson, *Different Like Coco* by Elizabeth Matthews, and *The Egg* by Shelley Gill.

Independent Practice: Invite students to try out this strategy with a piece of writing. When students come to writing conferences, ask them to be ready to explain how they used the dash to create a list, add a dramatic pause to the sentence to announce important information, create a summary, or replace commas of apposition.

Reflection: After students share their pieces containing dashes, ask them to reflect on what they did.

How did using this strategy help your piece?

How do you think your piece improved by using the dash?

Was it easy or difficult to insert dashes into your writing? Explain.

What is the difference between using the dash and using the parenthesis to set off information within a sentence?

When could you use dashes again?

Your Turn Lesson 3

Crafting Compound Sentences

Compound sentences are independent clauses that are linked together through the use of a coordinating conjunction. As we work to help students combine sentences to make them longer and more interesting, we must also make them aware of the words (conjunctions) and punctuation they need to get the job done. Jeff Anderson (2005) is a great source for information on the use of the comma and coordinating conjunctions in compound sentences.

Hook: *Just Me and 6,000 Rats: A Tale of Conjunctions* by Rick Walton is a great book that not only tells a story but also highlights the use of conjunctions. After your students enjoy the story, return to it and have them focus on the conjunctions. Pull out the examples of compound sentences and list them on the board. For example:

> *The elevators were crowded, but the people were very nice. We had a ball, yet the players didn't appreciate our trying to help.*

Another excellent book for this lesson is *If You Were a Conjunction* by Nancy Loewen. Ask the students to tell you what they notice about the sentences in this book. You can also use examples from any other text the students are familiar with. Try to include enough examples that the students see that two sentences can be combined to make a compound sentence through the use of the words *for, and, nor, but, or, yet,* and *so* (Jeff Anderson uses the acronym FANBOYS to remember these common conjunctions). Students should also notice that a comma comes before the use of the conjunction in a compound sentence. You might also discuss with the students when each word would be most appropriate. For example, use *and* when you are connecting similar ideas; use *but* for ideas that contrast.

Purpose: *Writers, today I am going to show you how you can take simple sentences and make them more interesting by combining them to make compound sentences. We'll use what we learned about commas and conjunctions to help us.*

Brainstorm: With the class, brainstorm some simple sentences about a common experience such as a field trip, a season, school, or a topic currently under study. For example, if the class is studying butterflies, the sentences might include the following:

> A butterfly is an insect.
> Butterflies can be many different colors.
> A butterfly has three main body parts.
> There are thousands of kinds of butterflies.
> Birds and frogs eat butterflies.
> Some butterflies are named for their colors.
> Some butterflies are poisonous to other animals.

Brainstorm lots of sentences so you will have a rich pool of ideas from which to choose.

Model: Show the students how you can combine some of the sentences to make a compound sentence. Think aloud as you do this, pointing out how you choose which conjunction would work best, how you are sure to add the comma, and how you might use a pronoun in place of a noun to make the sentence have a more appealing sound. In the example about butterflies, you could create the following:

> A butterfly is an insect, so it has three main body parts. Birds and frogs eat butterflies, but some butterflies are poisonous to other animals.

Shared/Guided Writing: Students can work as a class or in pairs or small groups to combine other sentences from the list into compound sentences. These can be charted, shared, and discussed.

Independent Writing: Have students return to a notebook entry or a piece of writing they are currently working on to revise for compound sentences. They could also use some of the sentences created in the lesson to write a paragraph around a topic. Remind them that not all the sentences in their piece should be compound, however. It is important to maintain a mix of sentence length that will contribute to the rhythm of the piece.

Reflection: After sharing their work, students can reflect on what they learned. The following questions can help guide this thinking:

What have you learned about crafting a compound sentence?

How can combining two short sentences into one longer sentence improve a piece of writing?

How could you use the strategy of listing simple sentences when you write other pieces?

Your Turn Lesson 4

Revising with Proper Nouns

Proper nouns are an essential writing tool used to add specificity and the voice of authority. This lesson demonstrates how students can develop an understanding of the importance of including proper nouns as they revise their informational writing. Because students are also learning about proper nouns, the lesson is a good example of how the teaching of grammar and conventions can be linked to the teaching of style.

Hook: Return to several mentor texts and focus on the author's use of proper nouns. *City of Snow* by Linda Oatman High, *Fireboat* by Maira Kalman, *Edna* by Robert Burleigh, *Saving Manatees* by Stephen Swinburne, and *How Big Is It? A Big Book All About Bigness* by Ben Hillman are good choices. If possible, display pages on a visualizer or document imager so students can also notice the use of capitalization. Discuss with students possible reasons why the author used specific names (identify them as proper nouns if you need to) and how it affects the writing. These ideas can be charted or recorded in individual writer's notebooks for future reference.

Purpose: *Writers, today I'm going to show you how using proper nouns can help you be a better writer. Proper nouns tell the reader that you really know what you are talking about—that you are an authority. Proper nouns also help you to give the reader a clearer picture of what you are writing about because they are more specific.*

Brainstorm: Since it is best to begin with what students know, think of a place they are very familiar with as a class. It may be the neighborhood where your school is located or the town or city where you live. Brainstorm specific things you might see as you walk through that area and record them on chart paper. Your list might include things such as the Acme, West Goshen Park, Mrs. Johnson's giant oak tree, Lincoln Avenue, Fidelity Bank, Maier's Bread Factory, St. Matthew's Church, and Murphy's Toy Store. As you record them, think out loud about why you are using capitalization.

Model: Write a short piece that describes the things you see as you walk through the neighborhood. Keep it general so you and the students can go back and revise later. For example, you might begin with something like this:

> As I walk through the neighborhood by the school I pass by the giant tree in the next yard. At the end of the block I cross the street, pass the bank, and quickly arrive at the park.

(This is just a sample; you would probably want to make your draft a little longer).
Reread the whole piece and ask the students if they think it gives a clear picture of the neighborhood. Hopefully, they will see that using general words could give readers very different mind pictures. Then, go back and start to revise by replacing some of the general nouns with the proper nouns from the brainstormed list.

Shared/Guided Writing: After modeling a few revisions, you will soon find that the students will begin to offer the words you need. This makes a natural transition into shared writing. As a class, you could then choose another familiar place (maybe the classroom or another room in the school) and write a description using proper nouns. Another option is to ask students to envision their bedroom or another room in their home. Hold a guided conversation with one or two students in front of the class and ask them to describe their room, guiding them to replace general nouns with more specific, proper nouns.

Independent Writing: Have students return to a notebook entry or a piece of writing they are currently working on and revise it to include some proper nouns. They could also choose to write the description of their bedroom or another room in their home that was part of the shared writing experience.

Reflection: Ask students to share the revisions they made in whole or small groups; then have them reflect on how it went.

How do you recognize a proper noun in a text?

How do you choose which words to capitalize?

Did the use of proper nouns improve your piece? How so?

When might it be important to use proper nouns? Why?

How are proper nouns different from more general nouns?

How does the use of proper nouns make you a better writer?

A Treasure Chest
of Books

We now invite you into our library of wonderful nonfiction books. Although we have listed many books, we know there are thousands of others. You may have your own favorites that you use every year with your students. After reading this book, perhaps you will revisit them and discover new ways to use them to teach your writers about the qualities of good writing.

Take the time to grow your collection slowly. In this way, you will be sure to have the books that you truly love and that will meet your purposes and goals for the writers in your classroom. Choose books that will capture the interest of your students and that will give them the models they need to write in different genres. Choose books, too, that will challenge your students and help them take risks—try out new things—so that they will be better writers tomorrow than they are today.

As with any collection, take time to examine the books each year. As your classes change, so may your goals and priorities. Remember, writing cannot be taught in a year. Choose the books that will move your writers forward, and don't be afraid to change the books if they no longer serve your students or if you find better books to take their place.

We have made a conscious decision to use mostly picture books as our mentor texts for writing workshop. Our rationale is simple. Picture books can be read in one sitting and provide a perfect model for the kind of writing we want our students to do. Additionally, authors of picture books are word-smiths—they need to use exact language in order write in a concise way. Picture books also provide rich illustrations that will lure struggling writers and readers into studying the text and rereading it many times.

Picture books can be successfully used at all grade levels. In our work with teachers, we have met many professionals who use picture books successfully with students in middle school and high school. They have found that picture books allow their students to successfully explore and imitate the craft of the picture book authors.

We wish you luck on your journey with nonfiction mentor texts. Keep your eyes open and imagine the possibilities!

An Author's Voice:
Writing Nonfiction Well—Three Big Ideas

Wendy Towle
Author of *The Real McCoy: The Life of an African-American Inventor*

Dear Young Authors,

I am so pleased to be able to share some thoughts with you about my favorite genre, nonfiction. When written well, nonfiction can be as exciting and engaging as any piece of fiction. To me, writing nonfiction involves many of the same techniques of craft that we use when writing fiction.

First and foremost, you must find a topic that truly interests you. Before I wrote *The Real McCoy*, I was always intrigued by meanings of words and the origins of famous sayings. So, when I came across a tiny article about Elijah McCoy and his relation to the saying, "the real McCoy," I was fascinated and wanted to learn more. My own enthusiasm and passion for the topic I was writing about helped me share Elijah's story in a way that would make my readers interested in my topic.

That brings me to my second point—when you write nonfiction, you must make it interesting. Merely sharing facts makes for a boring report, not an interesting, engaging piece of writing. Even though you are writing to share information, you are still trying to tell a story. Think about how you will draw your readers into your piece—how will you weave your information into a story or journey that will inspire your readers to become as excited about your topic as you are? When I told Elijah's story, I wanted my readers to feel as though they were right there with him as he tinkered in his workshop and worked so hard on the railroads. I could only do this if I wrote in a way that included description that made Elijah come alive.

My last point is this—in order to be a successful writer of nonfiction, you must read a lot of nonfiction. Read as much as you can—in many different formats—and think about which pieces draw you in and which leave you flat. Read like a writer and make note of those techniques that authors use to help the reader become engaged with the text. Try some of those techniques in your own writing. Remember, you become a better writer by writing!

Good luck, young authors—

Wendy Towle

Chapter 2: Establishing the Topic and Point

Algie, Amy. 1998. *Bears*. Denver: Shortland.
A concept book for emergent readers; easy to determine the essential question: What do bears like to do?

Arnold, Caroline. 2007. *Super Swimmers: Whales, Dolphins, and Other Mammals of the Sea*. Watertown, MA: Charlesbridge.
Overriding topic and point is that all mammals can swim, although some are better at it than others. Specific topic—dolphins as speedy swimmers; dolphins as acrobats. (See also Gunzi's *The Best Book of Whales and Dolphins*.)

Arnosky, Jim. 2002. *All About Frogs*. New York: Scholastic.
Arnosky is established as an expert in the field of nonfiction children's books. He often includes his point of view in the final pages of his "All About" books.

Aruego, Jose, and Ariane Dewey. 2002. *Weird Friends: Unlikely Allies in the Animal Kingdom*. NY: Harcourt.
Explores the relationship between different pairs of animals; an excellent source for short text and fact-question-response.

Aston, Dianna. 2006. *An Egg Is Quiet*. San Francisco: Chronicle Books.
A point is made on each two-page spread; additional text and illustrations explain the point made.

———. 2007. *A Seed Is Sleepy*. San Francisco: Chronicle Books.
A point is made on each two-page spread; additional text and illustrations explain the point made.

Batten, Mary. 2008. *Please Don't Wake the Animals: A Book About Sleep*. Atlanta: Peachtree.
Introduction states the topic; conclusion states the point.

Beeler, Selby. 1998. *Throw Your Tooth on the Roof: Tooth Traditions from Around the World*. Boston: Houghton Mifflin.
Focuses on traditions/folklore concerning baby teeth.

le Bloas, Renee, and Jerome Julienne. 1997. *The Shark: Silent Hunter*. Watertown, MA: Charlesbridge.
Highly focused topics provided on each two-page spread.

———. 2004. *The Dolphin: Prince of the Waves*. Watertown, MA: Charlesbridge.
Each topic is covered in a two-page spread. Students can use the topics of super swimmers, social animals, and echo location to cross-reference with other dolphin books listed in the treasure chest.

Brenner, Martha. 1994. *Abe Lincoln's Hat*. New York: Random House.
Focuses on the fact that Lincoln kept important papers in his hat in order to help him remember the things he had to do.

Brown, Don. 2007. *Dolley Madison Saves George Washington.* New York: Houghton Mifflin.
   Focuses on one event in the life of Dolley Madison—how she saved a portrait of George Washington.

Brown, Margaret Wise. 1949. *The Important Book.* New York: HarperCollins.
   Provides a useful scaffold for focusing on important aspects of an event, thing, or person. Each important aspect can be developed into a longer piece.

Bruce, Lisa. 2004. *Yellow.* Chicago: Raintree.
   Introduces children to yellow things found in nature. This book can be used to explore an author's essential question.

Bryant, Jen. 2008. *A River of Words: The Story of William Carlos Williams.* Grand Rapids, MI: Eerdmans Books for Young Readers.
   A great text to reinforce to students the importance of writing about what you know.

Burleigh, Robert. 2003. *Into the Woods: John James Audubon Lives His Dream.* New York: Atheneum.
   Provides a great example of a sharp focus for a biography.

Cline-Ransome, Lesa. 2002. *Quilt Counting.* New York: North-South Books.
   Explains a process.

Cohn, Amy L., and Suzy Schmidt. 2002. *Abraham Lincoln.* New York: Scholastic.
   Makes the point that Lincoln was a big man, not just in stature but in the hearts of those who knew him.

Collard, Sneed B., III. 2002. *Leaving Home.* New York: Houghton Mifflin.
   An exploration into how, when, and why different animals leave home. The point is stated in the first sentence.

———. 2003. *The Deep-Sea Floor.* Watertown, MA: Charlesbridge.
———. 2006. *In the Deep Sea.* New York: Marshall Cavendish Benchmark.
———. 2008. *Teeth.* Watertown, MA: Charlesbridge.
   The point is stated in the introduction.

Crenson, Victoria. 2003. *Horseshoe Crabs and Shorebirds: The Story of a Food Web.* Tarrytown, NY: Marshall Cavendish.
   Makes the point in the author's note that measures should be taken to protect the horseshoe crab.

Davidson, Susanna. 2002. *Whales and Dolphins.* New York: Scholastic.
   Table of contents displays specific topics for study. Interesting points are made about dolphin intelligence, dolphins as social creatures, and how dolphins help people. Includes Internet links.

Davies, Nicola. 2001. *Bat Loves the Night.* Cambridge, MA: Candlewick.
   Focuses on one pipistrelle bat. Davies describes the nocturnal activities of Bat and makes the point in the title and in the last line of the book.

———. 2001. *One Tiny Turtle.* Cambridge, MA: Candlewick.
  Contains a great example of narrowing the focus in the beginning of the
  book. Davies went from reptiles to turtles to sea turtles to loggerheads in
  order to find her focus.

———. 2003. *Surprising Sharks.* Cambridge, MA: Candlewick.
  The title lets readers know that they might learn some surprising
  information about sharks, so that is the point of the book. Davies gives
  her point of view in the concluding pages—we should respect and
  protect sharks.

Dunphy, Madeleine. 2008. *The Peregrine's Journey: A Story of Migration.*
  Berkeley, CA: Web of Life Children's Books.
  Example of writing to the "one"; written in present tense.

Earle, Ann. 1995. *Zipping, Zapping, Zooming Bats.* New York: HarperCollins.
  Can be used for point-of-view poetry.

Edwards, Pamela Duncan. 1997. *Barefoot: Escape on the Underground
  Railroad.* New York: HarperCollins.
  Illustrates how to take a research topic and focus on one small aspect.

———. 2005. *The Bus Ride That Changed History: The Story of Rosa Parks.*
  New York: Houghton Mifflin.
  Author's note includes the point; effective repetition used throughout to
  state the point.

Fletcher, Ralph. 2007. *How to Write Your Life Story.* New York: HarperCollins.
  Gives advice to students on how to find a focus for autobiographical
  writing.

Frank, John. 2008. *Keepers: Treasure-Hunt Poems.* New York: Roaring
  Brook Press.
  Helps students find things to write about and where to look for them—
  at the beach, in the attic, at the flea market, even under the ground;
  point of view—what is considered a treasure?

Fritz, Jean. 1969. *George Washington's Breakfast.* New York: Coward-
  McCann.
  A great mentor text to demonstrate the mind-set of a researcher; shows
  how specific an essential question can be; demonstrates that answering
  one essential question often leads to asking another.

Gehman, Julianne. 2007. *Hummingbirds: Tiny but Mighty.* Akron, PA:
  Reading Matters.
  The point is made in the title and in the summary conclusion; the
  author's note reveals where the idea for the book originated.

Gill, Shelley. 1990. *Alaska's Three Bears.* Homer, AK: Paws IV Children's
  Books.
  The author reveals her point of view in the concluding sentence.

Golenbock, Peter. 1990. *Teammates*. New York: Harcourt.
Illustrates how to narrow a topic; the point is stated in the final sentences.

Gracestone, Katherine. 1998. *What Lays Eggs?* Denver: Shortland.
A simple concept book for emergent readers where the essential question is found in the title.

Grambo, Rebecca. 1997. *Defenses*. Chicago: Kidsbooks.
Each two-page spread explores a different animal defense system.

Gunzi, Christiane. *The Best Book of Whales and Dolphins*. 2001. Boston: Kingfisher.
Headings and subheadings help to focus the reader on different aspects of whales and dolphins, such as dolphins are acrobats, dolphins help humans, dolphins have extensive communication systems, and so on.

Harris, Caroline. 2005. *Whales and Dolphins*. Boston: Kingfisher.
Each two-page spread is built around a specific topic, including dolphins as clever hunters, how dolphins communicate, playful dolphins, and how dolphins use their senses.

Heinrichs, Ann. 2002. *Ants*. Minneapolis: Compass Point Books.
Short one-page chapters that each focus on one aspect of different kinds of ants.

High, Linda Oatman. 2004. *City of Snow: The Great Blizzard of 1888*. New York: Walker.
Includes an author's note that explains the seed of the idea for the book.

———. 2007. *The Cemetery Keepers of Gettysburg*. New York: Walker.
Includes an author's note that explains the seed of the idea for the book.

Hillman, Ben. 2007. *How Big Is It? A Big Book All About Bigness*. New York: Scholastic.
Explores the topic of size.

Hummon, David. 1999. *Animal Acrostics*. Nevada City, CA: Dawn Publications.
A multigenre approach that combines acrostic poetry and facts written in paragraph format at the bottom of the page. Provides an example for narrowing the focus.

Ireland, Karin. 1996. *Wonderful Nature, Wonderful You*. Nevada City, CA: Dawn Publications.
A multigenre approach that states the specific point on each two-page spread in italics. The point is supported through factual information written as advice. Offers lessons from nature.

Jenkins, Martin. 1997. *Chameleons Are Cool*. Cambridge, MA: Candlewick.
Explores the point made in the title.

Jenkins, Steve. 2004. *Actual Size*. Boston: Houghton Mifflin.
    Explores one topic—size—through illustrations and short text.

———. 2007. *Living Color*. Boston: Houghton Mifflin.
    Focuses on colors of animals—each section is dedicated to a different color
    and uses short text to describe how the different animals use that color.

Jenkins, Steve, and Robin Page. 2008. *Sisters and Brothers: Sibling
    Relationships in the Animal World*. New York: Houghton Mifflin.
    Focuses on the relationships between animal brothers and sisters; makes
    the point that sometimes the animal siblings are a lot like human siblings.

Kalman, Bobbie. 2003. *Dolphins Around the World*. New York: Crabtree.
    Organized by species; students can focus research around a specific type
    of dolphin.

———. 2005. *Camouflage: Changing to Hide*. New York: Crabtree.
    Demonstrates how to ask an essential question and organize key ideas
    around it.

Kaner, Etta. 1999. *Animal Defenses: How Animals Protect Themselves*.
    Tonawanda, NY: Kids Can Press.
    Explores the essential question of how animals defend themselves; a
    good source for short text that does not have to be read in order.

———. 2006. *Who Likes the Wind?* Tonawanda, NY: Kids Can Press.
    Great example of how students can narrow their topic by focusing on
    the things they wonder about; can be used to demonstrate how
    questioning leads to more focused research.

Kramer, Stephen. 1992. *Avalanche*. Minneapolis: Carolrhoda Books.
    Can be used to practice forming essential questions and still-wondering
    questions (those questions a reader still has after finishing a text).

Laminack, Lester. 2007. *Snow Day!* Atlanta: Peachtree.
    Humorous narrative (fictionalized story) demonstrating point of view of
    the characters; useful to create a persuasive or informational piece.

Lewis, J. Patrick. 2005. *Monumental Verses*. Washington, DC: National
    Geographic Society.
    Poetic verses about monuments; includes a poem of introduction and an
    epilogue that can be used to help students discover author's purpose and
    point of view. Includes an invitation to write.

Lopez, Gary. 2007. *Sharks*. Chanhassen, MN: The Child's World.
    Most pages begin with an essential question that is answered in one or
    two paragraphs.

MacAulay, Kelley, and Bobbie Kalman. 2006. *Dolphins and Other Marine
    Mammals*. New York: Crabtree.
    Makes the point that porpoises and dolphins are alike and different in
    many ways—can be used to compare/contrast. Other points about

dolphins include how they breathe (see also Caroline Arnold's *Super Swimmers*) and that they are strong swimmers.

Mayer, Cassie. 2008. *Water.* Chicago: Heinemann Library.
Part of a series of books on materials that ask essential questions and provide simple answers.

McGovern, Ann. 1966. *If You Grew Up with Abraham Lincoln.* New York: Four Winds Press.
Explores the differences in such things as transportation, clothing, school, and so on between present time and the time that Lincoln lived.

McGrath, Barbara Barbieri, and Peter Alderman. 2003. *Soccer Counts!* Watertown, MA: Charlesbridge.
This book is organized by numbers and focuses on how to play soccer. Each individual page can be presented as a focused piece of writing.

Muirden, James. 1998. *Seeing Stars.* Cambridge, MA: Candlewick.
Can be used to collect facts, questions, and responses about stars.

Mullin, Rita Thievon. 1998. *Who's for Dinner? Predators and Prey.* New York: Crown.
Focused chapters describing the food habits of different animals.

Murphy, Frank. 2003. *Thomas Jefferson's Feast.* New York: Random House.
Focuses on Thomas Jefferson's interest in food.

Nowacek, Stephanie, and Douglas Nowacek. 2006. *Discovering Dolphins.* St. Paul, MN: Voyageur.
Includes a table of contents that divides the book into three sections with specific topics within each section.

Peterson, Cris. 1996. *Harvest Year.* Honesdale, PA: Boyds Mills.
Explores the essential question of what foods are harvested during different months and in different places; uses the months of the year as an organizational scaffold.

Pringle, Laurence. 2000. *Bats! Strange and Wonderful.* Honesdale, PA: Boyds Mills.
Can be used to create a point of view.

Rice, David. 1997. *Lifetimes.* Nevada City, CA: Dawn Publications.
Explores the topic of how long certain animals and things exist.

Settel, Joanne. 1999. *Exploding Ants: Amazing Facts About How Animals Adapt.* New York: Atheneum.
Each one- to two-page spread presents highly focused and specific research with attention-getting titles.

Silverman, Buffy. 2000. *Bat's Night Out.* Katonah, NY: Richard C. Owen.
Can be used to write point-of-view poetry.

Simon, Seymour. 1995. *Sharks.* New York: HarperCollins.
States the point in the first page introduction.

———. 2001. *Animals Nobody Loves*. New York: North-South Books.
The purpose for writing and point of view are included in the introduction; individual selections are highly focused and often persuade the reader to consider a different point of view.

Souza, D.M. 2007. *Look What Whiskers Can Do*. Minneapolis: Lerner.
Highly focused topic around an essential question that looks to uncover a function or purpose.

Sway, Marlene. 1999. *Bats: Mammals That Fly*. New York: Franklin Watts.
Can be used for point-of-view poetry.

Swinburne, Stephen R. 1999. *Unbeatable Beaks*. New York: Henry Holt.
This book is all about bird beaks, so it provides a great example of focus for research. The point is made in the title. Contains a glossary that describes the beak and provides other factual information about thirty-nine different birds.

Tatham, Betty. 2004. *How Animals Play*. New York: Scholastic.
Researches one essential question. The chapters help to organize and divide the topic into manageable chunks.

Thomas, Keltie. 2004. *How Baseball Works*. New York: Firefly Books.
Within each general topic about baseball are very specific pieces that take different formats, including time lines, recipes, opinion articles, diagrams and labels, how-to's, and paragraphs of explanation. It is a great source of short texts that teachers can use to demonstrate a very specific topic with a controlling point.

Weber, Belinda. 2002. *Amazing Animal Homes*. Boston: Kingfisher/Universal.
Global point is stated in the introduction; each two-page spread can be used to help students narrow their topic and research.

———. 2004. *Animal Disguises*. Boston: Kingfisher.
An example of narrowing a topic around an essential question to provide a global structure for a book.

Whitehouse, Patricia. 2003. *Alligator*. Chicago: Heinemann Library.
Each two-page spread has an essential question, making it an excellent source for introducing this concept to young writers.

Winer, Yvonne. 2002. *Frogs Sing Songs*. Watertown, MA: Charlesbridge.
An example of a narrow focus around one point expressed in the title.

Winters, Kay. 2003. *Abe Lincoln: The Boy Who Loved Books*. New York: Simon and Schuster.
Makes the point that Lincoln's love of books influenced many aspects of his life.

Zolotow, Charlotte. 1993. *The Moon Was the Best*. New York: Greenwillow Books.
Makes the point through dialogue on the last page of the text.

Chapter 3: Building Content

Adler, David A. 2005. *Joe Louis: America's Fighter*. New York: Harcourt.
Use of anecdote; rich descriptions of setting; use of dialogue; time line example.

Anderson, Laurie Halse. 2008. *Independent Dames: What You Never Knew About the Women and Girls of the American Revolution*. New York: Simon and Schuster.
Use of inserts (extended captions) to add content; humorous speech bubbles; time line; additional information included in final pages along with an author's note and an illustrator's note.

Arnold, Caroline. 2007. *Super Swimmers: Whales, Dolphins, and Other Mammals of the Sea*. Watertown, MA: Charlesbridge.
Includes many features of nonfiction, including diagrams, labels, headings, and a glossary.

Arnosky, Jim. 2002. *All About Frogs*. New York: Scholastic.
Includes comparisons and examples of diagrams and illustrations with labels.

Batten, Mary. 2008. *Please Don't Wake the Animals: A Book About Sleep*. Atlanta: Peachtree.
Detailed explanations for each main idea; use of italics to highlight vocabulary.

Beeler, Selby. 1998. *Throw Your Tooth on the Roof: Tooth Traditions from Around the World*. Boston: Houghton Mifflin.
Builds content through diagrams, labels, and descriptions of kinds of teeth; includes an author's note.

Brennan-Nelson, Denise. 2003. *Penny: The Forgotten Coin*. Chelsea, MI: Sleeping Bear Press.
Embeds questions in explanations to build content and maintain interest.

Brenner, Barbara. 1997. *Thinking About Ants*. New York: Mondo.
Uses comparison to help visualize the size of an ant, listing to expand ideas, and drawings with labels.

Brown, Don. 2000. *Uncommon Traveler: Mary Kingsley in Africa*. Boston: Houghton Mifflin.
Uses quotes from Kingsley's journals to build content.

———. 2007. *Dolley Madison Saves George Washington*. Boston: Houghton Mifflin.
Use of quotes to build content.

Bryant, Jen. 2005. *Music for the End of Time*. Grand Rapids, MI: Eerdmans Books for Young Readers.
Builds content by including the thoughts of the character written in italics; includes an author's note.

————. 2008. *A River of Words: The Story of William Carlos Williams.* Grand Rapids, MI: Eerdmans Books for Young Readers.
Builds content with a sprinkling of dialogue; includes a time line that mirrors world events; illustrations include speech bubbles; author's note extends the content with information about the poet's life and writing.

Burleigh, Robert. 2003. *Into the Woods: John James Audubon Lives His Dream.* New York: Atheneum.
Uses quotations from Audubon's journals to add to content; includes facts about Audubon at the end of the book.

Cherry, Lynne. 1992. *A River Ran Wild.* New York: Harcourt Brace.
Includes pictures and labels, rich descriptions, maps, and a time line.

Christelow, Eileen. 2003. *Vote!* New York: Clarion Books.
Uses cartoons and speech bubbles to extend content; great time line example that extends her craft into a graphic organizer.

Cline-Ransome, Lesa. 2002. *Quilt Counting.* New York: North-South Books.
Builds content through explanations and descriptions.

Cole, Joanna. 1996. *The Magic School Bus Inside a Beehive.* New York: Scholastic.
Uses cartoons and speech bubbles to extend content through dialogue. Additional content built through sidebars in poster format, often using bullets to answer an essential question or support a key idea. Use of diagrams, labels, and riddles. Any of the Magic School Bus books can be used as examples of these different ways to build content.

Collard, Sneed B., III. 2000. *The Forest in the Clouds.* Watertown, MA: Charlesbridge.
Builds content with rich descriptions, statistics; includes a glossary and map.

————. 2008. *Teeth.* Watertown, MA: Charlesbridge.
Short text that contains a main idea on almost every page. Each idea is elaborated on with rich descriptions.

————. 2008. *Wings.* Watertown, MA: Charlesbridge.
Short text that contains a main idea on almost every page. Each idea is elaborated on with rich descriptions.

Collins, Mary. 2003. *Airborne: A Photobiography of Orville and Wilbur Wright.* Washington, DC: National Geographic.
Builds content with quotations and vivid descriptions.

Crenson, Victoria. 2003. *Horseshoe Crabs and Shorebirds: The Story of a Food Web.* Tarrytown, NY: Marshall Cavendish.
Uses rich descriptions to describe the life cycle of the horseshoe crab and its importance to migrating shorebirds. Builds content through descriptions, explanations, examples, definitions, and diagrams.

Crossingham, John. 2003. *Lacrosse in Action*. New York: Crabtree.
Builds content through diagrams, captions, and labels.

Curlee, Lynn. 2001. *Brooklyn Bridge*. New York: Atheneum.
Provides an example of an anecdote to build content.

Davidson, Susanna. 2002. *Whales and Dolphins*. New York: Scholastic.
Uses many features of nonfiction, including maps, photographs, graphs, headings and subheadings, and diagrams.

Davies, Nicola. 2003. *Surprising Sharks*. Cambridge, MA: Candlewick.
Contains diagrams with labels, captions that add information, and examples to build content.

———. 2007. *What's Eating You? Parasites—the Inside Story*. Cambridge, MA: Candlewick.
Builds content with explanations, headings, and labels. Incorporates humor through speech bubbles and illustrations.

Dray, Philip. 2008. *Yours for Justice, Ida B. Wells: The Daring Life of a Crusading Journalist*. Atlanta: Peachtree.
Includes two time lines that embed biographical information in the context of what was happening in the real world. Dialogue and quotes, descriptions and explanations; afterword.

Dunphy, Madeleine. 2008. *The Peregrine's Journey: A Story of Migration*. Berkeley, CA: Web of Life Children's Books.
Includes examples of maps, rich descriptions, and detailed explanations.

Earle, Sylvia. 2000. *Sea Critters*. Washington, DC: National Geographic Society.
Includes descriptions and illustrations with labels.

Edwards, Pamela Duncan. 2001. *The Boston Tea Party*. New York: G. P. Putnam's Sons.
Time line included in the final pages.

———. 2003. *The Wright Brothers*. New York: Hyperion.
Example of a time line on the end flaps.

———. 2005. *The Bus Ride That Changed History: The Story of Rosa Parks*. New York: Houghton Mifflin.
Includes a time line of events.

Ericson, Anton. 1994. *Whales and Dolphins*. Chicago: Kidsbooks.
Uses headings, photographs with captions, and explanations to build content.

Farris, Christine King. 2003. *My Brother Martin*. New York: Simon and Schuster.
Use of anecdote to reveal character traits.

Frank, John. 2008. *Keepers: Treasure-Hunt Poems*. New York: Roaring Brook Press.
Includes short, well-written descriptions.

Frasier, Debra. 2004. *The Incredible Water Show.* New York: Harcourt.
Contains speech bubbles, quotes from works of literature, and directions.

Fredericks, Anthony D. 2001. *Under One Rock: Bugs, Slugs, and other Ughs.*
Nevada City, CA: Dawn Publications.
Includes examples of field notes that highlight fantastic facts.

———. 2006. *On One Flower: Butterflies, Ticks and a Few More Icks.*
Nevada City, CA: Dawn Publications.
Includes examples of field notes that highlight fantastic facts.

Freedman, Russell. 1980. *They Lived with the Dinosaurs.* New York: Holiday House.
Short text that provides rich descriptions.

———. 1987. *Lincoln: A Photobiography.* New York: Clarion Books.
Builds content with explanations, examples, and primary source documents such as quotes included in the text from letters. Includes a sampling from many of Lincoln's speeches.

Fritz, Jean. 1976. *What's the Big Idea, Ben Franklin?* New York: Putnam.
Includes descriptions, explanations, and examples.

George, Jean Craighead. 2000. *How to Talk to Your Cat.* New York: HarperCollins.
An example of explanations to describe a process.

———. 1998. *Everglades.* 1995. New York: HarperCollins.
Rich descriptions and imagined dialogue to build content.

George, Lindsay Barrett. 1999. *Around the World: Who's Been Here?* New York: Greenwillow Books.
Diagrams, maps, drawings, and labels; additional information about animals on the last page.

Gibbons, Gail. 1992. *Stargazers.* New York: Holiday House.
Examples of illustrations and diagrams with labels.

———. 1997a. *The Honey Makers.* New York: William Morrow.
Contains examples of explanations and descriptions. Includes wow facts to build content and maintain interest, illustrations and diagrams with labels, and a time line.

———. 1997b. *The Moon Book.* New York: Holiday House.
Examples of illustrations and diagrams with labels, and use of a time line.

Giblin, James Cross. 1992. *George Washington: A Picture Book Biography.*
New York: Scholastic.
Author's note discusses the history behind the anecdote about Washington chopping down the cherry tree.

———. 1994. *Thomas Jefferson: A Picture Book Biography*. New York: Scholastic.
Includes a time line, a two-page spread with quotes from Thomas Jefferson as the primary document source, and a description of Monticello.

Gigliotti, Jim. 2007. *Smoke Jumpers*. Chanhassen, MN: The Child's World.
Builds content with photos, captions, and information in sidebars.

Gill, Shelley. 1990. *Alaska's Three Bears*. Homer, AK: Paws IV Children's Books.
Hooks facts to legends; rich description; examples and explanations offered.

Golenbock, Peter. 1990. *Teammates*. New York: Harcourt.
Use of anecdotes, examples, explanations, and descriptions.

Grimes, Nikki. 2002. *Talkin' About Bessie: The Story of Aviator Elizabeth Coleman*. New York: Orchard Books.
Examples of anecdotes; rich description; quotes.

Guiberson, Brenda. 1991. *Cactus Hotel*. New York: Henry Holt.
Builds content with rich descriptions that appeal to the senses and provide number facts; opens with a description of setting.

———. 1996. *Into the Sea*. New York: Henry Holt.
Builds content with rich descriptions that appeal to the senses and provide number facts.

Gunzi, Christiane. *The Best Book of Whales and Dolphins*. 2001. Boston: Kingfisher.
Uses features of nonfiction, including table of contents, glossary, index, maps, captions, and diagrams.

Halpern, Shari. 1992. *My River*. New York: Macmillan.
Uses illustrations to introduce young readers to some of the plants and animals that inhabit rivers.

Heinrichs, Ann. 2002. *Ants*. Minneapolis: Compass Point Books.
Includes a table of contents, index, and "Did You Know?" box.

Hillman, Ben. 2007. *How Big Is It? A Big Book All About Bigness*. New York: Scholastic.
Includes specific numbers in descriptions of objects.

Hiscock, Bruce. 2008. *Ookpik: The Travels of a Snowy Owl*. Honesdale, PA: Boyds Mills.
Rich descriptions; includes an author's note that gives more information on the snowy owl.

Hodgkins, Fran. 2007. *How People Learned to Fly*. New York: HarperCollins.
Speech bubbles, captions, charts and diagrams, labels, descriptions, and explanations.

Hopkinson, Deborah. 2006. *Sky Boys: How They Built the Empire State Building.* New York: Random House.
Explanations and the use of a time line to build content.

Iverson, Diane. 1996. *Discover the Seasons.* Nevada City, CA: Dawn Publications.
Uses poetry to add to content; includes explanations. A two-page spread of crafts and activities in the form of how-to paragraphs and bullets for steps is repeated for each season.

Jackson, Ellen. 1998. *Turn of the Century.* Watertown, MA: Charlesbridge.
Builds content with facts bulleted for each new century.

Jenkins, Steve, and Robin Page. 2008. *Sisters and Brothers: Sibling Relationships in the Animal World.* New York: Houghton Mifflin.
Short text on each page acts like a caption, sometimes adding imagined dialogue; rich descriptions; headings.

Kalman, Bobbie. 1998. *Colonial Times from A to Z.* New York: Crabtree.
An alphabet book that describes people and things from colonial times. Additional content is provided in captions, photos, and diagrams. Explanations use boldface print to highlight key vocabulary.

———. 2005. *Camouflage: Changing to Hide.* New York: Crabtree.
Offers rich descriptions, explanations, and examples. Includes boldfaced vocabulary defined in the context, photos, captions, and labels.

Kerley, Barbara. 2008. *What to Do About Alice? How Alice Roosevelt Broke the Rules, Charmed the World, and Drove Her Father Teddy Crazy!* New York: Scholastic.
Builds content through dialogue, anecdotes, and newspaper headlines in illustrations. Includes an Author's Note.

Kirkland, Jane. 2001. *Take a Backyard Bird Walk.* Lionville, PA: Stillwater.
Part of a series of Take a Walk books. Builds content through photos, charts, sidebars, captions, poems, anecdotes, and descriptions of places and animals. Encourages response through writing.

———. 2007. *Take a Beach Walk.* Lionville, PA: Stillwater.
Part of the Take a Walk book series.

———. 2008. *Take a Winter Nature Walk.* Lionville, PA: Stillwater.
Part of the Take a Walk book series.

Knight, Tim. 2003. *Fantastic Feeders.* Chicago: Heinemann Library.
Rich descriptions with use of numbers; compares unknown with something known; captions add content and extend the examples.

Koscielniak, Bruce. 2003. *Johann Gutenberg and the Amazing Printing Press.* Boston: Houghton Mifflin.
Includes talking captions (dialogue added to illustrations without speech buubles) and speech bubbles; explanations and examples; rich descriptions.

Kramer, Stephen. 1992. *Avalanche*. Minneapolis: Carolrhoda Books.
Use of anecdotes to build content.

———. 1992. *Lightning*. Minneapolis: Carolrhoda Books.
Use of anecdote to build content.

Kulling, Monica. 1999. *The Great Houdini: World-Famous Magician and Escape Artist*. New York: Random House.
Use of anecdotes and examples to build content; includes an excerpt from a newspaper article.

Leacock, Elspeth, and Susan Buckley. 2001. *Journeys in Time: A New Atlas of American History*. Boston: Houghton Mifflin.
Includes a table of contents; text box with bulleted facts; and maps with numbers that match paragraph explanations.

Leedy, Loreen. 2006. *Postcards from Pluto: A Tour of the Solar System*. New York: Holiday House.
Listing; speech bubbles opposite postcards offer additional facts about the planet, sometimes in a question and answer format.

Legg, Dr. Gerald. 1998. *From Seed to Sunflower*. Danbury, CT: Grolier.
Good examples of diagrams and illustrations with labels or captions.

Locker, Thomas. 1984. *Where the River Begins*. New York: Dial Books.
Rich descriptions in text and illustrations.

———. 2003. *John Muir: America's Naturalist*. Golden, CO: Fulcrum.
Uses quotes from Muir's journals to build content.

Lopez, Gary. 2007. *Sharks*. Chanhassen, MN: The Child's World.
Uses sidebars; incredible photography with captions; glossary and table of contents.

Lyon, George Ella. 2003. *Mother to Tigers*. New York: Atheneum.
Use of anecdote; author's note extends the content by giving more facts about Helen Delaney's life.

MacAulay, Kelley, and Bobbie Kalman. 2006. *Dolphins and Other Marine Mammals*. New York: Crabtree.
Examples of providing a definition within a sentence.

Malone, Peter. 2007. *Close to the Wind: The Beaufort Scale*. New York: G. P. Putnam's Sons.
Written as diary entries to explain the different numbers of the scale used to describe wind force; includes diagrams and a glossary.

Mann, Elizabeth. 1996. *The Brooklyn Bridge*. New York: Mikaya Press.
Use of anecdote and short biographies in sidebars; explanations and diagrams build content; content is provided in captions to photos and illustrations.

Markle, Sandra. 1996. *Creepy, Crawly Baby Bugs*. New York: Walker.
Builds content with labels, captions, and photographs; vocabulary is explained within the text; includes a glossary and an index.

Maruki, Toshi. 1980. *Hiroshima No Pika*. New York: Lothrop, Lee and Shepard Books.
Includes an author's note, rich descriptions, and sprinkles of conversations.

Matthews, Elizabeth. 2007. *Different Like Coco*. Cambridge, MA: Candlewick.
Talking captions; time line; quotes.

Matthews, Tom. 1998. *Light Shining Through the Mist: A Photobiography of Dian Fossey*. Washington, DC: National Geographic Society.
Uses quotes from Fossey's journals and letters; examples of photographs and captions, maps, time line, and anecdote; rich descriptions; includes an afterword.

McGrath, Barbara Barbieri, and Peter Alderman. 2003. *Soccer Counts!* Watertown, MA: Charlesbridge.
A counting book that explains the history and rules of soccer.

McNamara, Ken. 2006. *It's True! We Came From Slime*. Buffalo, NY: Firefly Books.
Extends content through the use of cartoons and talking captions to add humor.

Melmed, Laura Krauss. 2003. *Capital! Washington D.C. From A to Z*. New York: HarperCollins.
Contains an interesting time line with drawings to extend content.

Micucci, Charles. 1995. *The Life and Times of the Honeybee*. New York: Houghton Mifflin.
Examples of time lines and calendars in creative formats.

———. 2003. *The Life and Times of the Ant*. Boston: Houghton Mifflin.
Factual information about ants; builds content through calendars, diagrams, labels, examples, explanations, and descriptions.

Miller, Debbie S. 2000. *River of Life*. New York: Houghton Mifflin.
Rich descriptions of setting; glossary provides additional information on animals and plants mentioned in the text.

———. 2003. *Arctic Lights Arctic Nights*. New York: Walker.
Describes different arctic animals' activities throughout each month— each short description is a snapshot of setting; glossary provides additional content.

Murphy, Frank. 2002. *George Washington and the General's Dog*. New York: Random House.
Uses an anecdote to demonstrate the honesty of George Washington; primary sources are revealed in the author's note.

———. 2003. *Thomas Jefferson's Feast.* New York: Random House.
Use of anecdotes.

Nelson, Ray Jr., and Douglas Kelly. 1995. *Greetings from America: Postcards from Donovan and Daisy.* Portland, OR: Flying Rhinoceros.
Builds content with explanations of word origins.

Noble, Trinka Hakes. 2007. *The Pennsylvania Reader.* Chelsea, MI: Sleeping Bear Press.
Includes a time line, explanations, examples, descriptions, and number facts.

O'Connor, Jane. 2003. *The Perfect Puppy for Me!* New York: Penguin Putnam.
Builds content through pictures and labels; sidebars; anecdotes; charts and labels; and recipes.

Peterson, Cris. 1996. *Harvest Year.* Honesdale, PA: Boyds Mills.
Each page explains the harvesting activities throughout the United States for that month; uses the power of three to provide examples; additional content is provided in the captions that accompany the photographs.

Rappaport, Doreen. 2001. *Martin's Big Words.* New York: Hyperion.
Includes a time line in the form of a list of important dates in the life of Martin Luther King Jr.

———. 2008. *Abe's Honest Words: The Life of Abraham Lincoln.* New York: Hyperion.
Builds content through the use of excerpts from Lincoln's letters and speeches.

Riley, Susan, ed. 2002. *World's Greatest Marbles Games.* Minneapolis: Compass Labs.
Builds content with sidebars that include interesting facts; also includes diagrams and labels.

Rockwell, Anne. 2006. *Why Are the Ice Caps Melting? The Dangers of Global Warming.* New York: HarperCollins.
Includes speech bubbles, diagrams with labels and explanations, and questions and answers.

Romanek, Trudee. 2005. *Switched On, Flushed Down, Tossed Out: Investigating the Hidden Workings of Your Home.* New York: Annick Press.
Cartoon-like drawings with speech bubbles to extend content; "did you know" boxes; case files including facts, questions, and theories.

Ryan, Pam Muñoz. 2001. *Hello Ocean.* Watertown, MA: Charlesbridge.
Rich descriptions using the senses.

Ryder, Joanne. 1993. *The Goodbye Walk.* New York: Lodestar Books.
Rich descriptions using senses and specific examples; provides an explanation of what a goodbye walk is.

Sayre, April Pulley. 2005. *Stars Beneath Your Bed: The Surprising Story of Dust*. New York: Greenwillow Books.
Lists examples to build content; additional information in the back about how dust helps to create sunsets.

Schuett, Stacey. 1995. *Somewhere in the World Right Now*. New York: Alfred A. Knopf.
A note to the reader at the beginning of the book builds content by explaining time zones; rich descriptions.

Schulman, Janet. 2008. *Pale Male: Citizen Hawk of New York City*. New York: Alfred A. Knopf.
Includes rich descriptions; examples of anecdotes; and explanations.

Settel, Joanne. 1999. *Exploding Ants: Amazing Facts About How Animals Adapt*. New York: Atheneum.
Contains explanations, descriptions, and examples; includes captions, photographs, headings, and subheadings.

Silver, Donald M. 1993. *One Small Square: Backyard*. New York: McGraw-Hill.
This is one in a series of many One Small Square books. Builds content with rich descriptions, diagrams, captions, labels, and sidebars.

Simon, Seymour. 2003. *Spiders*. New York: HarperCollins.
Examples of rich descriptions that help the reader visualize; use of numbers and comparisons.

———. 1989. *Whales*. New York: Crowell.
Builds content through rich descriptions that include facts and numbers.

Skog, Jason. 2008. *Citizenship*. Mankato, MN: Capstone.
A mentor text for graphic literacy; examples of speech bubbles to enhance cartoons and text; fact boxes; includes a glossary and a time line.

Smith, David J. 2002. *If the World Were a Village: A Book About the World's People*. Towanda, NY: Kids Can Press.
Builds content through number words, statistics, and lists.

Stewart, David. 2001. *You Wouldn't Want to Sail on the Titanic! One Voyage You'd Rather Not Make*. Danbury, CT: Franklin Watts.
Use of cartoon-like drawings and speech bubbles to extend content; headings, captions, table of contents, index, and glossary; rich descriptions; statistics; examples and explanations; has an interesting addition in the form of handy hints throughout the book.

Swain, Gwenyth. 2002. *Pennsylvania*. Minneapolis: Lerner.
Includes maps and captions; boldface vocabulary explained within the body of the text; annotated "places to visit" and "outstanding Pennsylvanians" lists; recipe; and fun facts.

Swanson, Diane. 2005. *The Wonder in Water*. Buffalo, NY: Firefly Books.
Builds content with descriptions, examples, and wow facts.

————. 2001. *Burp! The Most Interesting Book You'll Ever Read About Eating*. Tonawanda, NY: Kids Can Press.
Examples of descriptions and explanations to build content; features of nonfiction including diagrams with labels and headings.

Swinburne, Stephen. 2005. *Turtle Tide*. Honesdale, PA: Boyds Mills.
Rich descriptions that appeal to the senses.

————. 2006. *Wings of Light: The Migration of the Yellow Butterfly*. Honesdale, PA: Boyds Mills.
Rich descriptions that appeal to the senses; includes an author's note that provides additional information about the cloudless sulphur butterfly.

Tagholm, Sally. 2001. *The Complete Book of the Night*. New York: Kingfisher.
Headings and subheadings (each subheading contains an introduction); captions and labels; table of contents and index.

Theodorou, Rod, and Carole Telford. 2000. *Lizards and Snakes*. Crystal Lake, IL: Rigby.
Builds content through explanations and examples; includes features of nonfiction such as boldface words and captions.

Thimmesh, Catherine. 2006. *Team Moon: How 400,000 People Landed Apollo 11 on the Moon*. New York: Houghton Mifflin.
Extends content through quotes, photos, and captions; rich descriptions throughout.

————. 2004. *Madam President: The Extraordinary, True (and Evolving) Story of Women in Politics*. New York: Houghton Mifflin.
Examples of quotes that come from primary source documents; time line; use of dialogue in the form of speech bubbles to extend thinking about key concepts and promote a personal connection.

Thomas, Keltie. 2004. *How Baseball Works*. New York: Firefly Books.
Provides examples of how to build content in a variety of ways: descriptions, explanations, time lines, diagrams, photos, and anecdotes.

Thomas, Peggy. 2008. *Farmer George Plants a Nation*. Honesdale, PA: Boyds Mills.
Builds content with rich descriptions and excerpts from Washington's diaries; includes a time line and additional information on the final pages.

Towle, Wendy. 1993. *The Real McCoy: The Life of an African-American Inventor*. New York: Scholastic.
Builds content through examples, explanations, use of anecdote, and descriptions.

Venezia, Mike. 1997. *Leonard Bernstein*. New York: Children's Press.
Use of anecdote to build content; also builds content through humorous illustrations in cartoon format to illustrate a fact.

———. 2008. *Faith Ringgold*. New York: Children's Press.
Builds content through humorous illustrations in cartoon format to illustrate a fact; additional content found in captions.

Weber, Belinda. 2004. *Animal Disguises*. Boston: Kingfisher.
Short paragraphs offer further explanations to the main idea presented on each two-page spread.

Wick, Walter. 1997. *A Drop of Water*. New York: Scholastic.
Builds content through explanations; examples of wow facts.

Winters, Kay. 2003. *Abe Lincoln: The Boy Who Loved Books*. New York: Simon and Schuster.
Use of anecdotes.

Zolotow, Charlotte. 1993. *The Moon Was the Best*. New York: Greenwillow Books.
Content is developed through specific examples and descriptions of places, objects, and people.

Chapter 4: Introductions and Conclusions

Allen, Judy. 2000. *Are You a Spider?* New York: Kingfisher.
Creates a "What if . . .?" scenario in the beginning by asking readers to imagine that they are something else.

Anderson, Laurie Halse. 2002. *Thank You, Sarah: The Woman Who Saved Thanksgiving*. New York: Simon and Schuster.
Sharing-a-secret beginning; conclusion includes a listing of character traits and returns to the title.

Arnosky, Jim. 1999. *All About Owls*. New York: Scholastic.
An example of a question lead.

Aruego, Jose, and Ariane Dewey. 2002. *Weird Friends: Unlikely Allies in the Animal Kingdom*. New York: Harcourt.
An example of a comparison lead.

Atkins, Jeannine. 1999. *Mary Anning and the Sea Dragon*. New York: Farrar, Straus and Giroux.
Beginning creates a scene; ends with Mary hearing the words of her father.

Batten, Mary. 2008. *Please Don't Wake the Animals: A Book About Sleep*. Atlanta: Peachtree.
Introduction states the topic; conclusion states the point; beginning and ending act as bookends—same sentence is repeated.

Beeler, Selby. 1998. *Throw Your Tooth on the Roof: Tooth Traditions from Around the World*. Boston: Houghton Mifflin.
Introduction begins and ends with a question and creates a scene.

Brennan-Nelson, Denise. 2003. *Penny: The Forgotten Coin.* Chelsea, MN: Sleeping Bear Press.
    Story lead; facts about the penny appear in the middle of the story, almost as an interrupter.

Bridges, Ruby. 1999. *Through My Eyes.* New York: Scholastic.
    Quotations from a variety of people placed in side bars and captions add content; rich descriptions of places and people; personalized accounts.

Brown, Don. 2000. *Uncommon Traveler: Mary Kingsley in Africa.* Boston: Houghton Mifflin.
    An example of an introduction that uses setting.

———. 2007. *Dolley Madison Saves George Washington.* New York: Houghton Mifflin.
    Introduction focuses on what everybody says about George Washington (a what-people-say beginning); conclusion describes a hope or wish for the future that has come true.

Bryant, Jen. 2005. *Music for the End of Time.* Grand Rapids, MI: Eerdmans Books for Young Readers.
    Begins with a snapshot of setting.

Buckley, Annie. 2007. *Hero Girls.* Chanhassen, MN: The Child's World.
    Has a combination question and definition lead; summary conclusion is found in the last paragraph.

Burleigh, Robert. 1991. *Flight: The Journey of Charles Lindbergh.* New York: Philomel Books.
    An example of a lead that recounts what people say about the subject (in this case, Charles Lindbergh).

———. 2000. *Edna.* New York: Orchard Books.
    Beginning creates a sense of era.

———. 2007. *Stealing Home: Jackie Robinson: Against the Odds.* New York: Simon and Schuster Books for Young Readers.
    Good information to create a summary/conclusion using the way we are known.

Chapman, Gillian, and Pam Robson. 1991. *Making Books: A Step-by-Step Guide to Your Own Publishing.* Brookfield, CT: Millbrook.
    Has an introduction that invites the reader to use the book to learn how to publish his or her work.

Christelow, Eileen. 2003. *Vote!* New York: Clarion Books.
    Begins with a "What if . . .?" scenario.

Clinton, Catherine. 2008. *Phyllis's Big Test.* New York: Houghton Mifflin.
    Begins with an introduction of explanation; conclusion is in the form of an epilogue.

Coles, Robert. 1995. *The Story of Ruby Bridges*. New York: Scholastic.
The introduction is a quote from Ruby's mother.

Collard, Sneed B., III. 2008. *Teeth*. Watertown, MA: Charlesbridge.
Short introduction; ends with a question.

Davies, Nicola. 2001. *Bat Loves the Night*. Cambridge, MA: Candlewick.
A narrative-informational structure; facts are included in a different font on the same page.

———. 2001. *One Tiny Turtle*. Cambridge, MA: Candlewick.
A narrative-informational structure; facts are included in a different font on the same page.

———. 2003. *Surprising Sharks*. Cambridge, MA: Candlewick.
Begins with a question and puts the reader right in the setting for the book—the ocean inhabited by sharks.

Dingle, Derek. 1998. *First in the Field: Baseball Hero Jackie Robinson*. New York: Hyperion.
Good information to create a sense of era and summary/conclusion using the way we are known.

Farris, Christine King. 2003. *My Brother Martin*. New York: Simon and Schuster.
Opens with an anecdote.

Fritz, Jean. 1991. *Bully for You, Teddy Roosevelt!* New York: G. P. Putnam's Sons.
Opens with a question answered by a summary list.

George, Jean Craighead. 1995. *Everglades*. New York: HarperCollins.
Story lead—creates a story around the information to be delivered, and the story continues throughout the book.

Gerstein, Mordicai. 2003. *The Man Who Walked Between the Towers*. Brookield, CT: Roaring Brook Press.
Opens with an amazing fact.

Gibbons, Gail. 1983. *Sun Up, Sun Down*. Orlando: Harcourt.
Opens by describing an action.

———. 1990. *Beacons of Light: Lighthouses*. New York: William Morrow.
Beginning creates a scene to help bring the reader into the moment.

———. 1993. *Spiders*. New York: Holiday House.
An example of a compare/contrast lead.

———. 1995. *Sea Turtles*. New York: Holiday House.
An example of a definition lead.

———. 1997. *The Honey Makers*. New York: William Morrow.
Beginning creates a scene to help bring the reader into the moment; ending returns to the title.

———. 2002. *Behold . . . the Unicorns!* New York: HarperCollins.
Definition lead; concludes with a list of characteristics of the unicorn.

Golenbock, Peter. 1990. *Teammates.* New York: Harcourt.
Beginning creates a sense of era; ends with a primary source—a quote.

Goodman, Susan E. 2006. *All in Just One Cookie.* New York: HarperCollins.
A narrative-informational structure; a story that includes facts about the ingredients used to make the cookies.

Guiberson, Brenda Z. 1991. *Cactus Hotel.* New York: Henry Holt.
Opens with a scene that includes setting, characters, and action as well as an amazing fact; conclusion returns to the title.

Hansen, Joyce. 2007. *Women of Hope: African Americans Who Made a Difference.* New York: Scholastic.
Opens with an anecdote.

Hearne, Betsy. 1997. *Seven Brave Women.* New York: Greenwillow Books.
Effective introduction uses a summary list of events followed by an alternative point of view. Conclusion presents a summary list and a wish for the future.

Heiligman, Deborah. 2002. *Honeybees.* Washington, DC: National Geographic Society.
Beginning poses a question to connect with readers.

Heinrichs, Ann. 2003. *Frogs.* Minneapolis: Compass Point Books.
Includes short passages about the physical characteristics, movement, feeding habits, and habitats of frogs that can be used to model many different lessons. This book is part of a series that also includes books about ants, bees, birds, butterflies, fish, grasshoppers, and ladybugs.

Hiscock, Bruce. 2008. *Ookpik: The Travels of a Snowy Owl.* Honesdale, PA: Boyds Mills.
Introduction explains the idea for the book and how it led to research.

Hodgkins, Fran. 2007. *How People Learned to Fly.* New York: HarperCollins.
Introduction combines a question with a "What if . . .?" or imagine-the-possibilities lead; summary conclusion wraps to the beginning.

Ireland, Karin. 1996. *Wonderful Nature, Wonderful You.* Nevada City, CA: Dawn Publications.
Introduction is a series of questions.

Jackson, Ellen. 1998. *Turn of the Century.* Watertown, MA: Charlesbridge.
Has an introduction that combines a definition lead with questions and interesting comparisons; concludes with an author's note.

Jenkins, Martin. 1997. *Chameleons Are Cool.* Cambridge, MA: Candlewick.
An example of a compare/contrast lead.

———. 1999. *The Emperor's Egg.* Cambridge, MA: Candlewick.
Begins with a description of setting.

Jenkins, Steve. 2006. *Almost Gone: The World's Rarest Animals.* New York: HarperCollins.
An example of a "What if . . .?" introduction.

———. 2007. *Living Color.* New York: Houghton Mifflin.
Includes a lead sentence in the form of a list and includes instructions for how to navigate the book.

Jenkins, Steve, and Robin Page. 2001. *Animals in Flight.* Boston: Houghton Mifflin.
An example of an imagine lead.

Kalman, Maira. 2002. *Fireboat: The Heroic Adventures of the John J. Harvey.* New York: G. P. Putnam's Sons.
Beginning creates a sense of era.

Kitchen, Bert. 1992. *Somewhere Today.* Cambridge, MA: Candlewick.
Each page of text uses a "somewhere today" lead to create interest. It matches the illustration on the opposite page.

Koscielniak, Bruce. 2003. *Johann Gutenberg and the Amazing Printing Press.* Boston: Houghton Mifflin.
An example of an imagine lead with a question/answer format; the conclusion tells the effect that the printing press had on the world, written as a thank-you.

Kramer, Stephen. 1992. *Lightning.* Minneapolis: Carolrhoda Books.
Beginning creates a scene to draw the reader in; conclusion is a series of unanswered questions.

Krull, Kathleen. 1996. *Wilma Unlimited: How Wilma Rudolph Became the World's Fastest Woman.* New York: Harcourt.
Beginning creates a sense of era.

Kulling, Monica. 1999. *The Great Houdini: World-Famous Magician and Escape Artist.* New York: Random House.
The conclusion is built around what the person is most known for—in this case, magic.

Lester, Julius. 1998. *From Slave Ship to Freedom Road.* London: Puffin Books.
An example of an action lead.

Levine, Ellen. 2007. *Henry's Freedom Box.* New York: Scholastic.
Opens with an amazing fact.

Levine, Shar, and Leslie Johnstone. 2005. *Kitchen Science.* New York: Sterling.
Interesting introduction that serves to pull the reader in to trying the science experiments described throughout the book.

Lopez, Gary. 2007. *Sharks*. Chanhassen, MN: The Child's World.
Creating-a-scene introduction; has a summary conclusion with author's point of view.

Lyon, George Ella. 2003. *Mother to Tigers*. New York: Atheneum.
Begins with an imagine lead.

Markle, Sandra. 2004. *Owls*. Minneapolis: Carolrhoda Books.
An example of a definition lead.

Maruki, Toshi. 1980. *Hiroshima No Pika*. New York: Lothrop, Lee and Shepard Books.
An example of a weather lead combined with actions. The conclusion is an example of using a powerful statement that sums up the purpose of telling the story.

McKissack, Patricia C., and Frederick L. 2003. *Days of Jubilee: The End of Slavery in the United States*. New York: Scholastic.
Introduction and conclusion use primary sources.

McNamara, Ken. 2006. *It's True! We Came From Slime*. Buffalo, NY: Firefly Books.
Compare/contrast lead in Chapter 1.

Micucci, Charles. 1995. *The Life and Times of the Honeybee*. New York: Houghton Mifflin.
Begins with a snapshot of the honeybee as a valuable insect.

———. 2003. *The Life and Times of the Ant*. New York: Houghton Mifflin.
Concludes by describing characteristics of the ant.

Mochizuki, Ken. 1993. *Baseball Saved Us*. New York: Lee and Low Books.
Includes an author's note, sprinkles of dialogue, and rich descriptions.

Murphy, Frank. 2000. *The Legend of the Teddy Bear*. Chelsea, MN: Sleeping Bear Press.
Beginning develops a sense of era and creates a feeling of nostalgia; conclusion incorporates a primary source (a letter from Teddy Roosevelt) and a sentence that lists the characteristics of the teddy bear.

———. 2002. *Always Inventing: The True Story of Thomas Alva Edison*. New York: Scholastic.
Combination lead—snapshot of setting and compare/contrast.

———. 2002. *George Washington and the General's Dog*. New York: Random House.
Sharing-a-secret lead; uses a true story to illustrate the honesty of George Washington.

———. 2003. *Thomas Jefferson's Feast*. New York: Random House.
Sharing-a-secret lead.

————. 2005. *Babe Ruth Saves Baseball!* New York: Random House.
Sharing-a-secret lead; conclusion repeats the introduction and ends with the title.

Nowacek, Stephanie, and Douglas Nowacek. 2006. *Discovering Dolphins*. St. Paul, MN: Voyageur.
Example of a definition lead.

Peterson, Cris. 1996. *Harvest Year*. Honesdale, PA: Boyds Mills.
Uses listing and appeal to the senses as strategies for the lead paragraph; includes a summary conclusion that relates to the title and makes a personal connection.

Pringle, Laurence. 2000. *Bats! Strange and Wonderful*. Honesdale, PA: Boyds Mills.
Introduction is written in the second person.

Robinson, Sharon. 2001. *Jackie's Nine: Jackie Robinson's Values to Live By*. New York: Scholastic.
Creates a summary/conclusion using the way we are known.

Ryan, Pam Muñoz. 1999. *Amelia and Eleanor Go for a Ride*. New York: Scholastic.
Sharing-a-secret beginning.

————. 2002. *When Marian Sang*. New York: Scholastic.
Both the beginning and the conclusion reflect what the subject is most known for—singing.

Ryder, Joanne. 1982. *The Snail's Spell*. New York: Penguin.
Creates a "What if . . .?" scenario in the beginning by asking readers to imagine that they are something else.

Rylant, Cynthia. 2006. *The Journey: Stories of Migration*. New York: Scholastic.
Example of a compare/contrast introduction; has a labeled summary conclusion.

Sayre, April Pulley. 2005. *Stars Beneath Your Bed: The Surprising Story of Dust*. New York: Greenwillow Books.
Begins with a snapshot of setting combined with a definition.

Schuett, Stacey. 1995. *Somewhere in the World Right Now*. New York: Alfred A. Knopf.
Provides a wonderful scaffold to lead into an informational piece about a place, a biome, or an occupation.

Settel, Joanne. 1999. *Exploding Ants: Amazing Facts About How Animals Adapt*. New York: Atheneum.
Has an introduction that offers an explanation for the content of the book.

Silver, Donald M. 1993. *One Small Square: Backyard.* New York: McGraw-Hill.
This is one in a series of many One Small Square books. Introductions
may create or describe a scene; conclusions offer reflection on the
importance of nature.

Simon, Seymour. 1986. *Stars.* New York: William Morrow.
An example of a definition lead.

———. 2000. *Out of Sight: Pictures of Hidden Worlds.* New York: North-
South Books.
Conclusion is a series of unanswered questions.

———. 2001. *Animals Nobody Loves.* New York: North-South Books.
A well-written introduction that uses questions as leads and sets a well-
defined purpose for reading; includes questions to promote thinking
after reading.

Stewart, David. 2001. *You Wouldn't Want to Sail on the Titanic! One Voyage
You'd Rather Not Make.* Danbury, CT: Franklin Watts.
Contains an introduction written as a "What if . . .?" lead in the second
person; conclusion in the form of an aftermath, including a wraparound
to the introduction.

Stone, Tanya Lee. 2008. *Elizabeth Leads the Way.* New York: Henry Holt.
Begins with a "What if . . .?" lead.

Stonehouse, Bernard. 2000. *Partners.* New York: Scholastic.
Introduction uses a compare/contrast format.

Swinburne, Stephen. 2006. *Wings of Light.* Honesdale, PA: Boyds Mills.
Begins by creating a scene.

Szabo, Corinne. 1997. *Sky Pioneer: A Photobiography of Amelia Earhart.*
New York: Scholastic.
Introduction and conclusion use primary sources—quotes from Amelia
Earhart.

Tagholm, Sally. 2001. *The Complete Book of the Night.* New York:
Kingfisher.
Introduction is a description of nightfall; conclusion is a description of
dawn—the end of the night; each section also has an introduction
written in various formats.

Thimmesh, Catherine. 2006. *Team Moon: How 400,000 People Landed
Apollo 11 on the Moon.* New York: Houghton Mifflin.
Introduction is built around two strategies, creating a scene and creating
a sense of era; wraps around to creating a scene in conclusion.

Theodorou, Rod, and Carole Telford. 2000. *Lizards and Snakes.* Crystal
Lake, IL: Rigby.
Example of a definition lead found on the first two pages, which are
labeled "Introduction."

Thomson, Sarah. 2005. *Imagine a Day*. New York: Atheneum.
A useful book to create an imagine or "What if . . .?" lead.

Weber, Belinda. 2004. *Animal Disguises*. Boston: Kingfisher.
Example of a definition lead.

Wilkes, Angela. 2002. *Rain Forest*. New York: Kingfisher.
Begins with a question that is answered with a definition.

Winters, Kay. 2003. *Abe Lincoln: The Boy Who Loved Books*. New York: Simon and Schuster.
Begins with a detailed description; conclusion is a list of characteristics.

Yolen, Jane. 1996. *Welcome to the Sea of Sand*. New York: G. P. Putnam's Sons.
Opens with a description of setting.

Chapter 5: Writing to Persuade

Allen, Judy. 2002. *Are You an Ant?* New York: Kingfisher.
Provides facts to support arguments about ants.

Anderson, Laurie Halse. 2002. *Thank You, Sarah: The Woman Who Saved Thanksgiving*. New York: Simon and Schuster.
Demonstrates the power of writing and having sound reasons or arguments in order to persuade.

Arnosky, Jim. 2002. *All About Frogs*. New York: Scholastic.
An example of a voice change from third person to first person to offer a point of view.

Babbitt, Natalie. 1975. *Tuck Everlasting*. New York: Farrar, Straus and Giroux.
Can be used to introduce written response from the point of view of a character or the student as a persuasive argument developed from a pro/con chart.

Blume, Judy. 1972. *Tales of a Fourth Grade Nothing*. New York: Dutton.
Can be used to help students develop arguments. They can take on the persona of a character and develop pro/con arguments to argue their case.

———. 1980. *Superfudge*. New York: Dutton.
Can be used to help students develop arguments. They can take on the persona of a character and develop pro/con arguments to argue their case.

Brenner, Barbara. 1997. *Thinking About Ants*. New York: Mondo.
Provides facts to support arguments about ants.

Brown, Marc. 1983. *Arthur's Thanksgiving*. New York: Little, Brown.
A good example of the importance of forming your arguments based on what you know about your audience.

Brown, Ruth. 1991. *The World That Jack Built*. New York: Dutton.
Simple text and richly detailed drawings work together to convince the reader of the importance of caring for the environment.

Cherry, Lynne. 1992. *A River Ran Wild*. New York: Harcourt Brace.
An informational, persuasive piece that offers facts and vivid descriptions; discusses forms of real world persuasion such as petitions, letters, and protests.

Cronin, Doreen. 2000. *Click, Clack, Moo: Cows That Type*. New York: Simon and Schuster.
Demonstrates the power of writing.

Friend, Robyn. 2007. *A Clean Sky: The Global Warming Story*. Marina Del Ray, CA: Cascade Pass.
Presents a clear point of view with supporting arguments.

Gehman, Julianne. 2007. *Hummingbirds: Tiny but Mighty*. Akron, PA: Reading Matters.
States the author's point of view in the title and in the last sentence of the text.

George, Jean Craighead. 1995. *Everglades*. New York: HarperCollins .
Demonstrates use of a questioning technique through a narrative format to persuade the reader.

Gibbons, Gail. 1992. *Recycle: A Handbook for Kids*. Boston: Little, Brown.
Uses facts, statistics, features of print, effective repetition, and exclamation marks to convince readers to recycle.

Graves, Donald. "Summer Squash." In *Baseball, Snakes, and Summer Squash: Poems About Growing Up*. Honesdale, PA: Boyds Mills.
Can be used to list pro/con arguments.

Grimes, Nikki. 2002. *Talkin' About Bessie: The Story of Aviator Elizabeth Coleman*. New York: Orchard Books.
Offers many points of view through different voices.

Hirschi, Ron. 1990. *Spring*. New York: Penguin.
One in a series of books on the seasons that can be used to list pro/con arguments for each season as the best. Other books in the series are *Winter* (1990), *Fall* (1991), and *Summer* (1991).

Hoose, Phillip, and Hannah Hoose. 1998. *Hey, Little Ant*. Berkeley, CA: Tricycle.
Shows different points of view; examples of persuasive arguments.

James, Simon. 1991. *Dear Mr. Blueberry*. New York: Simon and Schuster.
Can be used to show how arguments must be supported by fact; demonstrates that persuasive arguments may not always change someone's mind.

Jenkins, Steve. 2006. *Almost Gone: The World's Rarest Animals*. New York: HarperCollins.
Provides an example of a "What if . . .?" lead that can be used as a grabber for a persuasive piece.

Kellogg, Steven. 1971. *Can I Keep Him?* New York: Penguin.
Arguments against keeping a variety of pets.

Kitchen, Bert. 1992. *Somewhere Today*. Cambridge, MA: Candlewick.
An example of a lead that can be imitated as a grabber lead for a persuasive piece.

Laminack, Lester. 2007. *Snow Day*. Atlanta: Peachtree.
Offers a point of view through the use of humor.

Lollis, Sylvia. 2003. *Should We Have Pets?* New York: Mondo.
Defines persuasive writing; great examples of supporting arguments with facts; encourages the evaluation of arguments; a great book about persuasive writing written by a group of second graders.

Lopez, Gary. 2007. *Sharks*. Chanhassen, MN: The Child's World.
Uses facts in several sections that are persuasive in nature.

Mass, Robert. 1993. *When Summer Comes*. New York: Henry Holt.
Can be used to list pro/con arguments for summer as the best season.

Micucci, Charles. 2003. *The Life and Times of the Ant*. New York: Houghton Mifflin.
Provides facts to support arguments about ants.

Naylor, Phyllis Reynolds. 1991. *Shiloh*. New York: Dell.
Offers opportunities for response to literature written from the viewpoint of one or several of the characters; spin-off persuasive piece concerning animal rights.

Noble, Trinka Hakes. 2004. *The Scarlet Stockings Spy*. Chelsea, MI: Sleeping Bear.
A tie to the curriculum with historical fiction that can be used to write persuasively from the point of view of the main character or the student.

———. 2007. *The Pennsylvania Reader*. Chelsea, MI: Sleeping Bear.
Appropriate content to build a point of view about living in the Pennsylvania colony.

O'Connor, Jane. 2003. *The Perfect Puppy for Me!* New York: Penguin.
Provides facts that can be used in persuasive arguments for a pet (dog); possibilities for counterarguments and different points of view.

Okimoto, Jean Davies. 2007. *Winston of Churchill: One Bear's Battle Against Global Warming*. Seattle: Sasquatch Books.
Demonstrates different ways arguments can be presented.

Orloff, Karen Kaufman. 2004. *I Wanna Iguana*. New York: G. P. Putnam's Sons.
    Written in letter format; presents arguments and counterarguments.

Palatini, Margie. 2003. *The Perfect Pet*. New York: HarperCollins.
    Presents reasons for getting a pet; can be used for evaluating arguments.

Pluckrose, Henry. 1994. *Changing Seasons*. Chicago: Children's Press.
    Can be used to list pro/con arguments for seasons.

Prelutsky, Jack. 1990. "Belinda Blue." In *Something Big Has Been Here*. New
    York: Greenwillow Books.
    Can be used to list pro/con arguments.

Rockwell, Anne. 2006. *Why Are the Ice Caps Melting? The Dangers of
    Global Warming*. New York: HarperCollins.
    Provides facts about global warming that could be used to write a
    persuasive piece.

Rylant, Cynthia. 2000. *In November*. New York: Harcourt.
    Can be used to list pro/con arguments for fall as the best season.

Salisbury, Graham. 1994. *Under the Blood-Red Sun*. New York: Delacorte.
    Through the characters, myriad points of view are presented.

Schulman, Janet. 2008. *Pale Male: Citizen Hawk of New York City*. New
    York: Alfred A. Knopf.
    Examples of forms of persuasive writing.

Silverstein, Shel. 1974. "Sarah Cynthia Sylvia Stout Would Not Take the
    Garbage Out." In *Where the Sidewalk Ends*. New York: Harper and Row.
    Can be used to list pro/con arguments.

Snihura, Ulana. 1998. *I Miss Franklin P. Shuckles*. New York: Annick Press.
    Can be used to list pro/con arguments for friendship.

Spinelli, Eileen. 2004. *I Know It's Autumn*. New York: HarperCollins.
    Can be used to list pro/con arguments for autumn as the best season.

———. 2007. *Where I Live*. New York: Dial Books.
    Can be used to chart the different points of view of the characters.
    Students could take on the persona of a character and write about why
    or why not Diana's family should move.

Stead, Tony, and Judy Ballester. 2002. *Should There Be Zoos? A Persuasive
    Text*. New York: Mondo.
    Persuasive arguments with opposing points of view written by children.

Swain, Gwenyth. 2002. *Pennsylvania*. Minneapolis: Lerner.
    Offers facts about Pennsylvania that can be used to support arguments
    about the state; part of the Hello USA series on each of the fifty states
    plus Puerto Rico and Washington, D.C.

Thomson, Sarah. 2005. *Imagine a Day*. New York: Atheneum.
    An example of an imagine lead that can be used as a grabber for a
    persuasive piece.

Uegaki, Chieri. 2003. *Suki's Kimono*. Towanda, NY: Kids Can Press.
    Represents various culturally based points of view.

Van Laan, Nancy. 2000. *When Winter Comes*. New York: Atheneum.
    Can be used to list pro/con arguments for winter as the best season.

Viorst, Judith. 1988. *The Good-Bye Book*. New York: Macmillan.
    A good book to use for evaluating arguments.

———. 1990. *Earrings!* New York: Macmillan.
    A good book to use for evaluating arguments.

———. 1995. *Alexander, Who's Not (Do You Hear Me? I Mean It!) Going to Move*. New York: Atheneum.
    A good book to use for evaluating arguments.

Wells, Rosemary. 1998. *Yoko*. New York: Hyperion.
    An example of a culturally based point of view.

———. 2008. *Otto Runs for President*. New York: Scholastic.
    Bumper stickers, slogans, and buttons as forms of persuasive writing; written for a younger audience.

White, E.B. 1952. *Charlotte's Web*. New York: Harper and Row.
    Can be used to chart pro/con arguments for selecting a friend.

Winters, Kay. 2008. *Colonial Voices: Hear Them Speak*. New York: Dutton.
    A collection of poems that expresses the different points of view of various colonists concerning the Boston Tea Party; includes a glossary and historical notes.

Yep, Lawrence. 1995. *Hiroshima*. New York: Scholastic.
    Offers perspectives around a compelling topic.

Zolotow, Charlotte. 1972. *William's Doll*. New York: HarperCollins.
    An example of a gender-based point of view.

———. 1992. *The Seashore Book*. New York: HarperCollins.
    Can be used to provide facts about the seashore that can be used to write a persuasive piece.

The following books were used in the examples of book reviews:

Cazet, Denys. 1990. *Never Spit on Your Shoes*. New York: Orchard Books.
Clark, Margaret Goff. 1980. *Freedom Crossing*. New York: Scholastic.
dePaola, Tomie. 1997. *Strega Nona*. New York: Aladdin.
Horowitz, Ruth. 2000. *Crab Moon*. Cambridge, MA: Candlewick.
Jenkins, Martin. 1999. *The Emperor's Egg*. Cambridge, MA: Candlewick.
Kehret, Peg. 1996. *Small Steps: The Year I Got Polio*. Morton Grove, IL: Albert Whitman.
Lester, Helen. 1988. *Tacky the Penguin*. Boston: Houghton Mifflin.
MacLachlan, Patricia, and Emily MacLachlan. 2003. *Painting the Wind*. New York: HarperCollins.

Osborne, Mary Pope. 1995. *Afternoon on the Amazon.* New York: Random House.

Scott, Liz, and Jay Scott (with help from Alex Scott). 2004. *Alex and the Amazing Lemonade Stand.* Wynnewood, PA: Paje.

Willems, Mo. 2006. *Don't Let the Pigeon Stay Up Late!* New York: Hyperion.

Chapter 6: Nonfiction Writing in the Real World (and Other Interesting Formats to Engage Student Writers)

Ada, Alma Flor. 1994. *Dear Peter Rabbit.* New York: Aladdin.
Examples of a friendly letter format.

Allard, Denise. 1997. *Postcards from the United States.* New York: Raintree Steck-Vaughn.
Demonstrates postcard content and format, including postscript; combines facts with personalized statements.

Ammon, Richard. 2001. *Amish Horses.* New York: Atheneum.
Can be used to pull out topics for creating a narrative recipe.

Armstrong, Jennifer. 2001. *Thomas Jefferson: Letters from a Philadelphia Bookworm.* New York: Winslow.
A series of fictitious letters written to Thomas Jefferson; includes research done with primary source documents to imagine what the letters might have contained and/or looked like. Part of the Dear Mr. President series.

Arnosky, Jim. 1999. *Crinkleroot's Nature Almanac.* New York: Simon and Schuster.
A real-world format that offers nature facts. Includes examples of how-to writing, nature journaling, and life cycles.

Beery, Barbara. 2006. *Pink Princess Cookbook.* Layton, UT: Gibbs Smith.
Children's cookbook that includes photographs.

Brown, Lisa. 2006. *How to Be.* New York: HarperCollins.
Provides a scaffold for simple advice beginning each sentence with a verb.

Bryant, Jen. 2005. *Georgia's Bones.* Grand Rapids, MI: Eerdmans Books for Young Readers.

———. 2008. *A River of Words: The Story of William Carlos Williams.* Grand Rapids, MI: Eerdmans Books for Young Readers.
Illustrator's note by Melissa Sweet discusses the research and her techniques.

Buckley, Annie. 2007. *Hero Girls.* Chanhassen, MN: The Child's World.
A great model for writing hero essays; also provides ideas for real-world projects.

Bull, Jane. 2002. *The Cooking Book*. New York: DK.
    Recipes include pictures and easy-to-follow directions; offers advice.

Bunting, Eve. 1999. *Butterfly House*. New York: Scholastic.
    Includes an afterword from the author on how to raise a butterfly.

Campbell, Janis, and Cathy Collison. 2005. *G Is for Galaxy: An Out of This World Alphabet*. Chelsea, MI: Sleeping Bear Press.
    An example of an ABC format in rhyme. Each page contains additional information about the subject.

Caney, Steven. 1985. *Steven Caney's Invention Book*. New York: Workman.
    Provides step-by-step directions for easy-to-do home projects.

Chapman, Gillian, and Pam Robson. 1991. *Making Books: A Step-by-Step Guide to Your Own Publishing*. Brookfield, CT: Millbrook.
    A how-to book using headings, subheadings, pictures, and labels to demonstrate how to make books.

Clark, Diane C. 1989. *A Kid's Guide to Washington, D.C.* New York: Harcourt Brace.
    Useful format for teaching students how to write guides with "Did you know . . .?" and "helpful hints" formats.

Collins, Mary. 2003. *Airborne: A Photobiography of Wilbur and Orville Wright*. Washington, DC: National Geographic.
    Examples of primary source documents employed in writing to enhance content; how-to explanations are embedded in text.

Cooney, Barbara. 1994. *Only Opal: The Diary of a Young Girl*. New York: Philomel Books.
    Provides examples for young writers of observations and wonderings that could be included in a diary; includes an author's note that explains the origin of the diary.

Crossingham, John. 2003. *Lacrosse in Action*. New York: Crabtree.
    Offers many step-by-step directions and explanations.

Danneberg, Julie. 2003. *First Year Letters*. Watertown, MA: Charlesbridge.
    Provides an example of the friendly letter format.

Dodge, Abigail Johnson. 2008. *Around the World Cookbook*. New York: DK.
    Easy-to-follow directions with photographs from around the world; includes sections on utensils, setting up, and cleaning up.

Dray, Philip. 2008. *Yours for Justice, Ida B. Wells: The Daring Life of a Crusading Journalist*. Atlanta: Peachtree.
    Contains examples of primary source documents.

Edwards, Pamela Duncan. 2001. *Boston Tea Party*. New York: Putnam.
    An easy scaffold for recipe writing; "ingredients" are added and repeated using the familiar scaffold of "The House That Jack Built."

Eldin, Peter. 2007. *The Most Excellent Book of How to Be a Magician.* Mankato, MN: Stargazer Books.
Great how-to book on magic tricks; uses numbered steps and includes practical tips.

Ewald, Wendy. 2002. *The Best Part of Me: Children Talk About Their Bodies in Pictures and Words.* New York: Little, Brown.
An example of using photographs to inspire writing.

Fletcher, Ralph. 2007. *How to Write Your Life Story.* New York: HarperCollins.
Offers strategies to get started with autobiographical writing; includes examples of interview format.

Forman, Michael H. 1997. *From Wax to Crayon.* New York: Children's Press.
Details the sequence of steps in making crayons; can be used for procedural or how-to writing.

Frank, John. 2007. *How To Catch a Fish.* New York: Roaring Brook Press.
Each page provides an example of a how-to piece written in a poetic style.

———. 2008. *Keepers: Treasure-Hunt Poems.* New York: Roaring Brook Press.
Links with the use of primary source documents and writing about the past in the section "In the Attic."

Frasier, Debra. 2004. *The Incredible Water Show.* New York: Harcourt.
Writing about water and its properties as a school play; uses a creative format to provide important information.

Frazee, Marla. 2006. *Walk On! A Guide for Babies of All Ages.* New York: Harcourt.
Presents advice on how to take your first steps, with implications for children and adults who are embarking on a new journey or phase of life.

Fritz, Jean. 1969. *George Washington's Breakfast.* New York: Coward-McCann.
Demonstrates the use of primary sources to answer the essential question that is being researched; a great mentor text to demonstrate the mind-set of a researcher.

George, Jean Craighead. 2000. *How to Talk to Your Cat.* New York: HarperCollins.
An example of explanations to describe a process.

George, Lindsay Barrett. 1999. *Around the World: Who's Been Here?* New York: Greenwillow Books.
Examples of the letter format; embedded clues to answer a riddle.

Gibbons, Gail. 1990. *How a House Is Built.* New York: Holiday House.
Offers an explanation with a step-by-step sequencing; includes transition words.

———. 1992. *Recycle: A Handbook for Kids.* Boston: Little, Brown.
Offers a step-by-step solution to the problem of trash.

Gigliotti, Jim. 2007. *Smoke Jumpers.* Chanhassen, MN: The Child's World.
A great mentor text for writing about a career; uses features of nonfiction; could be used to create interview questions.

Gold, Rozanne. 2006. *Kids Cook 1-2-3: Recipes for Young Chefs Using Only 3 Ingredients.* New York: Bloomsbury.
Recipes are divided into foods for different times of the day; simple directions; description of each dish is persuasive in nature; appetizing titles for each dish.

Gomi, Taro. 2006. *My Friends=Mis Amigos.* San Francisco: Chronicle Books.
Can be used to help young writers think of something they learned to do from someone else and how to explain it for procedural writing.

Gravett, Emily. 2006. *Meerkat Mail.* New York: Simon and Schuster.
Provides models of real postcards.

Haas, Jessie. 2002. *Appaloosa Zebra: A Horse Lover's Alphabet.* New York: Greenwillow Books.
Uses alliteration in an ABC format to present information about horses.

Hay, Donna. 2000. *Cool Kids Cook.* New York: HarperCollins.
Includes an introduction; easy step-by-step directions with pictures; safety and time-saving tips; and pictures and descriptions of tools needed.

Hearne, Betsy. 1997. *Seven Brave Women.* New York: Greenwillow Books.
A mentor text to help students create a family history using common threads to connect the generations; includes an author's note.

Hodgkins, Fran. 2007. *How People Learned to Fly.* New York: HarperCollins.
Contains a how-to paragraph for making a paper airplane.

Hoose, Phillip, and Hannah Hoose. 1998. *Hey, Little Ant.* Berkeley, CA: Tricycle.
Can be used to write letters to authors about what students have learned in order to persuade characters to act in a certain way.

Hopkinson, Deborah. 1997. *Birdie's Lighthouse.* New York: Atheneum.
Imagined diary entries based on experiences of true lighthouse heroines of the 1800s; includes an author's note.

Hummon, David. 1999. *Animal Acrostics.* Nevada City, CA: Dawn Publications.
Includes a how-to for writing an acrostic poem.

Iverson, Diane. 1996. *Discover the Seasons.* Nevada City, CA: Dawn Publications.
Recipe writing and how-to paragraphs; offers many step-by-step directions and explanations.

Katz, Susan. 2004. A *Revolutionary Field Trip: Poems of Colonial America*. New York: Simon and Schuster.
Provides an example of a creative format (verse) for reporting about history.

Kirkland, Jane. 2001. *Take a Backyard Bird Walk*. Lionville, PA: Stillwater.
Great examples of how to take notes about nature.

———. 2005. *Take a City Nature Walk*. Lionville, PA: Stillwater.
A good source for children living in the city for how to observe and identify nature.

———. 2007. *Take a Beach Walk*. Lionville, PA: Stillwater.
An excellent resource (as are the other Take a Walk books) to demonstrate what constitutes a field guide; offers help and suggestions for observing and recording nature at the beach.

Koscielniak, Bruce. 2003. *Johann Gutenberg and the Amazing Printing Press*. Boston: Houghton Mifflin.
How-to descriptions for making ink, pouring type, and printing—all in various formats.

Kuntz, Lynn, and Jan Fleming. 1997. *American Grub: Eats for Kids from All Fifty States*. Layton, UT: Gibbs Smith.
Recipes from every state; includes list of equipment needed as well as ingredients; helpful illustrations.

Leedy, Loreen. 2000. *Mapping Penny's World*. New York: Henry Holt.
Provides examples of different kinds of maps to help students create their own; examples are embedded in a friendly, narrative format.

———. 2006. *Postcards from Pluto: A Tour of the Solar System*. New York: Holiday House.
Postcard format with postscripts as well as addresses displayed and a stamp for each planet; facts included within personalized messages.

Levine, Shar, and Leslie Johnstone. 2005. *Kitchen Science*. New York: Sterling.
A book of science experiments written as recipes; includes explanations of what the experiment demonstrated.

Lobel, Anita. 1990. *Alison's Zinnia*. New York: Mulberry Books.
Uses alliteration in an ABC format; each page introduces the next letter by ending with a word that starts with that letter.

———. 1994. *Away from Home*. New York: Greenwillow Books.
Uses alliteration in an ABC format.

McCarthy, Meghan. 2008. *Astronaut Handbook*. New York: Alfred A. Knopf.
Offers a guide to becoming an astronaut; written in student-friendly language in the second person.

Moss, Marissa. 2000. *Hannah's Journal: The Story of an Immigrant Girl.* New York: Harcourt.
Provides an example of creating journal entries based on a real person.

Murphy, Frank. 2002. *George Washington and the General's Dog.* New York: Random House.
Includes an example of a primary source document that led the author to write this book.

Nelson, Ray Jr., and Douglas Kelly. 1995. *Greetings from America: Postcards from Donovan and Daisy.* Portland, OR: Flying Rhinoceros.
Provides format for writing and addressing postcards; examples of how to combine facts with more personal information.

Noble, Trinka Hakes. 2007. *The Pennsylvania Reader.* Chelsea, MI: Sleeping Bear Press.
Many different formats for students to imitate, including poetry in rhyming couplets, riddles, counting rhymes, letters written in the persona of a colonial child, and reader's theater.

Paul, Ann Whitford. 1999. *All By Herself: 14 Girls Who Made a Difference.* New York: Harcourt.
Poetry to highlight famous women and their courage; useful in writing for Women's History Month to illicit interview questions.

Polacco, Patricia. 2007. *The Lemonade Club.* New York: Philomel Books.
A book based on real-world events, as most of Patricia Polacco's books are; can be used as part of an author study, and students can write postcards or letters to the author.

Rappaport, Doreen. 2001. *Martin's Big Words.* New York: Hyperion.
Includes an author's note and an illustrator's note that explain where the ideas for how to write the book came from.

Ricciuti, Edward, and Margaret W. Carruthers. 1998. *National Audubon Society First Field Guide: Rocks and Minerals.* New York: Scholastic.
A good example of what a field guide looks like; includes directions about how to navigate it.

Riley, Susan, ed. 2002. *World's Greatest Marbles Games.* Minneapolis: Compass Labs.
Provides a simple scaffold for giving directions.

Rockwell, Anne. 1973. *Games (and How to Play Them).* New York: Thomas Y. Crowell.
Directions for playing simple games; written in paragraph format.

Romanek, Trudee. 2005. *Switched On, Flushed Down, Tossed Out: Investigating the Hidden Workings of Your Home.* New York: Annick Press.
Includes unique format of case files created with facts, questions, and theories.

Ruurs, Margriet. 1996. *A Mountain Alphabet*. Plattsburgh, New York: Tundra Books.
Uses alliteration in an ABC format.

Sabin, Ellen. 2008. *The Greening Book: Being a Friend to Planet Earth*. New York: Watering Can Press.
Myriad formats including helpful hints, "Did you know . . .?" information, practical tips, and how-to.

Schuett, Stacey. 1995. *Somewhere in the World Right Now*. New York: Alfred A. Knopf.
Useful scaffold to begin a travel guide or brochure. The scaffold could also be used to compare/contrast.

Schulman, Janet. 2008. *Pale Male: Citizen Hawk of New York City*. New York: Alfred A. Knopf.
Uses narrative to capture a true-life story; illustrations display newspaper headlines and protest signs; contains an author's note describing the seed of the idea and information about hawks and New York City's parks.

Schwartz, David M. 1998. *G Is for Googol: A Math Alphabet Book*. Berkeley, CA: Tricycle.
An ABC book with tons of detailed information about the concept presented on each page.

Scott, Liz, and Jay (with help from Alex Scott). 2004. *Alex and the Amazing Lemonade Stand*. Wynnewood, PA: Paje.
A book that recounts a real-world event; can inspire class projects that would include writing a press release, advertisements, newspaper articles, and community newsletters.

Shore, Diane Z., and Jessica Alexander. 2006. *This Is the Dream*. New York: HarperCollins.
Provides an interesting and familiar scaffold (the house that Jack built) to talk about a real-world issue.

Silver, Donald M. 1993. *One Small Square: Backyard*. New York: McGraw-Hill.
This is one in a series of many One Small Square books. It gives detailed suggestions for exploring nature and recording discoveries in a notebook.

Spinelli, Eileen. 2007. *Where I Live*. New York: Dial Books.
Can be used to inspire recording observations in nature journals/ notebooks and writing poetry about nature.

Steckel, Richard, and Michele Steckel. 2004. *The Milestones Project: Celebrating Childhood Around the World*. Berkeley, CA: Tricycle.
A collection of milestone stories from students and authors to document childhood experiences around the world. Includes real-world themes, such as birthdays, lost teeth, friends, school, haircuts, glasses, and pets.

Stewart, David. 2001. *You Wouldn't Want to Sail on the Titanic! One Voyage You'd Rather Not Make.* New York: Franklin Watts.
Can be used to create guides with helpful hints.

Stewart, Sarah. 1997. *The Gardener.* New York: Farrar, Straus and Giroux.
Provides examples of the friendly letter format.

Swain, Gwenyth. 2002. *Pennsylvania.* Minneapolis: Lerner.
Examples of an annotated "places to visit" and "outstanding Pennsylvanians" list; recipe; fun facts.

Swinburne, Stephen. 2006. *Saving Manatees.* Honesdale, PA: Boyds Mills.
Connections to the real world include photographs of signs, the author working with the manatees, and references to laws; suggests resources for further reading; manatee facts, sometimes presented in lists, offer directions or paragraphs of explanations.

Tagholm, Sally. 2001. *The Complete Book of the Night.* New York: Kingfisher.
Provides examples of A to Z format, practical tips, and a how-to; also provides sidebars that lend themselves to compare/contrast structure.

Teague, Mark. 2002. *Dear Mrs. LaRue: Letters from Obedience School.* New York: Scholastic.
A mentor text for the friendly letter format; examples of headlines and feature articles for real-world news reporting.

———. 2004. *Detective LaRue: Letters from the Investigation.* New York: Scholastic.
A mentor text for the friendly letter format; examples of headlines and feature articles for real-world news reporting.

Thomas, Keltie. 2004. *How Baseball Works.* New York: Firefly Books.
Breaks up the process of how to play baseball into more manageable chunks; can be used as a model for writing a how-to for one aspect of a more complex process.

Webb, Sophie. 2004. *Looking for Seabirds: Journal from an Alaskan Voyage.* Boston: Houghton Mifflin.
A series of notebook entries that provides examples of scientific writing, including maps, diagrams, charts, drawings with labels, and graphs.

Weil, Carolyn Beth. 2006. *Williams-Sonoma Sweet Treats.* New York: Free Press.
Recipe book with easy-to-follow, step-by-step directions; lists ingredients and tools needed.

White, Kelly, ed. 2003. *The Girls' Life Guide to Being the Best You!* New York: Scholastic.
Can be used as a mentor text for a survival guide.

Wild, Margaret. 1994. *Our Granny.* Boston: Houghton Mifflin.
A great model for compare/contrast structure to create real-world text.

Williams, Vera. 1981. *Three Days on a River in a Red Canoe*. New York: Greenwillow Books.
Includes examples of recipes, step-by-step directions, and chronicles of a trip.

Wilson, Karma. 2007. *How to Bake an American Pie*. New York: Simon and Schuster.
An example of a recipe or how-to format; uses the language of recipes in a rhyming format but applies it to a broader concept, in this case, America.

Woodruff, Elvira. 1998. *Dear Austin: Letters from the Underground Railroad*. New York: Alfred A. Knopf.
Story told through letter format.

Zalben, Jane Breskin. 1999. *To Every Season: A Family Holiday Cookbook*. New York: Simon and Schuster.
A cookbook organized around holidays. In addition to recipes, each holiday has a short explanation about its origin and history.

Zolotow, Charlotte. 1992. *This Quiet Lady*. New York: HarperCollins.
A work of fiction that can serve children who would like to write a focused family history with drawings and/or photographs. It shows writers how to pick out important events to highlight.

———. 1993. *The Moon Was the Best*. New York: Greenwillow Books.
Provides a scaffold to describe a place as a series of unique snapshots.

Zschock, Martha Day. 2006. *Journey Around Philadelphia From A to Z*. Beverly, MA: Commonwealth Editions.
Provides an example of an ABC format that can be used for writing about real-world issues; includes an interesting layout with a code at the bottom of each page.

Chapter 7: Voice, Syntax, and Conventions in Nonfiction

Ajmera, Maya, Michael Regan, and the Global Fund for Children. 2000. *Let the Games Begin!* Watertown, MA: Charlesbridge.
Creates a conversational voice by asking questions and offering advice.

Allen, Judy. 2000. *Are You a Spider?* Boston: Kingfisher.
Written in the persona of a spider; second person narration; variety of sentence structures; use of ellipses and hyphenated adjectives.

———. 2002. *Are You an Ant?* Boston: Kingfisher.
Written in the persona of an ant; second-person narration; humor; dashes; strong verbs and exact nouns. This book is one in a series of Backyard Books.

Anderson, Laurie Halse. 2002. *Thank You, Sarah: The Woman Who Saved Thanksgiving.* New York: Simon and Schuster.
Written in a friendly voice with a touch of sarcasm; use of ellipses and variation in print.

———. 2008. *Independent Dames: What You Never Knew About the Women and Girls of the American Revolution.* New York: Simon and Schuster.
Written in a friendly voice with a touch of sarcasm; use of parentheses and dashes.

Aston, Dianna. 2006. *An Egg Is Quiet.* San Francisco: Chronicle Books.
Examples of metaphors; poetic voice.

———. 2007. *A Seed Is Sleepy.* San Francisco: Chronicle Books.
Examples of metaphors; poetic voice.

Bouchard, David. 1994. *The Colours of British Columbia.* Vancouver, BC: Raincoast Books.
Rhyming couplets describe the colors found in British Columbia; most pages alternate between verses written in the second person and the first person; use of the repeated refrain "I remember . . ."

———. 1995. *If You're Not from the Prairie.* New York: Simon and Schuster.
Rhyming verse about the prairie; contains the repeated refrain "If you're not from the prairie . . .," which can be used as a scaffold; can be used to study italics and other print conventions.

———. 1996. *Voices from the Wild: An Animal Sensagoria.* San Francisco: Chronicle Books.
A series of poems about animals, organized around the senses. Some poems are written in first person and some in second person. The book is framed by poems posing a series of questions to the reader, inviting response. The final pages offer additional information about each of the animals featured.

———. 1997. *Prairie Born.* Custer, WA: Orca.
Prairie memories written as verse and organized around the seasons; contains a repeated refrain.

Brenner, Barbara. 1997. *Thinking About Ants.* New York: Mondo.
Creates a conversational voice by asking questions and offering advice.

Bryant, Jen. 2005. *Georgia's Bones.* Grand Rapids, MI: Eerdmans Books for Young Readers.
A rhythmic and lyrical biography of Georgia O'Keefe; provides examples of dashes, word pairs, and dialogue.

———. 2005. *Music for the End of Time.* Grand Rapids, MI: Eerdmans Books for Young Readers.
Provides examples of dialogue, ellipses, and dashes.

————. 2008. *A River of Words: The Story of William Carlos Williams.*
Grand Rapids, MI: Eerdmans Books for Young Readers.
Examples of onomatopeia, alliteration, and proper nouns; use of ellipses,
dashes, and colons.

Burleigh, Robert. 2000. *Edna.* New York: Orchard Books.
Offers examples of proper nouns, dashes, dialogue, and parentheses.

————. 2003. *Into the Woods: John James Audubon Lives His Dream.* New
York: Atheneum.
Assumes the voice of Audubon through an imaginary conversation with
his father; examples of specific verbs and nouns, dashes, use of rhyme,
parentheses, and onomatopoeia.

Camper, Cathy. 2002. *Bugs Before Time: Prehistoric Insects and Their
Relatives.* New York: Simon and Schuster.
Provides examples of exact nouns and verbs, dashes, proper nouns,
variation of print, and exclamatory sentences.

Clark, Margaret Goff. 1980. *Freedom Crossing.* New York: Scholastic.
Words or phrases from this book can be used to create found poetry.

Cleary, Brian P. 1999. *A Mink, a Fink, a Skating Rink: What Is a Noun?*
Minneapolis: Millbrook.
One in a series of books that explains and gives examples of a particular
part of speech. Other books focus on adjectives, adverbs, verbs, and
prepositions.

Collard, Sneed B., III. 2000. *The Forest in the Clouds.* Watertown, MA:
Charlesbridge.
Written in a conversational voice; similes; onomatopoeia.

————. 2002. *Leaving Home.* New York: Houghton Mifflin.
Simple text that speaks directly to the reader in a conversational way.

Davies, Nicola. 2001. *Bat Loves the Night.* Cambridge, MA: Candlewick.
Personalizes the subject by using Bat as a name; beautiful word choice,
including similes and strong verbs.

DeGross, Monalisa. 1994. *Donovan's Word Jar.* New York: HarperCollins.
A fictional book that can be used to get young writers interested in word
collecting.

Dray, Philip. 2008. *Yours for Justice, Ida B. Wells: The Daring Life of a
Crusading Journalist.* Atlanta: Peachtree.
Examples of commentary dashes; proper nouns for specificity; strong
verbs; use of colon and commas of apposition; variety of sentence types.

Edwards, Pamela Duncan. 1997. *Barefoot: Escape on the Underground
Railroad.* New York: HarperCollins.
Variety of sentence structure and rhythm of language provides
background information for writing a lyric summary.

Ferris, Jeri. 1988. *Go Free or Die: A Story About Harriet Tubman.*
Minneapolis: Carolrhoda Books.
Variety of sentence structure and rhythm of language provides
background information for writing a lyric summary.

Florian, Douglas. 2007. *Comets, Stars, the Moon, and Mars.* New York:
Harcourt.
A collection of poems about objects in space; includes an annotated
glossary with additional factual information.

Frasier, Debra. 2000. *Miss Alaineus: A Vocabulary Disaster.* New York:
Harcourt.
A picture book that can be used to get students interested in words and
word meaning.

———. 2004. *The Incredible Water Show.* New York: Harcourt.
Use of exclamations (often interjections), variation in print sizes, ellipses,
colon, and onomatopoeia; particular nomenclature (e.g., Pirates);
commentary dashes.

Fredericks, Anthony D. 2001. *Under One Rock: Bugs, Slugs, and Other
Ughs.* Nevada City, CA: Dawn Publications.
Opens with a letter in the voice of a spider; whispering parentheses;
hyphenated adjectives; commentary dashes; alliteration; rhyme and
rhythm.

———. 2006. *On One Flower: Butterflies, Ticks and a Few More Icks.*
Nevada City, CA: Dawn Publications.
Opens with a letter in the voice of a stink bug; whispering parentheses;
hyphenated adjectives; commentary dashes; alliteration; rhyme and
rhythm.

Freedman, Russell. 1987. *Lincoln: A Photobiography.* New York: Clarion
Books.
An example of how an author can bring an historical figure to life and
write with voice.

Frost, Helen. 2008. *Monarch and Milkweed.* New York: Atheneum.
A life-cycle book; creates interest and personalizes the subject matter by
using Monarch and Milkweed as names; contains examples of
semicolons, commas, dashes, and ellipses.

Ganeri, Anita. 1995. *I Wonder Why the Sea Is Salty and Other Questions
About the Ocean.* Boston: Kingfisher.
Contains examples of dashes.

Garland, Sherry. 2000. *Voices of the Alamo.* New York: Scholastic.
Demonstrates how a writer can develop a book through many different
voices; closely associated with point of view.

Gershwin, George, DuBose Heyward, Dorothy Heyward, and Ira Gershwin.
1999. *Summertime*. New York: Simon and Schuster.
The book is the song "Summertime" from *Porgy and Bess,* with
beautiful illustrations by Mike Wimmer; provides a model for a song
that can be used for writing lyric summaries.

Gibbons, Gail. 1997. *The Moon Book.* New York: Holiday House.
Gives facts about the moon that can be embedded into poetry; variety of
sentences and sentence beginnings; strong verbs and adjectives.

———. 2002. *Behold . . . the Unicorns!* New York: HarperCollins.
Use of proper nouns for specificity; foreign words to add flavor;
hyphenated adjectives; use of apostrophe; commas of apposition and in
a series; commentary dashes; use of ellipses.

Giblin, James Cross. 1994. *Thomas Jefferson: A Picture Book Biography.*
New York: Scholastic.
Provides examples of strong verbs, proper nouns, dashes, variation in
sentence structure and length.

Gigliotti, Jim. 2007. *Smoke Jumpers.* Chanhassen, MN: The Child's World.
Whispering parentheses; hyphenated adjectives; commentary dashes;
exact nouns; asks questions to create and maintain interest; use of
quotation marks to denote that the word or phrase has a special meaning.

Gill, Shelley. *The Egg.* Watertown, MA: Charlesbridge.
Provides examples of the use of the dash.

Hearne, Betsy. 1997. *Seven Brave Women.* New York: Greenwillow Books.
Use of commentary dashes, whispering parentheses, conventions of
print, colons, and proper nouns for specificity.

Heller, Ruth. 1988. *Kites Sail High: A Book About Verbs.* New York: Grosset
and Dunlap.
One in a series of books that each explain a specific part of speech.

High, Linda Oatman. 2004. *City of Snow: The Great Blizzard of 1888.* New
York: Walker.
Provides examples of hyphenated adjectives, specific verbs (often in
pairs), similes, personification, use of proper nouns, colons, and
alliteration.

———. 2007. *The Cemetery Keepers of Gettysburg.* New York: Walker.
Provides examples of similes, adjective pairs, commentary dashes, a
sprinkle of dialogue, proper nouns, hyphenated adjectives, and
alliteration.

Hillman, Ben. 2007. *How Big Is It? A Big Book All About Bigness.* New
York: Scholastic.
Use of questions and parentheses to establish a conversational voice;
dashes; proper nouns; use of colon.

Hiscock, Bruce. 2008. *Ookpik: The Travels of a Snowy Owl*. Honesdale, PA: Boyds Mills.
Examples of strong verbs, onomatopoeia, and variety of sentence structures; lots of opportunities to explore grammar and conventions by studying sentences.

Hoberman, Mary Ann. 2004. *Yankee Doodle*. New York: Little, Brown.
Provides a model for a song that can be used for writing lyric summaries.

Hopkinson, Deborah. 1997. *Birdie's Lighthouse*. New York: Atheneum.
Written in an imagined voice—the collective voice of many lighthouse heroines; dashes; appeal to senses; strong verbs and special vocabulary.

———. 2006. *Sky Boys: How They Built the Empire State Building*. New York: Random House.
Written in the second person; examples of print variations; use of commas, colons, semicolons, strong verbs, and similes.

Howard, Elizabeth Fitzgerald. 1999. *Virgie Goes to School with Us Boys*. New York: Simon and Schuster.
Told through the voices of black children attending a Quaker school after the Civil War.

Hummon, David. 1999. *Animal Acrostics*. Nevada City, CA: Dawn Publications.
A great book to teach the importance of word choice; contains examples of hyphenated adjectives, exact adjectives, use of colon, strong verbs, varying punctuation, and commentary dashes.

Iverson, Diane. 1996. *Discover the Seasons*. Nevada City, CA: Dawn Publications.
Strong verbs; poetry.

Jackson, Ellen. 1998. *Turn of the Century*. Watertown, MA: Charlesbridge.
Use of proper nouns; writing in the persona of another; similes; hyphenated and exact adjectives and nouns; appeal to the senses; commas in a series; exclamations; commentary dashes.

Jenkins, Martin. 1997. *Chameleons Are Cool*. Cambridge, MA: Candlewick.
Written in a humorous and lighthearted voice; examples of parentheses, hyphenated adjectives, dashes, and ellipses.

Jenkins, Steve, and Robin Page. 2001. *Animals in Flight*. Boston: Houghton Mifflin.
Provides examples of dashes, colons, adjective placement, and exact nouns and verbs.

Kalman, Maira. 2002. *Fireboat: The Heroic Adventures of the John J. Harvey*. New York: G. P. Putnam's Sons.
Offers examples of proper nouns, variation in print, and dialogue.

Keating, Frank. 2006. *Theodore*. New York: Simon and Schuster.
Written in the first person; contains actual quotations from Theodore Roosevelt.

Kennedy, Jimmy. 2000. *The Teddy Bears' Picnic*. New York: Aladdin.
Provides a model for a song that can be used for writing lyric summaries.

Kerley, Barbara. 2008. *What to Do About Alice? How Alice Roosevelt Broke the Rules, Charmed the World, and Drove Her Father Teddy Crazy!* New York: Scholastic.
Examples of print variations; use of ellipses, epithets, colons, exact and proper nouns, and dashes; quotation marks used for many different purposes.

Kirkland, Jane. 2001. *Take a Backyard Bird Walk*. Lionville, PA: Stillwater.
One in a series of Take a Walk books that establishes a conversational tone with the reader through the use of second-person voice.

Koscielniak, Bruce. 2003. *Johann Gutenberg and the Amazing Printing Press*. Boston: Houghton Mifflin.
Use of parentheses to provide explanations and create a conversational tone.

Kramer, Stephen. 1992. *Lightning*. Minneapolis: Carolrhoda Books.
Use of questions, italics, and parentheses.

Leedy, Loreen. 2006. *Postcards from Pluto: A Tour of the Solar System*. New York: Holiday House.
Whispering parentheses; commentary dashes; variation in print; humor in speech bubble offered by each planet; riddles; poems; picture writing (rebus).

Lewis, J. Patrick. 2005. *Monumental Verses*. Washington, DC: National Geographic Society.
A collection of different types of poems about some of the great monuments of the world; can be studied for word choice or conventions.

Loewen, Nancy. 2007. *If You Were a Conjunction*. Minneapolis: Picture Window Books.
Explains the use of conjunctions with sample sentences.

Markle, Sandra. 1996. *Creepy, Crawly Baby Bugs*. New York: Walker.
Written in a conversational tone with questions and advice.

Maruki, Toshi. 1980. *Hiroshima No Pika*. New York: Lothrop, Lee and Shepard Books.
Provides examples of strong adjectives and verbs, dashes, proper nouns, and similes.

Matthews, Elizabeth. 2007. *Different Like Coco*. Cambridge, MA: Candlewick.
Use of foreign language (French) to add authenticity and flavor; hyphenated adjectives and proper nouns for specificity; strong adjectives; alliteration; use of commentary dashes; quotation marks to highlight words that have a hidden meaning; similes; adjective pairs.

McGee, Marni. 2006. *Winston the Book Wolf*. New York: Walker.
A picture book that can be used to interest students in words.

Miller, Debbie S. 2000. *River of Life*. New York: Houghton Mifflin.
Establishes a conversational tone by asking the reader questions; written in the present tense; use of onomatopoeia, strong verbs, and commas.

Murphy, Frank. 2000. *The Legend of the Teddy Bear*. Chelsea, MN: Sleeping Bear Press.
Use of proper nouns, ellipses, and quotation marks for conversation.

———. 2001. *Ben Franklin and the Magic Squares*. New York: Random House.
Use of italics, exclamation marks, commas, ellipses, parentheses, and dashes.

———. 2002. *George Washington and the General's Dog*. New York: Random House.
Use of dashes, italics, proper nouns, and end punctuation.

———. 2002. *Always Inventing: The True Story of Thomas Alva Edison*. New York: Scholastic.
Use of dashes, quotation marks, commas, and exclamation marks.

———. 2003. *Thomas Jefferson's Feast*. New York: Random House.
Written in a conversational tone; establishes voice through the use of whispering parentheses.

———. 2005. *Babe Ruth Saves Baseball!* New York: Random House.
Use of dashes, exclamation marks, commas, proper nouns, and quotation marks.

O'Connor, Jane. 2003. *The Perfect Puppy for Me!* New York: Penguin Putnam.
Proper nouns; voice through unique language and humor; sentence variety; commentary dashes; interjections.

Orloff, Karen Kaufman. 2004. *I Wanna Iguana*. New York: G. P. Putnam's Sons.
Adjectives used to describe the boy relate to the argument he is giving; parentheses; ellipses; dialogue; variety of sentence types.

Peterson, Cris. 1996. *Harvest Year*. Honesdale, PA: Boyds Mills.
Includes proper nouns, commas, ellipses, hyphenated adjectives, similes, and alliteration.

Pollock, Penny. 2001. *When the Moon Is Full*. New York: Little, Brown.
A companion book to Cynthia Rylant's *Long Night Moon*; can be used to study word choice, particularly verbs and adjectives; contains additional information about the moon on the final pages.

Prap, Lila. 2005. *Why?* La Jolla, CA: Kane/Miller.
Used to create interest in riddle writing and humor.

Pringle, Laurence. 2000. *Bats! Strange and Wonderful.* Honesdale, PA: Boyds Mills.
Introduction is written in the second person.

Ransford, Sandy. 1995. *Otter.* Boston: Kingfisher.
Provides examples of the use of the dash.

Ryder, Joanne. 1982. *The Snail's Spell.* New York: Penguin.
Written in the second person; invites the reader to imagine himself or herself as a snail.

———. 1989. *White Bear, Ice Bear.* New York: William Morrow.
Written in the second person; examples of personification, specific adjectives, effective repetition, strong verbs, adjective placement, and dashes.

———. 1993. *The Goodbye Walk.* New York: Lodestar Books.
Written in the second person; examples of adjectives placed after the noun, similes, hyphenated adjectives, ellipses, dashes, colons, and strong verbs.

Rylant, Cynthia. 2004. *Long Night Moon.* New York: Simon and Schuster.
Poems about the full moon in each of the twelve months; can be used to study word choice, particularly verbs and adjectives; a companion book to Penny Pollock's *When the Moon Is Full.*

———. 2006. *The Journey: Stories of Migration.* New York: Scholastic.
Use of dashes, parentheses, colons, italics, proper nouns, specific verbs, exact adjectives, and exclamatory sentences.

Schroeder, Alan. 1996. *Minty: A Story of Young Harriet Tubman.* New York: Dial Books.
Variety of sentence structure and rhythm of language provide background information for writing a lyric summary.

Schuett, Stacey. 1995. *Somewhere in the World Right Now.* New York: Alfred A. Knopf.
Uses present tense to describe what is happening in different parts of the world at one specific time; uses the repeated refrain "Somewhere in the world right now . . ." that can be used as a scaffold.

Schwartz, David M. 1998. *G Is for Googol: A Math Alphabet Book.* Berkeley, CA: Tricycle.
An ABC book with lots of voice—check it out!

Siebert, Diane. 1991. *Sierra.* New York: HarperCollins.
Written in first person from the viewpoint of the mountain; examples of colons and semicolons.

Silver, Donald M. 1993. *One Small Square: Backyard.* New York: McGraw-Hill.
One in a series of many One Small Square books, all examples of writing in the second person.

Stewart, Melissa. 2008. *When Rain Falls*. Atlanta: Peachtree.
Strong verbs and vivid adjectives; repeated refrain "When rain falls on . . ." provides a scaffold.

Stockdale, Susan. 2008. *Fabulous Fish*. Atlanta: Peachtree.
Simple text—can be used to teach parts of speech (nouns, verbs, adjectives).

Swanson, Diane. 2005. *The Wonder in Water*. Buffalo, NY: Firefly Books.
Contains many examples of dashes.

Swinburne, Stephen. 1998. *Moon in Bear's Eyes*. Honesdale, PA: Boyds Mills.
Onomatopeia, strong verbs, variety of sentence beginnings and length, and use of commas; hyphenated adjectives.

———. 2005. *Turtle Tide*. Honesdale, PA: Boyds Mills.
Provides examples of the use of dashes.

———. 2006. *Saving Manatees*. Honesdale, PA: Boyds Mills.
Written in a very conversational tone; use of proper nouns and dashes.

———. 2006. *Wings of Light*. Honesdale, PA: Boyds Mills.
Written in the present tense; examples of the use of proper nouns and hyphenated adjectives.

Thimmesh, Catherine. 2006. *Team Moon: How 400,000 People Landed Apollo 11 on the Moon*. New York: Houghton Mifflin.
Uses parentheses to make a complex subject more reader friendly, adding a conversational tone or voice; uses dashes.

Towle, Wendy. 1993. *The Real McCoy: The Life of an African-American Inventor*. New York: Scholastic.
Provides examples of the use of the dash, proper nouns, and commas.

Walton, Rick. 2007. *Just Me and 6,000 Rats: A Tale of Conjunctions*. Layton, UT: Gibbs Smith.
Highlights conjunctions in sentences; can be used to study the place of conjunctions within a sentence and the punctuation needed when they are used.

Weatherford, Carole Boston. 2006. *Moses: When Harriet Tubman Led Her People to Freedom*. New York: Hyperion.
Variety of sentence structure and rhythm of language provide background information for writing a lyric summary.

White, Kelly, ed. 2003. *The Girls' Life Guide to Being the Best You!* New York: Scholastic.
Use of questions to establish a conversational tone.

Wick, Walter. 1997. *A Drop of Water*. New York: Scholastic.
Contains examples of dashes, commas, and semicolons.

Wild, Margaret. 1994. *Our Granny*. Boston: Houghton Mifflin.
Use of ellipses, lists with strong verbs and specific adjectives, and humor.

Winters, Kay. 2008. *Colonial Voices: Hear Them Speak.* New York: Dutton.
Poems written in the voices of different colonists; has examples of
variations of print, proper nouns, sprinkling of dialogue, and ellipses.

Yolen, Jane. 1998. *The Originals: Animals That Time Forgot.* New York:
Philomel Books.
A collection of story poems about many unusual animals; can be studied
for word choice or conventions.

Zolotow, Charlotte. 1992. *This Quiet Lady.* New York: HarperCollins.
Effective repetition, hyphenated adjectives, exact nouns, and adjectives
placed after the noun.

———. 1993. *The Moon Was the Best.* New York: Greenwillow Books.
Specific adjectives, similes, exact nouns, and personification.

Afterword

Today nonfiction writing is more important than ever. After all, it is closely tied with the majority of reading and real-world writing our students will be doing when they leave school to embark on careers and daily living. Often, we find that nonfiction writing included challenging forms of discourse for our students. We, as teachers, have not always found the teaching of nonfiction writing to be joyful or rewarding.

If we look to the literature, we can find stellar examples of nonfiction with voice. We can find varying formats rich in vocabulary, sentence structures, and language that often sounds more like poetry than prose. Gone are the days of voiceless nonfiction writing. Authors write passionately from their points of view and to specific target audiences. The Information Age has placed at their fingertips a colorful array of specific, accurate, and compelling facts and changing perspectives to unfold past, present, and future worlds.

Most nonfiction writers could be likened to scientists. They use their keen powers of observation and their natural curiosity about their world to write with an enthusiasm that reels in readers of all ages. This is what we want for our young writers—the ability to act on their curiosity about their world and share their passion and new discoveries through the written word. Rachel Carson also had this desire for children everywhere. In *The Sense of Wonder* (1998), she writes:

> *If I had influence with the good fairy who is supposed to preside over the christening of all children, I should ask that her gift to each child in the world be a sense of wonder so indestructible that it would last throughout life.* (54)

Perhaps by giving our students wonderful mentor texts and opportunities to write about the things that dazzle them, inspire them, and cause them to question their world, we can make Rachel Carson's wish come true. So, the journey cannot be taken alone. Students need the support of their mentors, both published authors and their teachers, as they travel down new roads. We hope this book will be packed in your travel bag to help you imagine new possibilities for nonfiction writing. Rachel Carson reminds us of the power and magic of mentorship when she says:

> *If a child is to keep alive his inborn sense of wonder . . . he needs the companionship of at least one adult who can share it, rediscovering with him the joy, excitement and mystery of the world we live in.* (1998, 55)

• • •

The following poem was written by Bruce Bloome, a fourth-grade teacher in the Upper Moreland School District. Bruce used the scaffold of *If You're Not from the Prairie* by David Bouchard to write this poem specifically for our book. Thank you, Bruce.

If you're not from a reading/writing classroom, you can't know mentor writing.

You just can't know mentor writing.

You can't know the wise and wondrous ways that writers use to wind their messages into fine threads, which they weave into beautiful quilts that cover their topic and warm the reader to the content.

You can't know the power of proper nouns and the vitality of verbs, carefully placed to create a picture, emphasizing the important elements, embracing the subject matter, and involving the reader.

You can't know the magnificence of the masterfully crafted metaphor, strengthening the framework of passages and serving as a scaffold that the writer can stand upon to refine and revise the message.

If you're not from a reading/writing classroom, you can't know mentor writing.

If you're not from a reading/writing classroom, you can't know awesome authors.

You just can't know awesome authors.

You can't know Rylant's tales of life in Appalachia, literate recollections of a youth spent in the mountains, passing on a heritage before it fades from memory.

You can't know Davies's narratives, tracking a tiny turtle through its tumultuous trail through life, or pondering the plight of a polar bear as it struggles to survive.

You can't know Cherry, advocating awareness and activism for the environment, a true-life environmentalist educating everybody, and enlisting them in her cause.

You can't know Yolen, Miller, Burleigh, Simon, and so, so many more, as they use the written word to inform, engage, and inspire us all.

If you're not from a reading/writing classroom, you can't know awesome authors.

If you're not from a reading/writing classroom, you can't know the power of nonfiction literature.

You unfortunately can't know the power of nonfiction literature.

You can't know the essentially essential need to use the storyteller's voice to share stories of science and social studies, living, real-life subjects that should never be stifled by lifeless text.

You can't know the illumination that illustrative text and illustrations provide to ignite the imagination, and create a desire for learning, lighting the learner's way towards further discovery.

You can never know the joy, the jubilation, and the journey that an integrated, literature-based learning experience can provide for the teacher and the student, the mentor and the mentee, as they share the art of artisans and are apprentices to the masters of the written word.

If you're not from a reading/writing classroom, where awesome authors reside and where their words resonate, reinforce, and refine the educational experience, you don't know mentor writing.

You simply can never know mentor writing.

Anderson, Jeff. 2005. *Mechanically Inclined: Building Grammar, Usage, and Style into Writer's Workshop.* Portland, ME: Stenhouse.

Angelillo, Janet. 2002. *A Fresh Approach to Teaching Punctuation.* New York: Scholastic.

Calkins, Lucy McCormick, with Shelley Harwayne. 1991. *Living Between the Lines.* Portsmouth, NH: Heinemann.

Calkins, Lucy McCormick, and Laurie Pessah. 2003. "Nonfiction Writing: Procedures and Reports." In *Units of Study for Primary Writing: A Yearlong Curriculum.* Portsmouth, NH: Heinemann.

Carson, Rachel. 1998. *The Sense of Wonder.* New York: HarperCollins. (Orig. pub. 1956.)

DiPardo, Anne, and Pat Schnack. 2004. "Expanding the Web of Meaning: Thought and Emotion in an Intergenerational Reading and Writing Program." *Reading Research Quarterly* 39: 14–37.

Dorfman, Lynne R., and Rose Cappelli. 2007. *Mentor Texts: Teaching Writing Through Children's Literature, K–6.* Portland, ME: Stenhouse.

Duke, Nell, and V. Susan Bennett-Armistead. 2003. *Reading and Writing Informational Text in the Primary Grades.* New York: Scholastic.

Ehrlich, Amy. 2003. *Rachel: The Story of Rachel Carson.* New York: Harcourt.

Fishman, Andrea. 1988. *Amish Literacy: What and How It Means.* Portsmouth, NH: Heinemann.

Fletcher, Ralph. 1993. *What a Writer Needs.* Portsmouth, NH: Heinemann.

———. 2007. *How to Write Your Life Story.* New York: HarperCollins.

Fletcher, Ralph, and JoAnn Portalupi. 2001. *Writing Workshop: The Essential Guide.* Portsmouth, NH: Heinemann.

Graves, Donald H. 1994. *A Fresh Look at Writing.* Portsmouth, NH: Heinemann.

Harwayne, Shelley. 2008. *Returning to the Good Old Days of Writing Workshop.* Keynote address. Celebrate Literacy Conference. West Chester, Pennsylvania, June 24, 2008.

Harvey, Stephanie. 1998. *Nonfiction Matters: Reading, Writing, and Research in Grades 3–8.* Portland, ME: Stenhouse.

Hoyt, Linda. 2002. *Make It Real: Strategies for Success with Informational Texts.* Portsmouth, NH: Heinemann.

Kletzien, Sharon Benge, and Mariam Jean Dreher. 2004. *Informational Text in K–3 Classrooms: Helping Children Read and Write.* Newark, DE: International Reading Association.

Kristo, Janice V., and Rosemary A. Bamford. 2004. *Nonfiction in Focus: A Comprehensive Framework for Helping Students Become Independent Readers and Writers of Nonfiction.* New York: Scholastic.

Lane, Barry. 1993. *After THE END: Teaching and Learning Creative Revision.* Portsmouth, NH: Heinemann.

———. 1999. *Reviser's Toolbox.* Shoreham, VT: Discover Writing Press.

———. 2003. *51 Wacky We-Search Reports: Face the Facts with Fun.* Shoreham: VT: Discover Writing Press.

Lane, Barry, and Gretchen Bernabei. 2001. *Why We Must Run With Scissors: Voice Lessons in Persuasive Writing 3–12.* Shoreham, VT: Discover Writing Press.

Lee, Harper. 1960. *To Kill a Mockingbird.* New York: Warner Books.

McEwen, Christian, and Mark Statman, eds. 2000. *The Alphabet of the Trees: A Guide to Nature Writing.* New York: Teachers and Writers Collaborative.

Peterson, Ralph L. 2007. *Grand Conversations: Literature Groups in Action.* New York: Scholastic.

Pike, Kathy, and Jean Mumper. 2004. *Making Nonfiction and Other Informational Texts Come Alive: A Practical Approach to Reading, Writing, and Using Nonfiction and Other Informational Texts Across the Curriculum.* Boston: Pearson Education.

Plotnik, Arthur. 2007. *Spunk & Bite: A Writer's Guide to Bold, Contemporary Style.* New York: Random House.

Portalupi, JoAnn, and Ralph Fletcher. 2001. *Nonfiction Craft Lessons: Teaching Information Writing K–8.* Portland, ME: Stenhouse.

Ray, Katie Wood. 1999. *Wondrous Words: Writers and Writing in the Elementary Classroom.* Urbana, IL: National Council of Teachers of English.

Robb, Laura. 2004. *Nonfiction Writing: From the Inside Out.* New York: Scholastic.

Romano, Tom. 2000. *Blending Genre, Altering Style: Writing Multigenre Papers.* Portsmouth, NH: Heinemann.

———. 2004. *Crafting Authentic Voice.* Portsmouth, NH: Heinemann.

Routman, Regie. 2000. *Conversations: Strategies for Teaching, Learning, and Evaluating.* Portsmouth, NH: Heinemann.

———. 2003. *Reading Essentials: The Specifics You Need to Teach Reading Well.* Portsmouth, NH: Heinemann.

———. 2005. *Writing Essentials: Raising Expectations and Results While Simplifying Teaching.* Portsmouth, NH: Heinemann.

Ruddell, Martha Rapp. 2008. *Teaching Content Reading and Writing.* Hoboken, NJ: John Wiley and Sons.

Schur, Joan. 2007. *Eyewitness to the Past: Strategies for Teaching American History in Grades 5–12.* Portland, ME: Stenhouse.

Stead, Tony. 2002. *Is That a Fact? Teaching Nonfiction Writing K–3.* Portland, ME: Stenhouse.

Viorst, Judith. 1972. *Alexander and the Terrible, Horrible, No Good, Very Bad Day.* New York: Atheneum.

Index

Page numbers followed by an *f* indicate figures.